GREATEST MOMENTS
IN
LSU
FOOTBALL HISTORY

Edited by Francis J. Fitzgerald

From the sports pages of the

PUBLISHER: DAVID C. MANSHIP
EXECUTIVE EDITOR: LINDA C. LIGHTFOOT
MANAGING EDITOR: JIM WHITTUM
EXECUTIVE SPORTS EDITOR: BUTCH MUIR
SPORTS EDITOR: SAM KING
DIRECTOR OF PHOTOGRAPHY: MICHAEL HULTS
LIBRARY DIRECTOR: JILL ARNOLD
GRAPHICS EDITOR: PAUL SANDAU
MARKETING DIRECTOR: LINDA WUNSTEL

ACKNOWLEDGMENTS: This book would not have been completed on time without the hard work and resourceful efforts of Jill Arnold, *The Advocate's* library director, and her top-notch staff — Laurie Christensen, Judy Jumonville, Christopher Miller, Sheila Varnado, Margaret Forrest and Dianne Muchow — who assisted me in finding the difficult photos in their archives and the microfilm newspaper stories that were not easy to locate at other libraries, and Butch Muir's excellent sports staff — Sam King, Scott Rabalais, Robin Fambrough, Scott Gremillion, Joe Macaluso, Sheldon Mickles, Joseph Schiefelbein, Glenn Guilbeau, Tony Brown, Gary English, Matt Randolph, Ben Reed, Bonner Ridgeway, T.J. Simoneaux and David Constantine. Also, the Southwestern Bell Cotton Bowl, the FedEx Orange Bowl, the Nokia Sugar Bowl, the Chick-Fil-A Peach Bowl, the CompUSA Florida Citrus Bowl, *The Birmingham News*, *The South Bend Tribune* and T. J. Ribs, who assisted in providing key photos for this book, and Herb Vincent and his media relations staff at LSU.

ISBN: 1-58261-510-1
Produced by Epic Sports, Birmingham, Ala.
Book Design by Richard Epps, Detroit.
Cover Design by Kerri Baker, Champaign.
Photo imaging by Philip Webb, Detroit.

Typefaces: Janson, Giza

Published in association with *The Advocate* by:

Sports Publishing L.L.C.
804 North Neil Street
Champaign, IL 61820
(217) 363-2072
http://www. sportspublishingllc.com

GREATEST MOMENTS
IN

FOOTBALL HISTORY

EDITED BY FRANCIS J. FITZGERALD

From the sports pages of the

SPORTS
PUBLISHING
INC.

■ LSU fans rocked Tiger Stadium during the Bengals' 1988 victory over Auburn. A campus seismograph proved it to be the loudest stadium in the country.

■ LSU quarterback Tommy Hodson (13) flings a rocket pass against Alabama in the Tigers' 19-18 win in 1988.

■ Jerry Stovall is congratulated by Alabama coach Paul (Bear) Bryant after LSU's 20-10 win in 1982.

■ Charlie McClendon is LSU's winningest coach with a record of 137-59-7 during 18 seasons.

■ **THE NIGHT THE CLOCK STOPPED:** LSU's 17-16 win over Ole Miss in 1972.

■ The 1958 Tigers were named National Champions after an 11-0 season.

■ Governor Huey Long took five trains and 5,000 students to back the Tigers in their 1934 game against Vanderbilt.

■ The Tigers defeated Michigan State, 45-26, in the 1995 Independence Bowl to cap Gerry DiNardo's first season.

DEDICATION

This book is dedicated to Bo Rein, who never had the opportunity to coach in Tiger Stadium.

■ Billy Cannon (20) rambles for big yardage against arch-rival Tulane.

1958: When LSU Owned the College Football World

By Sam King
The Advocate

Except for the passing of summer and the arrival of football, there was little to cheer about in Louisiana in the early days of September 1958. Forty years ago, it seemed like Louisiana led the nation in everything bad and brought up the rear in all that was good. Air conditioning was a household pipe dream; television was still a nightly attraction in show rooms of furniture stores across the state.

■ LSU coach Paul Dietzel and his star halfback, Billy Cannon.

Football might have been bad, but politics was worse. The governor (Earl Long) was teetering between stripping and "flipping" — trying to stay with stripper Blaze Starr and stay out of a mental institution — being admitted to the latter on June 15, 1959.

The economy was down, but promised to get better. You couldn't say the same for LSU's football team.

The Tigers had lost four of their final five games in 1957, marking their fourth straight losing season and third under 34-year-old coach Paul Dietzel, who likely questioned his job security at the time. LSU was ranked no better than No. 37 (UPI) and No. 33 (AP) in the major polls and was young and inexperienced. It had 31 underclassmen and only two seniors who would play. It sorely lacked depth.

Not only did Dietzel have to replace All-America fullback Jimmy Taylor, but the entire right side of the offensive line. He

had some outstanding players for his first team, but after that, only some who could play offense and others who could play only defense.

"Frankly, it takes a different type of player for offense and defense," said Dietzel. "On offense, you need kids that are smart, that aren't too fast, but are quick. On defense, you need players that are semi-wild, very aggressive and very fast."

He wanted to be two teams deep, but that seemed unlikely. Dietzel and his staff huddled. They made a decision that would stand the football world on its kicking tee. They would have three teams. The starters, the best players, would play both ways and be on the White Team. The remainder would compose the Go Team, which played only offense, and the others were the wild defensive specialists who composed the famed and ever-so popular Chinese Bandits.

Dietzel and Tigers everywhere loved those Chinese Bandits,

■ **The White Team: LSU's 1958 starting offensive and defensive team.**

who entered the game to the tune of a specially written song.

"The White team was good, but allowed the opponent 3.2 yards per carry," said Dietzel. "But, the Bandits gave up only .9 yards per carry.

"They really weren't that good, but they didn't know it. They were so wound up and were s-o-o-o wild. I never understood why there was so much gang tackling, but their speed was all the same and they all got to the ball at the same time."

And a tip of the coolie hat to you.

Coach Charles McClendon, who was in charge of the defense (there were no coordinators in those days), said, "the Bandits just got stronger and stronger and stronger.

"They didn't know they weren't a good football team — nobody ever told them. They were 100 percent go-getters."

Dietzel said he had been thinking about a move to provide more depth since Ole Miss thrashed the Tigers, 46-17, in 1956.

"That's what got us going. We could not play both ways with just one team. They just wore us out," said Dietzel. "Our first team could play them to a standstill, but got tired. We just didn't have enough depth.

"Now, everybody was very alert because they knew they had to play," said Dietzel. "The morale was fantastic because of that."

Possibly the greatest asset was the unbelievable amount of Louisiana talent that migrated to LSU. Then, if you were worth your salt, you didn't even consider going out of state to play. If you left, your family and just about everyone who liked

you were ostracized. Schools and communities, no matter how small or how large, took great pride in the fact that one of their own was playing at LSU.

Unquestionably, this team was Louisiana's — and would become its proudest possession.

"There was a tremendous feeling about what that team brought to the state," recalled Chinese Bandits defensive back Merle Schexnaildre during the 30-year celebration of the championship.

"The team was everybody's and everyone who was there knows and understands what I'm talking about.

"It was a source of pride for our state. There's not a day that goes by when someone or something doesn't remind me of that year."

Dietzel struck a mother lode of talent, the type that comes along only once every three or four generations. He put it to use very wisely.

The 33 spots on the 1958 Tiger squad were filled with 24 players from Louisiana, including three starters — Istrouma and University High halfbacks Billy Cannon and Johnny Robinson and Baton Rouge High quarterback Warren Rabb — in the backfield who grew up in the shadows of Tiger Stadium.

"That was one of the most unique things I've ever seen," said Dietzel recently. "Having three starting backs from one town is almost unbelievable — and they were all outstanding.

"Robinson," he surmised, "was the most underrated football player we had. He was such a good athlete. He was overshadowed by the fact Cannon was an All-American and won the

■ The Chinese Bandits were a specialized defensive team who held opposing offenses to .9 yards per carry in 1958.

Heisman Trophy — but Billy deserved that."

The three-team concept wasn't all the innovative Dietzel improvised.

The success Ole Miss had experienced with the winged-T offense had Dietzel thinking about yet another change. He had already swapped the Tigers offense from the Split-T to the double winged-T.

After hearing Iowa coach Forest Evashevski speak at a spring coaching clinic here, Dietzel was convinced to go to the winged-T. Evashevski loaned Dietzel his Iowa game film and helped install the offense.

Ironically, when the season unfolded it was LSU that beat out Iowa for the No. 1 honor.

And what a year it was — the year of all years, a season to always remember.

Cannon would become everybody's All-American. Dietzel would become National Coach of the Year. The Chinese Bandits would become a legend in their own time and Tiger Stadium became Death Valley, deafening and frightening to all opponents — none of whom left victorious the next two years.

The LSU bandwagon picked up a crowd in a hurry, playing to sellout crowds later in the season. It was Mardi Gras and New Year's Eve all rolled into one.

"When it started, it was more or less a routine season," recalled Hart Bourque, a Chinese Bandit back. "As the season went on, the enthusiasm and attention grew. People got more and more involved. They not only came (to the games), but they got more into the playing of the games. It was great."

Although it was three or four games into the season before the hysteria and hoopla really began, LSU's home attendance jumped

from an average of 49,659 per game the previous year to 59,315.

It was hard-working people in a hard-working community pulling hard for their Tigers — and they were THEIR Tigers in every sense of the word.

"Baton Rouge was always a blue collar community," recalls Cannon. "There were some rich and affluent people, but basically it was blue collar. The fans were just fantastic.

"In our era they dressed up to go to the ball games. Football season was a social season. It coincided with Halloween, Thanksgiving and Christmas. It was a very good time of the year."

Cannon stopped and laughed a little.

"I thought it was pretty good then, but they're making movies about that era now and telling me it was better than I thought," said Cannon.

The incredible happenings early in the season may have left players and coaches wondering what was going to unfold. Lightning struck and injured some players and trainer Marty Broussard a week before the first game. The stands would collapse in the second quarter of a game against Alabama in Mobile, Ala., and Rabb's father would die late in the morning just hours before LSU's first home game.

It began on the Saturday before LSU opened at Rice, when a bolt of lightning struck in Bernie Moore Stadium and knocked the fillings out of the teeth of three freshmen. Across the street at Alex Box Stadium, the "big" bolt hit.

"I could see it coming from the side of my eyes. It came through the goal posts and I just felt myself being raised up. It hit me and knocked me about 30 yards," recalled Broussard, who was knocked unconscious, had two discs ruptured, sus-

■ The Tigers defeated Alabama and their new coach, Paul (Bear) Bryant, 13-3, in 1958.

tained a broken fibula in his left leg and suffered scalp blisters when his cap burned up.

LSU was impressive in a 26-6 win in the opener against Rice, its offense having its way with the Owls and the defense extremely aggressive. It marked Dietzel's first win over the Owls in four tries.

Coach Paul (Bear) Bryant, who was just starting to rebuild Alabama's football fortunes and met LSU the next week, watched the game.

"I was impressed by the quarterback play of LSU and the fine running of little Don Purvis. Of course, Cannon is always a threat and tough to contain," said Bryant.

LSU vaulted to No. 13 in the AP poll and No. 16 in the UPI poll with the triumph.

The play of the Chinese Bandits led LSU to its 13-3 victory over Alabama a week later. Dietzel put the Bandits in after Alabama recovered a fumble near the goal. Thrice they denied the Tide any ground and forced a field goal into the north stadium seats — which collapsed seconds later sending hundreds of fans into a heap.

Bandit lineman Emile Fournet called the contest, "The game in which the Chinese Bandits were born.

"Bear Bryant had a heck of a team and Alabama recovered a fumble deep in our territory. Instead of leaving the Go Team in on defense, Dietzel sent in the Bandits," said Fournet, of Bogalusa.

"Alabama had the ball with first-and-goal at the three and we stopped them. That convinced the coaches and everyone else that we could play."

LSU moved to No. 13 in the AP poll, but slipped to No. 17 in the UPI.

A damper was put on the home opener for Rabb, whose dad, Amos, died late that morning. However, Rabb played — and played superbly, completing 5 of 6 passes for 88 yards and

ran for a 9-yard touchdown as LSU posted the 20-6 victory.

"Warren played the finest football of his career. I know he wanted to. He had made up his mind to do it for his dad," said Dietzel.

LSU was still unable to crack the Top 10 of either poll, standing at No. 11 in the AP and No. 15 in the UPI poll.

A strong Miami team awaited LSU in the Sunshine State. An obviously much stronger Tiger team went in and knocked the wind out of the Hurricanes, 41-0.

Andy Gustafson said following the shelling. "Paul Dietzel told me a year ago that he was building for 1959. It looks like they've arrived a year early."

Indeed they had.

"That's the game that really started it (LSU's drive to a national championship)," recalls Dietzel. "It convinced us we had a pretty good football team. Everything worked well."

It was the first time LSU had won its first four games since 1937 and the loss was the worst for Miami since 1944. It was the first time Miami had been shutout since 1927.

"We went down there and the game was supposed to be a tossup," Bourque said. "The way we beat a team that was supposed to be our equal was the high point up until that time."

Cannon had noted, "After we beat Miami, the Eastern press realized we were a good football team."

Respect at last! LSU vaulted to No. 9 in both polls. LSU fans couldn't wait for the next game. LSU was for real. A record 65,000 fans would turn Tiger Stadium into the Death Valley we now know when LSU went against Kentucky, which lost by only 8-0 to No. 1-ranked and defending national champion Auburn the previous week. LSU's offense was awesome; its defense overwhelming.

"We just wilted down," said Kentucky coach Blanton Collier, whose team experienced the problems felt by the

■ **Billy Cannon sweeps left, looking for an opening in the Tulane secondary.**

Tigers only a year earlier.

"I don't know if anyone could beat LSU unless it had an off night," said Kentucky Gov. Happy Chandler after the Tigers' 32-7 romp.

LSU moved to No. 5 in the UPI poll and zoomed to No. 3 in the AP poll — the highest a Tiger team had climbed since 1937.

Depth-laden Florida gave LSU all it could handle a week later in Gainesville, however. Billy Cannon's 1-yard smash helped keep it even with Tommy Davis' 26-yard field goal, providing the winning margin in the 10-7 victory with only 2:59 remaining.

It's hard-fought victory helped LSU to its first No. 1 ranking in the AP poll, although it remained No. 5 in the UPI poll.

That set the scene for one of the wildest weeks in LSU history.

Arch-rival Ole Miss, undefeated, untied and ranked No. 6 in both polls, would come calling. It truly was one of those weeks in which "you had to be there" to believe the excitement and electricity.

Go Team center Max Fugler once recalled "that entire week

before the Ole Miss game was terrific.

"We were thinking of the Southeastern Conference championship, not the national championship. The way the entire student body, the community and the state got behind us was something I'll never forget," he said. "The students kept a fire burning on top of two mounds in front of the Field House the entire week. The game itself is indelible probably due to the crowd noise and the intensity. It was the only time I ever really heard the crowd noise while I was playing."

Ticket scalping flourished. Advertisements seeking tickets filled the papers and airwaves.

"Go to Hell, Ole Miss," banners were displayed throughout the city. Graffiti reading the same message was on walls, plate glasses and auto windows. The message was also blared on all radio stations. Coolie hats were all over the town. Football fever was rampant. It was all part of what was to be known as "Ole Miss Week" for years.

The LSU campus was bombed by "Go to Hell, LSU" pamphlets dropped from an airplane (a maneuver credited by the innovative Dietzel to fire up students, fans and his team). It worked.

Several thousand students rushed over to cheer the Tigers in practice. The next day, Ole Miss students cheered their team at practice in Oxford.

Ole Miss threatened first in the game, but one of LSU's many great south end zone goal-line stands denied the Rebels, who had first-and-goal to go on the LSU 2, and three chances to put it in from one foot away, but couldn't.

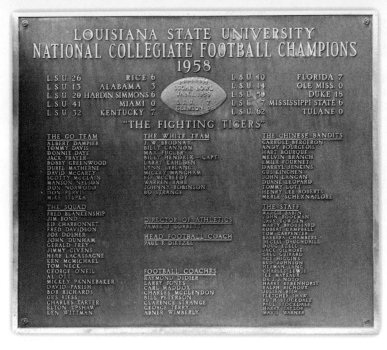

Only Tulane stood between LSU and a national championship, since the polls would be announced prior to the bowl games.

The game was no runaway early. LSU led by only 6-0 — but then scored 56 points in the final 30 minutes for a 62-0 romp in Sugar Bowl Stadium before the largest football crowd ever (85,000) in the South.

White Team guard Larry Kahlden said his highlight of the year "had to be the Ole Miss game. We stopped them four times on the goal line."

Fugler echoed the same thought as for his highlight in the championship season.

"The goal line stand easily," he quipped. "They started at the (LSU) 2 and ended up on the (LSU) 4."

LSU recovered a fumble and drove a short 21 yards for the first touchdown. Rabb looked for a receiver, but decided to run on fourth down at the five. He was met on the 2 by one Rebel, but was then hit by another player from behind who drove him into the end zone.

Durel Matherne, the Go Team quarterback, rolled in for the final score to ice away the 14-0 victory.

The win strengthened LSU's grip on No. 1 in the AP poll, but the coaches shunned LSU in the UPI poll, putting Army No. 1.

However, even the coaches couldn't deny LSU a No. 1 ranking the next week after the Tigers flattened Duke and quarterback Bob Brodhead, 50-18. It was a brilliant day for all the Tiger backs who helped LSU score 50 points for the first time since 1908.

The SEC title was now within reach, but the Tigers were only one slip away from failing. The water-logged field of Hinds Stadium against Mississippi State would have been an appropriate place to slip the following week.

It was one of the games which Dietzel still remembers vividly.

"We were in ankle-deep mud. It was one of the worst playing fields I've ever seen. We were literally up to our ankles in water," said Dietzel.

Recovering a Bulldogs' fumble, LSU trudged from the 34 to the 5 where the Tigers faced fourth down. Rabb hit Hendrix as he sloshed to the sideline for the touchdown. Davis' extra point provided the narrow 7-6 triumph over State.

It was the most points scored by LSU since 1936 when the Tigers slammed USL by 93-0.

The Go team and Chinese Bandits performed too well, particularly in the last quarter and Dietzel had to send the White team, the starters in for the final portion of the game.

"Tulane fans thought we had run the score up, but we were trapped by the substitution rule," said Dietzel. "Half way through the fourth quarter we had to play the White Team — so, here goes Cannon and Robinson and the others in.

"I didn't say run it up, but everything they did, they scored," said Dietzel.

Cannon, on the other hand, had a good laugh talking about that game. "Someone speared Scooter (Purvis) and I was the only 'live' back on the bench. He (Dietzel) had to send me in.

"He said, 'I want you to go out there and tell Durel (quarterback Matherne) to run the clock out, take the ball and fall on it,' " said Cannon. "I went in, called a toss left — to me — and went on in to make it 62-0.

"It was so funny," continued Cannon, "(Wave coach Andy) Pilney was on one sideline cussing Dietzel for everything in the book for running up the score. Dietzel was standing on the other (sideline) screaming, 'It wasn't me. I didn't call it.' "

On Dec. 1, LSU was proclaimed national champion. The appropriate celebrations for such an honor ensued with parties and celebrations and the production and sale of national championship license plates, bumper stickers, Coolie hats and trinkets of all kinds to commemorate the occasion. It was a crowning achievement for Dietzel and assistants Charles McClendon, George Terry, Carl Maddox, Larry Jones, Abner Wimberly and Bill Peterson.

The hard-earned 7-0 victory over Clemson in the Sugar Bowl would only be icing for the biggest cake in college football.

It was truly a year to remember.

Billy Cannon Wins Heisman Trophy

New York — *Dec. 9, 1959*

LSU's Billy Cannon, the two-time All-American, joined gridiron's immortal greats today when he was awarded the 25th Heisman Memorial Trophy, which is symbolic of the nation's outstanding football player of the year.

Vice President Richard Nixon made the presentation at The Downtown Athletic Club, which sponsors the award.

Cannon won the award on the vote of nearly 1,000 sportswriters throughout the nation. He received 1,929 votes while the runnerup, Richie Lucas of Penn State, was awarded with 613 votes.

The Tiger star topped all five sections in the voting and won by one of the largest margins in the history of the Heisman Trophy.

In making the award, Vice President Nixon said, "LSU had more than a Cannon; they had an atomic Cannon, the ultimate in weapons. He was the chief weapon in Tiger coach Paul Dietzel's arsenal of football weapons that included the White team and the Chinese Bandits."

The Vice President also said he watched Syracuse play UCLA and after checking records found out that they had the best offense and the best defense and were No. 1.

"In fact, they had everything but a Billy Cannon."

In presenting the trophy, Vice President said he was glad Cannon was a weight lifter so he could carry the trophy. The replica of the Heisman Trophy weighs 36 pounds and was silver plated this year in honor of its 25th year.

In accepting the award Cannon stated: It is a great honor but one I couldn't have gained without a lot of help and so I would like to thank my high school coach, Big Fuzzy Brown, who started me in football and taught me how to win and what it meant to win.

"I would also like to thank my mother and father, and my wife who put up with me during the football seasons.

"And most of all, I would like to thank my teammates who made it possible for me to get this honor and it was through their great efforts that I was able to win it."

Prior to the presentation of the award, Gen. Troy Middleton, the president of LSU, spoke briefly and said that LSU was proud of Cannon who was a fine athlete and a great young man who appreciated all that had been done for him.

Coach Paul Dietzel spoke briefly and said, "The coaching staff at LSU is proud of Cannon who had the tremendous desire to excel at everything he played. He also showed great humility and was a great pleasure to coach."

Attending the presentation award was Mr. and Mrs. Harvey Cannon, parents of the Tiger star, and his wife, Mrs. Dorothy Cannon.

■ **Vice President Richard Nixon and Billy Cannon.**

The presentation ceremonies were attended by a host of sports figures from all over the nation. The ceremonies were broadcast over a national network.

Cannon joins a host of former stars who gained the top recognition, including Jay Berwanger of Chicago, Doak Walker of SMU, Johnny Lujack of Notre Dame, Army stars Glenn Davis and Doc Blanchard and others.

For Cannon, the award climaxed a fabulous career that started at Istrouma High where he won All-American prep fame before entering LSU.

At LSU, Cannon became an all-time backfield great, rolling up a record rushing yardage for the Bengals in three years and twice gaining All-American honors.

Among the nationally known sportswriters were Tom Meany of New York, and Mel Allen, famed radio and TV broadcaster.

Cannon returns to Baton Rouge where he'll resume training with his Tiger teammates for their Sugar Bowl clash with Ole Miss.

Following his performance in the Sugar Bowl, Cannon will go to Honolulu to play in the Hula Bowl there on Jan. 10.

Cannon was recently drafted by the Los Angeles Rams of the National Football League and has announced his intentions to join that pro club. He was also drafted by Houston of the American Football League.

Hendrix & Davis Give LSU Edge Over Miss. St., 7-6

By Ted Castillo

The Advocate

Jackson, Miss. — *Nov. 15, 1958*

The LSU Golden Bengals had to take advantage of a fumble to come from behind and eke out a 7-6 victory over the rough and tough Mississippi State Maroons here tonight to protect their unblemished record, the only perfect record among the nation's collegiate greats.

State proved a tough and capable foe, scoring early in the second quarter after being thrust back three times by the valiant Tigers in the first period.

The Maroons went into the half with a 6-0 lead but LSU came back early in the third period to take advantage of Bubber Trammell's fumble on the State 34 to move for their touchdown in seven plays and Tommy Davis booted the extra point for what proved the winning margin.

Warren Rabb, the hard working Tigers quarterback, pitched the telling blow for the touchdown when he hit Red Hendrix in the end zone on fourth down for the touchdown.

Like State, LSU passed up earlier opportunities to score as they played most of the second quarter deep in the Maroons' territory.

The game, which kept the fans on their feet was climaxed in the fourth quarter with both elevens passing up scoring opportunities.

State had the first chance when J.E. Logan recovered a Billy Cannon fumble on the Tiger 16. The Maroons marched to the Bengal 10 and on fourth down Bobby Tribble missed a field goal, his second missed field goal of the night.

Billy Stacy, State's great quarterback, twice gave LSU scoring opportunities late in the fourth quarter. Once he fumbled on his 39 and LSU Hendrix recovered for the Bengals. A few minutes later, Stacy fumbled going through the middle and this time Rabb recovered for LSU at the Maroon 27.

This time a 15-yard penalty stymied the Tigers and the LSU first eleven held State deep in their own territory to windup the tingling gridiron fray.

It was the nation's No. 1 eleven's poorest performance of the season as they could never get a sustained drive going at any time in the game and they fumbled the wet and soggy ball at crucial times.

The Maroons were ready for the vaunted Bengals and their big mobile forward wall gave LSU trouble all night as they spilled the Tiger halfbacks before they could get going off their tricky winged-T attack.

LSU edged the Maroons in rushing yardage with 140 to 134 but the Maroons picked up 57 yards to 16 for LSU in the air to take the edge in total offense with 191 yards to 156 for LSU.

Tonight's game was played on a soggy and slick field that gave the passers trouble all night. A steady downpour a half hour before the game drenched the already soggy field.

Some 26,000 fans, a capacity turnout, witnessed the fumbling, bumbling, but hard fought play.

Tiger coach Paul Dietzel was forced to play his first team out for more minutes than in any other game this season and Coach Wade Walker of the Maroons kept his top unit in the game for the most part.

Billy Cannon, who was bothered all night keeping the ball under control, ran 13 times for 57 yards while big Tommy Davis picked up 35 yards on nine plays. Red Brodnax ran six times for 35 yards.

Bubber Trammell, the left halfback of the Maroons, was the top carrier for State with 44 yards in 10 carries.

The expected aerial duel between the Bengals' Rabb and the Maroons' Stacey failed to materialize as both teams stuck to the ground. Rabb connected on three of six passes for 16 yards but it was his telling scoring pass in the third period that put LSU back in the game.

Stacey completed three of 10 passes for 57 yards but was heavily rushed by the valiant Tigers' forward wall all night.

Both elevens put themselves in the hole time after time and again with fumbles, both losing the ball three times during the fray.

The expected kicking duel between State's Gil Peterson and LSU's Tommy Davis also failed to materialize as both were kicking deep in the foes territory and both had several kicks to roll over the goal. Cannon also kicked for LSU.

Probably the standout play for the Bengals was the hustle of Hendrix, who snagged the scoring pass from the hands of State defender and who recovered a crucial fumble.

Score by Periods

LSU	0	0	7	0 —	7
Mississippi State	0	6	0	0 —	6

■ **Tommy Davis' extra-point kick gave LSU the winning edge over Mississippi State.**

The game opened with State getting a chance when Davis punted short to his 46 and Stacy returned the Tiger 32, State drove to the Bengal 3 where a 15-yard penalty stymied them but only after Stacy had hit Jack Batte with a 20-yard pass to put the Maroons back on the Tigers doorstep at the LSU 3. A fourth-down pass by Gil Peterson failed to click.

A few minutes later, State took a short Tiger punt and rolled again from the LSU 38, this time to the Tiger 7 before they failed.

As the first quarter ended, State got still another try when Cannon fumbled on his 21 and State's Willie Daniels recovered. However, LSU held as the period ended and on the first play of the second quarter Tribble failed to kick his first try for a field goal.

State scored a few plays later when Donnie Dave fumbled on the Tiger 22 and the Maroons recovered. This time State moved in for their score, getting a first down at the 13. After Peterson picked up two yards, Stacy rolled out to his left and picked up good blocking to speed over the Tiger goal line after an 11-yard jaunt.

However, the Tigers finally cashed in on a break when Brodnax recovered Trammell's fumble on the State 34.

On a fine fake, Brodnax roared down the middle for 14 yards for a first down at the State 20. LSU moved the ball on short dashes to the 5. On fourth down, Rabb hit Hendrix in the end zone for the tying score. Davis kicked the extra point to give LSU its 7-6 win, but not before both elevens threatened in the final period.

It was LSU's 10th win in a row and their ninth straight this season.

The Tigers have only Tulane left as an obstacle to their first undefeated and untied record since 1908, some 50 years ago.

■ **Billy Cannon (20) sweeps left against a Clemson defense who spent the afternoon trying to corral him.**

Cannon's TD Pass to Mangham Seals LSU Win

By Bud Montet

The Advocate

New Orleans, La. — *Jan. 1, 1959*

The LSU Tigers, the nation's No. 1 football power, were hard pressed to protect their unblemished record today as an inspired and hard-hitting Clemson eleven held the vaunted Baton Rouge collegians to a 7-0 decision.

Clemson, who was a two to three-touchdown underdog prior to the game, gave the 25th Silver Anniversary Sugar Bowl turnout its best game in the past few years as they held the vaunted Bengals well in check most of the game and managed to stage the game's longest drive right after LSU scored.

For LSU the victory gave them their 12th straight victory, the longest winning streak in modern LSU history. It was also LSU's first Sugar Bowl win in five attempts. In previous Sugar Bowls, LSU lost to TCU, Santa Clara, twice, and Oklahoma.

Clemson kept the pressure on the Bengals throughout the game and LSU had to use a break late in the third period to get its lone score.

The scoring play came when on fourth down Clemson's center passed the ball back poorly on an attempted punt play and LSU's Duane Leopard recovered the ball at the Clemson 11.

LSU moved to the nine in two plays and then Durel Matherne handed off to Billy Cannon, who raced to his right and pitched to Mickey Mangham in the end zone for the score. Cannon added the extra point to put the Tigers up, 7-0, and that completed the scoring for the afternoon.

LSU missed the services of its All-SEC quarterback, Warren Rabb, who sustained a broken right hand near the end of the first half. With Rabb out, Tiger coach Paul Dietzel used Matherne the entire second half on his offensive units.

The fleet LSU attack was bothered by the slippery turf in the Sugar Bowl Stadium and Bengal backs slipped down a number of times. However, it was their inability to hang onto the ball in the first half that stymied LSU on a number of scoring opportunities.

Clemson's big forward wall gave the Bengals plenty of trouble all afternoon and their short plunges by a half dozen backs enabled the South Carolina Tigers to outgain the No. 1 eleven on the ground.

However, Clemson made but two sustained drives, moving to the LSU 26 where a fumble by George Usry halted the drive as LSU's Bo Strange recovered.

In the fourth period, Clemson made a determined bid to tie the game when they drove from their 16-yard line to the Tiger 24 where they gave up the ball on downs and LSU kept possession until the final whistle.

On the play before the final one of the game, a mild melee started among the players but was quickly broken up by the officials.

In the battle of the figures, Clemson gained an edge on LSU, picking up 195 yards on the ground to 134 for LSU. The Baton Rouge Bengals hit on four passes for 68 yards while Clemson hit on two for 23 yards.

Clemson didn't throw a pass until the fourth period as they were content to run for short gains behind their huge line.

LSU and Clemson both lost a pair of fumbles.

The Bengals lost three scoring opportunities in the second period with fumbles marring a pair of chances. Late in the first period, LSU drove from their 25 to the Clemson 25 for the first sustained drive of the game.

However, on the first play of the second half, Matherne fumbled and end Ray Masneri recovered for Clemson to end the threat.

A few minutes later the Bengals got another scoring chance when Clemson's Charlie Horne had a punt partially blocked and lost two yards on the boot with LSU getting possession on the Clemson 29-yard line.

LSU drove down to the Clemson 12 where Rabb missed on four straight passes.

The third time didn't prove lucky for LSU for a few minutes later they drove from their 44 to the Clemson 1-yard line where Red Brodnax fumbled going over the goal line. However, the officials ruled he had fumbled while still in the playing field and Clemson recovered in the end zone for a touchback and the South Carolina eleven got the ball back out on their 20.

Billy Cannon, LSU's great All-American back, was held well in check by the big Clemson line and the fleet Tiger gained

Score by Periods

LSU	0	0	7	0	— 7
Clemson	0	0	0	0	— 0

only 51 yards on 13 tries but it was his clutch touchdown pass to Mangham that gave LSU its victory.

Cannon won The Digby-Miller Memorial Trophy as the game's Most Valuable Player for his efforts.

LSU's Bo Strange, a sophomore tackle — playing against tackles that outweighed him 20 and 30 pounds — turned in a fine defensive game for LSU.

Also outstanding for the Bengals were center Max Fugler, end Mangham and Durel Matherne, who replaced the injured Rabb in the second half.

Clemson's hard driving backs — Rudy Hayes, Usry, Bob Morgan and Charlie Horne — all played well in sparking the Clemson attack. Up front, Jim Padgett and Lou Cordileone, a pair of huge tackles, stood out for the Mountain Tigers.

The first period was spent in a punting duel with LSU's Cannon getting the edge. Later in the period, LSU started their first drive from their 25. With the Go Team in the game, LSU marched steadily with Davis getting the drive going with an 11-yard plunge. Later, Matherne pitched to Scotty McClain for 26 yards and a first down at the Clemson 30.

LSU got to the Clemson 25 as the quarter ended and then on the first play of the second period Matherne fumbled and Masneri recovered for Clemson.

A few minutes later, LSU drove from the Clemson 29 to the 12. Taking the ball after a poor Clemson partially blocked kick at the 29, Brodnax rambled for nine yards and then Rabb hit Cannon with an eight-yard pass for a first down at the Clemson 12. Here Rabb missed on four passes in a row.

Midway in the period, LSU staged its longest sustained drive. Taking over on their 44, Rabb pitched 23 yards to Mangham to get the drive going.

The pass play gave LSU a first down at the Clemson 33. Rabb then kept for 15 yards and combined with Brodnax for 11 yards and a first down at the Clemson 8. Cannon got to the Clemson 1 on two tries and then Brodnax fumbled on the goal line.

In the third period, Clemson made it's first big march to the LSU 26 before fumbling. Then LSU came back to get their score but Clemson wasn't finished as they drove in the fourth period from their 16 to the Tiger 24 before giving up the ball.

LSU failed to exhibit the sharp winged-T attack that featured their play all season. No doubt the loss of Rabb proved a stunning blow.

For the first time this season Coach Dietzel mixed up his playing units.

Strange enough, LSU ended the season with but one able quarterback, Matherne, as Daryl Jenkins, the Bandit quarterback, didn't suit out, and Rabb was lost after the first half.

■ Billy Cannon's pass to Mickey Mangham in the end
zone ensured LSU's 11-0 national championship season.

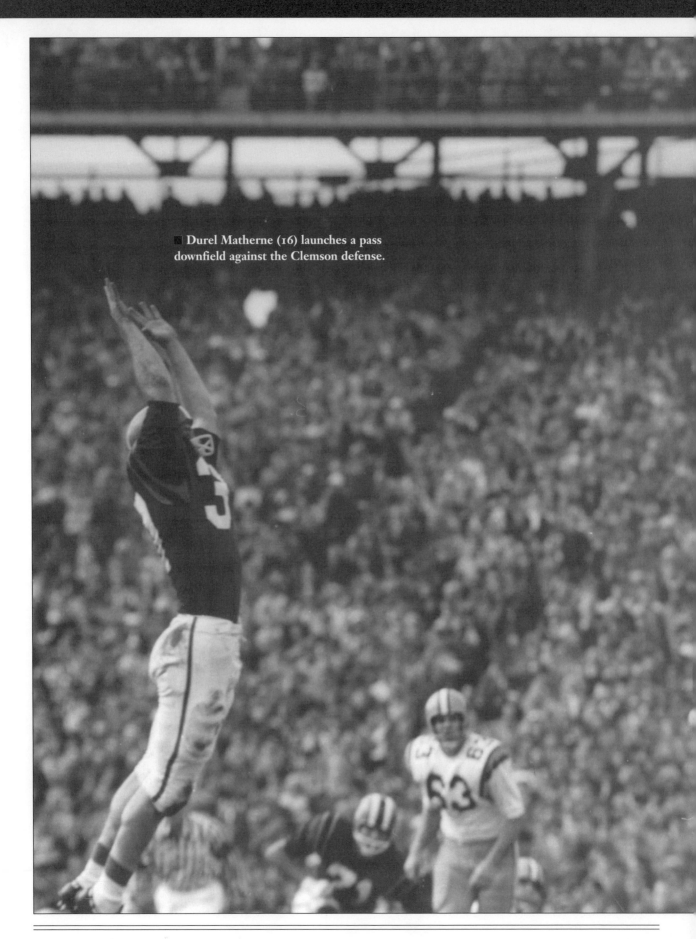

■ Durel Matherne (16) launches a pass downfield against the Clemson defense.

■ Billy Cannon's 89-yard punt return on Halloween night 1959 will forever be part of LSU folklore.

Cannon Gallops Past Rebs For 7-3 LSU Win

By Bud Montet
The Advocate

Baton Rouge, La. — *Oct. 31, 1959*

The defending national champion LSU Tigers proved to be a brilliant "clutch" eleven tonight when they roared with Billy Cannon to come from behind and hand Ole Miss a 7-3 setback — their first loss of the season. It was LSU's 19th straight victory without a loss.

Battling from behind all the way, LSU overcame the three-point deficit with 10 minutes left in the game when All-American Cannon grabbed a Jake Gibbs punt on his 11-yard line and, starting slowly, picked his way to the sidelines and twisted past a quartet of Ole Miss defenders to break loose at midfield and gallop on over for the lone touchdown of the game. It was a twisting, coolly-calculated run by the big Tiger back who finally broke loose to the roaring of 67,000 fans who jammed Tiger Stadium for Homecoming.

But Cannon's run just set the stage for the most thrilling 10 minutes of the game as the Rebels took the kickoff and marched from their 21 to inside the Tiger 2-yard line where the Tigers held them on fourth down with 18 seconds left in the game.

Coach Paul Dietzel had to call on his tired but game White eleven to go in and halt the threatening Rebels.

The Tiger's goal line stand of holding the Rebels from their seven with four downs to go duplicated their great stand of last year when they hurled back the Rebels to protect their lead.

Santa Claus looked as if he was coming early to the Ole Miss Rebels when LSU gave the Mississippians a "gift" of five scoring chances in the first half. Three fumbles paved the way for the Rebels to threaten, a questionable pass interference gave the visitors a chance, and a poor kick by Bandit end Gus Kinchen also gave the Rebs a shot at the Tiger goal.

Each time LSU threw back the challenge, but early in the first quarter the Rebs moved from their 40 to the Tiger 3 and Bobby Khayat booted a 23-yard field goal squarely through the uprights. It was Khayat's fourth field goal in 10 tries this season.

Later, Kinchen's 27-yard punt out of bounds gave the Rebels a shot and this time they were held at the 30.

The second quarter found the Rebs moving to the Tiger 22 where LSU center Johnny Langan knocked down a Rebel fourth down pass.

Ole Miss drove from their 39 to the LSU 22 a few minutes later and this time LSU halted a flurry of passes to take the ball away.

Big Earl Gros fumbled near the end of the first half on the LSU 29 to give the Rebels another shot and this time LSU rose up and halted the Mississippians on their eight.

LSU spent the entire third period in Rebel territory, moving to the Ole Miss 31 once before Wendell Harris missed a 37-yard attempt at a field goal. Later LSU moved to the 19 with big Gros missing a first down try by inches.

LSU came back to drive to the Rebel 35 where Cannon tried a fake punt and run on fourth down and was hauled down for a yard loss.

Then the Bengals exploded midway in the fourth period with Cannon making his sensational gallop, answering the Ole Miss critics who were rating their big fullback Charlie Flowers over the brilliant Cannon.

Cannon answered the critics with the greatest run in his Tiger career. It also allowed LSU to capture its 19th straight

Score by Periods

Ole Miss	3	0	0	0 —	3
LSU	0	0	0	7 —	7

victory, their seventh of this season, and probably kept the Bengals at the top the national rankings.

But while Cannon's long 89-yard gallop was the offensive fireworks it remained for the valiant goal line stand of the White Team to really climax the fierce battle, which was rated as the nation's number-one game of the week.

LSU's frequent fumbles in the first half — they lost the ball three times in four fumbles — kept the Bengals from getting under way.

Ole Miss picked up 160 yards on the ground to LSU's 142. In the air, LSU gained 29 yards and Ole Miss 19.

Cannon was the "big gun" for the Tigers in more ways than one. While it remained for his long touchdown gallop to prove the deciding factor, the hard-working youth packed the ball 12 times for 48 yards, which edged him over his rival Flowers, who carried for 35 yards in 10 tries.

Cannon proved a timely and clutch punter, booting four times for a 42-yard average.

Defensively, the Bengals played probably their greatest game of the year. Time after time they rose up to hurl back the Rebels within the shadow of their goal and their great "clutch" goal-line stand that saved the game was one of their finest efforts.

LSU started off brilliantly, moving from their 27 after the opening kickoff to the Rebel 40 where Donnie Daye fumbled and Ole Miss' Billy Brewer recovered for the Rebs at the 44-yard line. It was the first of three recoveries for Brewer, a fine defensive back.

Ole Miss senior quarterback, Bobby Franklin, set up the first Ole Miss threat when he booted 43 yards out on the Tiger 5-yard line.

Cannon ran the ball out to the 21 but fumbled and again Brewer pounced on it.

This time the Rebels moved in short dashes to the LSU 3-yard line where LSU held and Ole Miss coach Johnny Vaught sent in his kicking specialist, Khayat, who booted the field goal and gave the Rebels a 3-0 lead.

Ole Miss kept coming at the Tigers for the rest of the half, once moving to the 30 after a poor kick by Kinchen.

The tables turned in the third period with LSU's Cannon giving the Bengals a chance when he intercepted a Jake Gibbs' pass on the LSU 48 and returned it to the Rebel 36. LSU moved to the 31 where a passing flurry failed.

Again LSU moved this time with the Go Team performing steady and moving from their 3 to the Ole Miss 19, where Gros missed a first-down try by inches.

Still later in the period, the Bengals moved from their 49 to

■ **Warren Rabb (12) and Billy Cannon (20) double-team Ole Miss' Doug Elmore at the 1-yard line.**

the Rebel 35 where Cannon's fourth down fake punt play failed.

Despite the drama of the first three quarters it remained for the final 10 minutes to unroll as great a gridiron drama as ever witnessed in Tiger Stadium.

With defeat staring them in the face, the Tigers kept going and then Cannon changed the outlook with his sensational gallop, one of the greatest ever seen on a Tiger gridiron.

Then came the brilliant try by Ole Miss to keep going and get back in the game.

Ole Miss took their kickoff on their 32 and in steady marches, with Cowboy Woodruff furnishing most of the impetus,

moved to the LSU 7 for a first down. The Bengal White Team rose up and held Ole Miss' George Blair for a two-yard gain. Fleet Doug Elmore on a keeper play sped to the Tiger 2 and then Jimmy Anderson gained a half yard on third down.

Ole Miss' Elmore rolled out to the left but a trio of Bengals closed in on him at the LSU 1 and smashed him to the turf to halt the threat and save the game.

Hysteria gripped the 67,000 fans who jammed Tiger Stadium as only 18 seconds remained in the game and once again LSU had pulled one out of the fire.

Never in LSU history have the Bengal gridders treated their homecoming fans to such a drama packed contest.

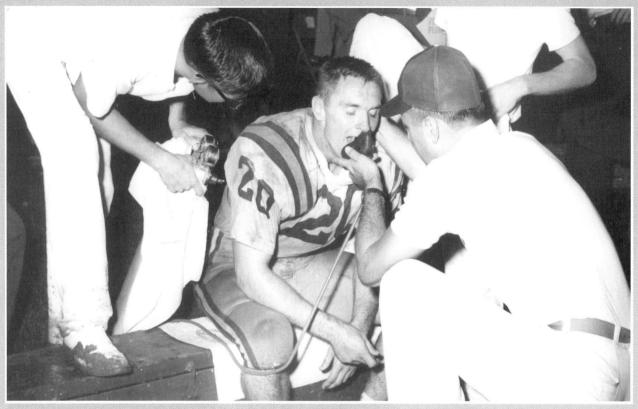

■ Following his epic punt return, Billy Cannon was administered oxygen on the sideline.

'But Big Billy Kept Going,' Tigers Recall

BY TED CASTILLO
The Advocate

Baton Rouge, La. — *Oct. 31, 1959*

"I thought Billy (Cannon) was down, then I looked up and that big animal was still going," declared LSU tackle Bo Strange after the Tiger All-American had pulled LSU off the floor with an 89-yard scoring sprint to give the Bengals their only touchdown in a 7-3 cliffhanger with Ole Miss tonight at Tiger Stadium.

"He ran over five men," Strange shouted above the dressing room din. "They thought he was down but big Billy kept going. When you need it, he's there. He won't get a hundred touchdowns against Podunk but he'll get one on somebody like Ole Miss."

Strange, like some other members of the White Team such as Ed McCreedy, Warren Rabb and Johnny Robinson said they felt they would hold the Rebels in the final minutes.

"I knew they'd have to pass to score," Robinson said, "but in a situation like that you don't know if you want them to come your way or go the other."

But Cannon and Mickey Mangham weren't as confident as their teammates.

"I was mighty afraid," Cannon said. And Mangham echoed his sentiments.

"They had me worried," the Tiger first-team terminal stated. "Ole Miss had the best line we've faced. TCU's backs were just as good but Ole Miss' line was better. I thought (Warren) Rabb played a whale of a game. He made the stop on their quarterback on fourth down when they got so close."

Describing part of his touchdown run while holding an ice pack to a bruised forehead, Cannon praised the blocking of this teammates.

"They really blocked for me, Johnny Robinson and Lynn LeBlanc and Scotty McClain and two or three others ... That's all I saw, all I could think about was hold that ball and don't fumble again," said the big Bengal back, who hugged the sidelines for more than half of his long gallop after breaking into the clear around the LSU 35. "I was mighty close to those chalklines," Cannon added.

Rebs Tie LSU on Late Field Goal, 6-6

By Bud Montet
The Advocate

Oxford, Miss. — *Oct. 29, 1960*

Score by Periods

LSU	0	0	6	0 —	6
Ole Miss	0	0	3	3 —	6

A last minute Ole Miss passing attack clutched victory right out of the hands of the gritty and determined LSU Tigers and Allen Green, the Rebels kicker, booted a 41-yard field goal with 13 seconds left in the game to give the vaunted Mississippians a 6-6 deadlock with the surprising Tigers.

Until the final minute and a half the Bengals covered the All-American prospect Jake Gibbs like a blanket but it was Gibbs' clutch passing that set up the field goal.

For LSU it was again a game of frustration as they watched the Rebels get two field goals to tie the score. It was the fourth game in a row where field goals either tied the score or won it for the opposition.

The Bengals stuck to the ground — they threw only two aerials — and pounded out 216 yards to 107 for the Rebs in rushing for their best ground offensive showing of the season.

Ole Miss struck through the air to pile up a net 107 yards — 52 yards of that came in the final two minutes of the game.

LSU threw just two passes, hitting on one for five yards.

The sparkling feature of the game was the running of the sophomore Go Team for LSU and the spirited defensive play of all Tiger gridders who held Ole Miss without a touchdown for the first time this season.

Gibbs, ranked as a crack runner as well as passer, was so well covered by the Bengals that he finished with a minus 13 yards.

While the Bengals turned in their season's top effort, again it was glaring errors that cost them the game. They drove to the Ole Miss 3 in the opening minutes of the first quarter when Wendell Harris missed an easy try at a field goal.

Then the Tigers' Earl Gros fumbled on the first scrimmage play of the second half to set up Green's first field goal. The Rebs moved to the Tiger 22 and Green booted his 38-yard kick to give the Rebels a 3-0 lead.

Green had previously missed one from the Tiger 13, the ball barely going wide of the posts.

Late in the game a questionable unsportsmanship 15-yard penalty by LSU gave the Rebels a chance to drive deep but they failed. The Rebs then got moving when LSU attempted to kill the clock and Jerry Stovall punted with one minute and 21 seconds left in the game.

Gibbs then came through to move the ball to the Tiger 25 and Green kicked the field goal that tied the game.

Often accused of being fangless, the Tigers rose up to answer their critics with their snarling offensive play. Stovall, the gifted sophomore halfback, led the squad with a net 96 yards on seven carries.

Charles Cranfield, the sophomore fullback, picked up 30 yards in six carries and once tumbled over the line to land on his feet and keep going for extra yardage. His fake into the middle on the Bengal touchdown was one of the finest of the afternoon as he teamed with Lynn Amedee to completely fool the Ole Miss defense.

Wendell Harris picked up 22 yards on nine carries and Donnie Daye garnered 24 in seven tries.

Ole Miss' top runner was Art Doty, a fast moving youth, who garnered 46 yards in 12 tries.

Gibbs continued his fine passing with seven completions in 18 attempts for 89 yards and almost half came on the clutch drive that enabled the Rebels to tie the score.

For the third straight year LSU has proven to be a spoiler of the Rebels. In 1958, they halted an undefeated Rebel eleven and again in 1959 they handed the Rebels their first defeat.

This year they couldn't quite match those efforts but they put a tie blot on the Rebel record after losing four straight games.

The Bengals, who haven't tasted victory since their season's opener against Texas A&M, weren't overly impressed with the Rebels' No. 2 ranking on the nation's grid lists. Against LSU, they turned in their finest offensive effort of the season but once more they were denied after getting within striking distance.

LSU had two opportunities in the opening quarter when they drove 77 yards to the Rebel 3 the first time they got their hands on the ball only to fail on the field goal try.

It was a fine 32-yard gallop by Stovall that set up this drive. On the first LSU scrimmage play he broke over left guard and cut back to his right and scooted to the Rebel 38 before he was hauled down.

Then in short bursts Stovall and Harris carried the ball to the Ole Miss 3 where the Rebels halted them and Harris missed the field goal attempt on fourth down.

A few minutes later Gene Sykes recovered Bill Roy Adams' fumble on the Rebel 32 and here the Rebels' Jim Dunaway broke through and blocked Harris' second attempt at a field goal.

Ole Miss got but one chance in the first half as they drove from the Tiger 48 to the five where LSU held them and Green missed his first try.

However, the big boy more than made up for it later with his two clutch field goals that kept the Rebels in the undefeated class.

The opening plays of the second half set the keynote as far as the Rebels were concerned. When Gros fumbled, his only appearance carrying the ball, Bookie Bolin, a Reb guard, recovered at the Tiger 24.

Ole Miss failed on two running plays and then Gibbs missed a pass into the end zone before Green stepped back and delivered a 39-yard field goal.

Stung by three straight losses as the results of field goals, the Bengals stormed back late in the period and drove to their 48 to score, their lone touchdown.

Tommy Neck set up the drive when he returned Gibbs' punt 22 yards to the Tiger 48. After missing a pass, Amedee handed off to Ray Wilkins, who gained a yard, and then Amedee stepped down the right sidelines for 15 yards and a first down at the Rebel 32.

Cranford danced through the middle for 10 yards and another first down, then picked up five more yards. Amedee followed up with a 5-yard pass to Wilkins — the Bengals' lone pass completion of the game — and on the final play of the third period Cranford drove to the Ole Miss 7.

Wilkins shook off tacklers for a six-yard gallop to the Rebel 2 and Cranford dove to the one. Then Amedee faked to Cranford, who made a great jump high onto the pile in the middle and the ball was handed off to Wilkins who scored over left tackle. Harris missed the extra point, which proved a crucial miss.

Ole Miss made one threat before they managed to get their

■ **The close contest between LSU and Ole Miss mirrored the fierce punting duel between Jerry Stovall and the Rebels' Jake Gibbs.**

tying field goal, but LSU halted them on their 37 when three of Gibbs' passes went astray.

The Bengals apparently had the game sewed up when Gibbs ran back Stovall's punt to his 31 with a minute and 21 seconds left.

Gibbs then tossed to Crespino for 15 yards to get the drive going. He lost six when hit hard by Billy Booth. However, Gibbs came back and connected on a pass to Crespino at the Rebel 49. He then tossed to Ralph Smith for 14 yards and a first down at the Tiger 35.

Gibbs' next pass to Crespino set the stage for Green's game-tying boot.

Feisty Bengals Swat Yellow Jackets, 10-0

By Bud Montet
The Advocate

Baton Rouge, La.— *Oct. 7, 1961*

A supposedly toothless Tiger ripped the hide off No. 3-ranked Georgia Tech's Yellow Jackets to take a stirring 10-0 victory tonight at Tiger Stadium before 66,000 roaring fans.

LSU dominated the game in the first half as they piled up a 10-point lead and then smashed all Tech efforts to come back.

After holding the Jackets to one first down in the first half, the Bengals went to sleep on a fake kick early in the third period and allowed Tech to complete a 44-yard pass from Bill Lothridge to Billy Williamson to mount a threat.

However, the Bengals rose up on their 1-foot line to toss Tech fullback Mike McNames for a two-yard loss on fourth down and Tech never threatened that close again.

All the scoring came in the second period when LSU exchanged fumbles with the Jackets. The Bengals drove to the Tech 19 early in the second period but Bo Campbell then fumbled and Williamson recovered for Tech at the 15.

The Jackets moved a bit but on fourth down Billy Lothridge went back to kick and dropped the ball and a host of Tigers swarmed him under on the Tech 16.

LSU went to work and big Earl Gros slammed over right guard for 12 yards and a first down at the Tech 4. Gros hit the middle for three yards and on the next play Jimmy Field faked to Gros and then sped off right tackle for the Tigers' touchdown.

Wendell Harris, the senior right half, added the extra point as the Tigers took a 7-0 lead with 6:02 left in the period.

LSU's next threat was set up a few minutes later when sophomore fullback, Buddy Hamic, intercepted a Stan Gann

■ **Jimmy Field piloted the Tigers to their only touchdown.**

Score by Periods

Georgia Tech		0	0	0	0 —	0
LSU		0	10	0	0 —	10

pass at midfield and raced it back for 21 yards to the Tech 29.

Lynn Amedee and the Go Eleven went to work and the ex-Istrouma High youth hit Ray Wilkins with a nine-yard pass and then kept for three yards and a first down at the Tech 17.

Amedee then pitched two straight ones into "left field," missing his receivers by tens of feet. Amedee gained eight yards and then Gros hit off the middle for four yards and a first down at the Jacket five.

LSU couldn't move and with time running out, Wendell Harris rushed into the game and booted a 22-yard field goal to give LSU a 10-0 lead.

Only nine seconds were left in the half when Harris booted the ball through the uprights.

The second half was mainly a punting duel between Jerry Stovall of the Bengals and Billy Lothridge of the Yellow Jackets.

LSU's defense completely halted the vaunted Tech's offense which had completely smothered Southern Cal and the Rice Owls, a team that humbled the Bengals in their opener.

It was the third time in the history of the rivalry that LSU has been able to trim the Yellow Jackets. It was LSU's second victory over Tech at Tiger Stadium, the first coming in 1957.

The Bengals completely dominated the game with the exception of Tech's drive at the start of the second half.

LSU piled up 11 first downs to nine for Tech and picked up a net rushing of 145 yards against 86 for Tech. LSU picked up 66 yards on the air and Tech got 70.

LSU pitched 11 aerials and completed five while Tech, supposedly a "hot" passing combine, pitched only 16 passes and completed six.

While the Bengals turned in their best offensive efforts of the season, it was their superb defensive work against the tricky Tech offense that eventually spelled victory.

The Bengals ends and linebackers turned in their best efforts of the season as they handled Tech's sprint-out and rolled-out passes in good shape.

Big Roy Winston turned in his best effort of the season as he consistently broke through to haul down Gann, the tricky Tech quarterback.

Also, Jack Gates, Billy Booth, Monk Guillot and Bob Flurry turned in fine defensive efforts as did the entire Chinese Bandit unit which had been below par during the two opening games.

■ Baton Rouge's Lynn Amedee quarterbacked the Go Team.

Others who looked good were Dan Hargett, Rodney Guillot and a host of other Tigers.

Big Earl Gros proved to be a hard-running fullback in the game as he led the Tiger rushers with 37 yards in eight tries while Harris picked up 30 yards in four tries and Wilkins got 24 in 5 tries.

Wilkins also proved the top Tiger pass receiver, grabbing three passes for 26 yards.

Mike McNames, the big fullback, was the top Tech ground-gainer who picked up 37 yards in nine tries. Williamson gained 32 yards in seven tries.

The touted Gann was held to three completions in eight tries his worst passing performance of the season. His completions gained but five yards.

His understudy, Lothridge, completed three of eight passes for 65 yards — most coming on his fake punt deal that was good for 44 yards to Williamson.

INTERCEPTION

SCHWENINGER (C)

31

40

HARRIS (LSU)

■ Loren Schweninger (31) intercepts an LSU pass and races for a 54-yard touchdown.

Tiger Defense Buries Colorado in Orange Bowl

By Bud Montet
The Advocate

Miami, Fla. — *Jan. 1, 1962*

With sheathed claws and hidden fangs the LSU Tigers still had a surprisingly easy time in downing the Colorado Buffaloes, 25-7, today before a crowd of only 62,391 fans who braved slight showers throughout the game.

Tossing away scoring chances time after time, the Bengals nevertheless managed to get three touchdowns, a field goal and a safety.

LSU had to come from behind after building up an early lead of 5-0 on Wendall Harris' field goal and a safety on a blocked kick by Gary Kinchen.

Colorado's lone touchdown came early in the second quarter when Loren Schweninger, the Buffalo fullback, grabbed a wobbly-tossed Jimmy Field pass on his 41 and sped unmolested down the sideline for 59 yards and the touchdown to take a 7-5 lead.

However, LSU came right back to march 82 yards for their first touchdown, with Charles Cranford going over from the Colorado 1 for the touchdown. On the extra-point play, LSU failed but they held a 11-7 first-half lead and were never threatened after that.

LSU scored twice in the third quarter as they built up their lead. Early in the period, LSU scored on a short 43-yard jaunt with Field going over from the Colorado 9 on a keeper play.

Late in the period, LSU backed the Buffaloes up to their goal line and Gene Sykes broke through to block Chuck McBride's attempted punt in the end zone and then fell on the ball for the third Tiger touchdown.

The Bengals didn't display their usual fine offensive effort and threw away several scoring chances.

Defensively, the Tigers lived up to their billing as they held the All-American end, Jerry Hillenbrand, well in check as a pass receiver and completely stopped the vaunted running of Colorado's Ted Woods and Bill Harris.

Colorado took to the air in an effort to best the Bengals and tossed 39 passes, a new Orange Bowl record.

But only once did the passing attack seriously threaten the Bengals.

It was LSU's second Orange Bowl victory and their third post-season triumph in the school's history.

Coach Paul Dietzel, who's rumored to leave Tigerland for West Point shortly, was carried off the field on the shoulders of his victorious youths.

Colorado failed to live up to its notice as an explosive football eleven and its All-Americans, guards Joe Romig and end Hillenbrand, didn't bother the Bengals.

LSU displayed an erratic passing game, hitting at will at times and then tossing interceptions.

It was no contest in the game statistics as LSU netted 206 yards on the ground to 30 for the Buffaloes and picked up 109 yards in the air to 105 for Colorado.

Colorado was able to complete only 12 of their 39 passes and most of those came late in the game when LSU sought to contain the long passes and gave the Buffs the short ones.

Ironically, not a single Colorado back netted yardage in double figures with their fullback Schweninger getting a net nine yards in five carries.

LSU's rushing was sparked by big Earl Gros who picked up 55 yards in ten carries. Field got 36 yards in eight attempts and

It was LSU's second Orange Bowl victory and their third post-season triumph in the school's history.

Score by Periods

Colorado	0	7	0	0	— 7
LSU	5	6	14	0	— 25

Harris got 26 yards in six tries.

Lynn Amedee connected on six of 12 passes for LSU while Field was successful on two of 6 tosses.

Weidner was the top aerial artist of the Buffs as he tossed 36 passes and connected on 11 for 98 yards.

LSU sputtered in the first quarter as they took the opening kickoff from their own 33 to the Colorado 14 where they bogged down and Harris booted a 30-yard field goal.

Colorado couldn't move the first time they got their hands on the ball and Kinchen's rush and block of McBride's punt resulted in a safety as the ball rolled out of the end zone.

LSU missed another scoring opportunity late in the first quarter when they drove to the Buffs' 28 and faltered.

Colorado came to life although they scored their lone touchdown before they got their first down.

In the first three minutes of the second quarter Field was trapped trying to pass, then uncorked a wobbly "wounded pigeon" that was gathered in by the fleet Schweninger, who scampered down the sidelines for 59 yards and a touchdown without anyone laying a hand on him.

LSU came right back to drive 78 yards with a 37-yard pass from Amedee to Ray Williams. It was the clutch play of the drive.

Wendell Harris set up the touchdown with a 14-yard scamper to the Buffs' 1-yard line. Cranford dove over on the next play for the Tigers' first score.

LSU got a quick touchdown in the first minutes of the third quarter when they almost blocked McBride's punt and the resulting punt rolled dead on the Colorado 42.

Moving on the ground, LSU got to the Colorado 21 where Field raced 12 yards around right end. He then added nine more on a sweep around left end for the Tigers' second touchdown.

LSU got another scoring chance late in the quarter when Woods fumbled and Sammy Odom recovered for LSU at the Colorado 49. The Bengals then marched to the Buffaloes' 19 where they gave up the ball, but a few seconds later Sykes made his great play and recovery on McBride's punt in the end zone and that wrapped up the scoring for both teams.

Colorado made their only sustained scoring threat early in the fourth quarter when they drove from their 42 where Woods recovered Gros' fumble. Colorado drove to the Tiger 11 where the threat failed.

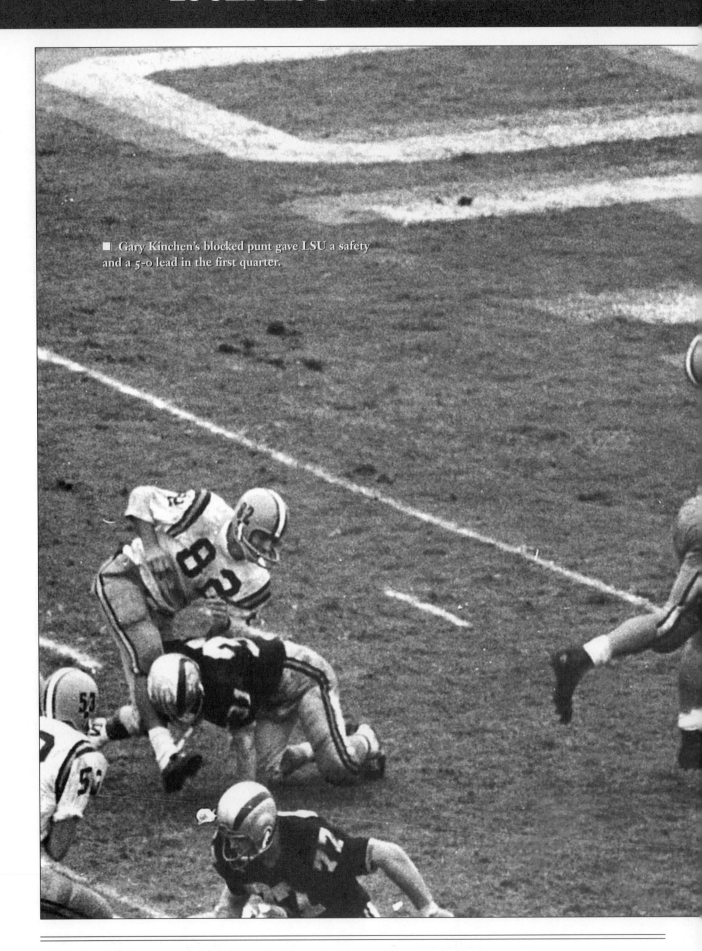

■ Gary Kinchen's blocked punt gave LSU a safety and a 5-0 lead in the first quarter.

Tigers Tame Longhorns, 13-0 in Cotton Bowl

By Bud Montet
The Advocate

Dallas, Tex.— *Jan. 1, 1963*

An alert LSU fighting Tiger eleven capitalized on fumble recoveries and pass interceptions to trounce the Texas Longhorns, 13-0, in a bruising battle that developed more offensive fireworks than anticipated.

It was the Bengals' second bowl victory in a row and was a fitting climax to Tigers coach Charlie McClendon finishing up his first year as head mentor of the LSU eleven.

Although Texas threatened twice in the game, LSU stayed in command from the time Lynn Amedee booted a 23-yard field goal. Amedee came back to get another field goal in the fourth period, this time a 37-yarder.

LSU's lone touchdown came on Jimmy Field's 23-yard gallop around left end after being rushed trying to find a receiver.

Amedee, the outstanding back of the game, proved to be the workhorse of the Tigers as his accurate toe accounted for the two field goals which now give him the all-time LSU record with seven in one year.

The Cotton Bowl record was a 22-yard field goal.

The lithe Baton Rougean also fired up the Tigers air with nine completions in 13 tries for 93-yards without an interception.

LSU's Jerry Stovall was a marked man as the tough Texas defenses keyed on him constantly. However, Stovall halted the final threat when he intercepted a Tommy Wade aerial deep in Tiger territory.

After that, Stovall managed to pick up 36 yards in 12 carries and played with all three units at one time or another.

Amedee, the Go Unit quarterback, walked off with the outstanding back of the game honors and joined Texas' Johnny Treadwell, the outstanding lineman, as the game's heroes.

Amedee, who for three years led the Bengals in total offense, finished his career in fine fashion. In the first half, Amedee hit on seven of nine passes for 74 yards.

In the scribes' voting, Amedee received 37 votes to four for Stovall and two for Jimmy Field, the White Team quarterback.

Treadwell received 20 votes while Bengals who received lineman votes were Jack Gates, another Tiger senior who

Score by Periods

LSU	0	3	7	3	— 13
Texas	0	0	0	0	— 0

played a fine game, Fred Miller, Ruffin Rodrique, Bill Truax, Jim Turner and Dennis Gaubatz.

The usual LSU defensive units played their usual hard-hitting ball and the host of White-shirted Bengals kept the Longhorns at bay most of the game.

Gates and Miller, along with Gaubatz, Rodrique, Buddy Hamic, Stovall, Gene Sykes, Dwight Robinson, and a host of others were responsible for the blanking of the Texas eleven.

Ironically, Stovall was in poor punting form but got some fine "LSU" bounces and came up with a brilliant 44-yard average.

His kicking rival, Ernie Koy of the famed Texas Koy family, averaged 47 yards and was largely instrumental in keeping the score down.

Koy kicked the Bengals back into the hole time after time.

LSU's other senior quarterback, Jimmy Field, had one of his finest days, scoring the lone touchdown and pitching four for eight passes for 39 yards. The Bengals' prime target was junior end Bill Truax, who grabbed three passes for 49 yards and late in the game caught a touchdown pass from Amedee but the play was nullified when LSU was caught with an ineligible receiver downfield.

LSU's win completed the SEC sweep of the New Year classics as Alabama downed Oklahoma and Ole Miss defeated Arkansas.

The first quarter wasn't five minutes old when LSU started a long drive from their 2 to the Longhorn 42 where they bogged down and had to kick.

Stovall and Koy then engaged in a fine kicking duel although LSU managed late in the period to get down to the Longhorns' 30-yard line.

Texas started the fireworks in the second quarter as they showed their best offensive drive of the day, going from their 15 to the Tiger 25 from where Tony Crosby tried a long field goal and missed badly.

LSU came right back to show their best offensive series of the game as they drove 80 yards and fought the fading seconds of the clock to get their first field goal with eight seconds left in the first period.

On the drive, Amedee's passing was the big factor and his

■ **LSU halfback Jerry Stovall huddles with his coach, Charlie McClendon, on the sidelines.**

22-yard toss to Truax set up the field goal.

After the Bengals moved to the Longhorns' 5, Amedee calmly booted the ball through the uprights with the clock ticking away.

LSU got a break on the second-half kickoff and made the most of it. Texas' Jerry Cook returned the punt back but was hit hard at his 34 and Amedee fell on the ball at that point.

An 11-yard Field-to-Gene Sykes pass set up the drive and two plays later Field faded to his right, seeking a receiver, but whirled and reversed his field, and raced to his left to go 22 yards for the lone touchdown of the game. On the sprint, Field made Texas' Joe Dixon miss him at the Longhorns' 5 as he neatly changed pace and side-stepped.

Amedee added the point-after, and LSU had a 10-0 lead.

Texas roared back and drove from their 32 to the Tiger 38 when a Johnny Genung passing attack failed.

The Bengals got a break near the end of the third period when a lineman tipped a Tommy Wade pass and Rodrique grabbed the ball for LSU at the midfield stripe.

LSU marched right down to the Longhorns' 7 with Jack Gates making a sensational diving catch of a Field-thrown aerial. However, LSU lost on successive plays as the period ended.

Texas started a march early in the fourth period as they moved to the LSU 32, where Hamic intercepted a Wade pass at the LSU 30.

The Bengals then took over and with Amedee pitching the ball moved to Texas' 22, where the Tiger star flipped a scoring pass to Truax only to have it nullified.

However after the penalty, Amedee ended the game's scoring with his second field goal for the afternoon.

Late in the fourth quarter, Koy kicked 72 yards dead on the LSU 2 to put the Bengals in a hole. After a short Stovall kick, the Longhorns drove to the Tiger 30 where Stovall intercepted a wild pass and LSU retained possession of the ball to the end of the game.

Following the game, tackle Red Estes and halfback Stovall signed pro contracts with the St. Louis Cardinals. LSU's convincing victory was a sweet one to Tigers coach McClendon and after the game the veteran mentor, serving his first year as LSU's head coach, had nothing but praise for his squad.

■ Charlie McClendon enjoys a victory ride following the Tigers' 13-0 win over Texas.

Two Minutes Told the Tale

By The Associated Press
The Advocate

Dallas— *Jan. 1, 1963*

"Two minutes in which Louisiana State scored 10 points proved the turning point of the Cotton Bowl football game," LSU coach Charlie McClendon observed today.

Louisiana State beat Texas, 13-0, and the victory was decisive since the Longhorns never got closer to LSU's goal line than the 25.

But it was that 2-minute period — part in the second quarter and part in the third — that vaulted LSU to its triumph.

LSU got another field goal late in the game, but Texas by then had been beaten down and disheartened by its mistakes and the unexpected strong LSU offense.

"I never felt safe with a 10-point lead going into the fourth quarter, because Texas has come back many times this year," said McClendon.

But it wasn't in the books this afternoon.

Texas coach Darrell Royal said, "I just didn't expect them to pass and catch like that. Their passing was tremendous and their receiving was great. They played fine football."

LSU tried 21 passes and completed 13 — an unusual output for the defense-minded Tigers.

But it was fumbling and pass interceptions that took the toll of the Longhorns' morale, Texas players admitted.

Bobby Gamblin, the Texas guard, said, "Anytime you fumble it's a mental letdown. But generally I don't think we played as well as we could."

McClendon declined to cite any one of his players as outstanding. "They were all outstanding and there were 18 seniors I was real proud of," he declared.

He said LSU passed more because of Texas' tight inside defense, which he praised. But he added that he thought Texas would pass more.

Pat Culpepper, the Texas linebacker, said the Tigers were the top team the Longhorns faced in quite a while.

Lynn Amedee, the LSU quarterback who was voted outstanding back of the game, said he was more sure of his second field goal than his first. He kicked a 23-yarder in the second period and a 37-yarder in the fourth quarter.

"I thought somebody might have tipped that first one," he said. This bettered the Cotton Bowl record by a yard.

■ LSU coach Edgar Wingard brought his Tigers to Havana to play in the first international football game.

LSU Routs Havana in Holiday Game

BY THE ASSOCIATED PRESS
The Advocate

Havana, Cuba— *Dec. 25, 1907*

The cadets of Louisiana State University, who are still on campus, not having gone home to spend the Christmas holidays with their families, are celebrating after receiving a cablegram from here, which announced that LSU had defeated the University of Havana, 56-0.

The LSU players expected and were confident that they would defeat the Havana team, but they did not expect to be able to pile up such a large score against the Cubans. The University of Havana is the largest institution of learning in Cuba. It has a number of former American players on its team and for this reason it should have been able to put up a good defense against LSU.

This game is the first international college football game ever played by an American team on foreign soil, the result was awaited with much interest. LSU draws thirty or forty students every year from Cuba.

■ Doug Moreau (80) pulls in a Pat Screen pass during the second half against the Orangemen.

Moreau Boots Tigers To 13-10 Win Over Syracuse

By Bud Montet
The Advocate

New Orleans, La. — *Jan. 1, 1965*

The gifted left toe of Doug Moreau spelled a hard-earned 13-10 victory for the LSU Tigers over the stubborn Syracuse Orangemen here today before 65,000 fans ... .

Moreau's 14th field goal of the season, an accurate 28-yarder with less than four minutes left in the game, broke a 10-all deadlock and gave LSU its second Sugar Bowl victory in seven appearances.

■ Syracuse's Floyd Little (44) teamed with Jim Nance in the Orangemen's fabled backfield.

The Tiger flanker set up his game winning effort by hauling down a long heave from quarterback Billy Ezell that was good for the Tigers' touchdown midway in the third quarter that tied the game when Ezell came right back to hit Joe Labruzzo with a "two-pointer" pass.

Moreau's fine efforts gained him the annual Fred Digby Most Valuable Player Award.

The Tigers played the first half with their usual disinterest in Sugar Bowl proceedings, and trailed, 10-2, going in at halftime.

Reversing their attitude in the second half the Bengals came

Score by Periods

LSU	2	0	8	3	— 13
Syracuse	10	0	0	0	— 10

to life and the first time they got their hands on the ball they marched 75 yards in seven plays and sustained the long drive despite a 15-yard penalty that threatened to mar their effort.

1965: LSU vs. Syracuse

■ On the sidelines, LSU coach Charlie McClendon listens to strategy from one of his players.

Syracuse's strong defensive tactics kept the Tiger running game completely bottled up in the first half and their good rushes forced the Tiger quarterbacks to hurry their throws with resulting poor efforts.

In the second half, the Bengals moved the big Orangemen to get their ground game going.

After LSU tied the game, Syracuse came back and sustained their longest drive to threaten to go ahead. The Orangemen drove from their 22 to the Tiger 13 where White Graves intercepted a Walley Mahle pass at the Bengals' 6.

In getting their winning three points, LSU drove from their 28 to the Syracuse 11 where a penalty marred the drive and Moreau then booted his 22-yarder for the victory.

Syracuse opened the game with a drive from midfield to the Tiger 7 where a 15-yard penalty pushed them back and Roger Smith booted a 23-yard field goal to put the Orangemen out in front, 3-0.

The Orangemen took advantage of a break near the end of the first period when their Dennis Reilly broke through and blocked a Buster Brown punt on the Tiger 45 and Syracuse's end, Brad Clarke, scooped up the ball on the Tiger 35 and raced over for the score. After the touchdown Smith added the point-after kick.

Between the two Syracuse scores, LSU managed to get a safety with big George Rice breaking through and hauling fleet Floyd Little down in the end zone.

■ LSU quarterback Billy Ezell (11) sprints for a first down.

■ **NO PLACE TO GO: Jim Nance (35) runs into a roadblock of LSU Tigers.**

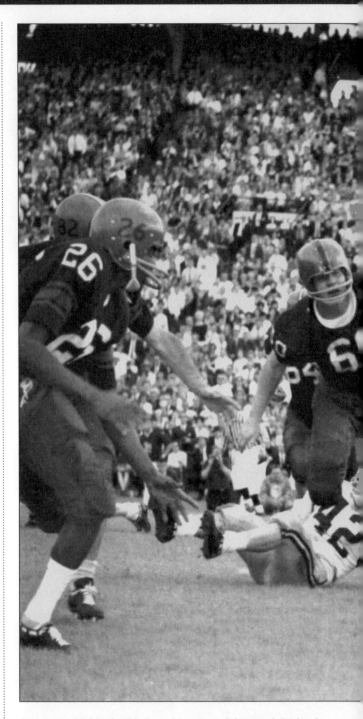

Brown's boot dead at the Syracuse 3 set up the play for the Tigers.

The Bengals held a slim lead in rushing with a net 161 yards to 151 for the Orangemen but picked up 199 yards in the air to only 52 for the Orangemen.

LSU hit on six of 15 aerials but two proved to be key plays, Ezell's long pass to Moreau for the Tiger touchdown and Pat Screen's 36-yard toss to Joe Labruzzo late in the final period set up the game-winning field goal.

Ezell's "two-pointer" pitch to Labruzzo also proved a key aerial in the game.

LSU passed up an early scoring opportunity when

Syracuse's Mahle fumbled on his 43-yard line and Richard Granier recovered for the Bengals midway through the period.

In the second quarter, a pair of short kicks by Syracuse's Rich King gave the Bengals good field position that they failed to exploit.

LSU's long touchdown drive featured short dashes by Labruzzo and fullback Don Schwab and a crucial first down 9-yard pass from Ezell to Labruzzo.

After marching to the Syracuse 40, LSU was guilty of a holding penalty and pushed back to their 43. On the next play, Ezell faked a pitch down the middle and then picked up Moreau at the Syracuse 30 and the fleet Tiger flanker gathered

in the pass without breaking stride and moved quickly to the Syracuse goal line. Moreau had beaten his defender by yards.

LSU's Schwab once again proved the workhorse of the backfield carrying the ball 17 times for a net 81 yards to outgain the fabled pair of Jim Nance and Floyd Little.

Gawain DiBetta ran 13 times and netted 18 yards while Labruzzo carried the ball 10 times and netted 25.

Ezell completed two of five passes for 67 yards and Screen pitched 10 passes and hit on four for 47.

Big Nance proved an erratic runner but managed to net 70 yards on 15 carries.

■ **Joe Labruzzo (22) sweeps outside against Syracuse. Labruzzo's running set up the game-winning field goal.**

Syracuse's regular quarterback, Mahle, started the game at right half and proved a troublesome runner, picking up a net 23 yards on seven carries.

The victory was a sweet one for the Bengals who have had their troubles in the Sugar Bowl in the past. It was the first meeting between LSU and Syracuse.

The Tigers' win was the second bowl victory for LSU coach Charlie McClendon in three tries as a head grid mentor.

■ Joe Labruzzo (22) scored both of the Tigers' touchdowns in the second quarter.

LSU Halts Hogs in Cotton Bowl, 14-7

By Bud Montet
The Advocate

Dallas, Tex.— *Jan. 1, 1966*

The Fighting Tigers of LSU who made a practice crusade of "Never 23" made good on the slippery turf of the Cotton Bowl when they bested the Arkansas Porkers, 14-7, and broke their win streak at 22.

Score by Periods

LSU	0	14	0	0	— 14
Arkansas	7	0	0	0	— 7

The clutch running of Joe Labruzzo, who scored both Bengal touchdowns in the second quarter, some fine offensive blocking by big Tiger tackle Dave McCormick and a sticky defense that never gave up although constantly threatened by the fleet Hogs were the big factors in the Bengals' upset victory.

■ **LSU's 14-7 win over Arkansas halted the Razorbacks' 22-game win streak.**

All during the pre-game practice sessions LSU coach Charlie McClendon dressed out his redshirt squads in red jerseys, numbered 23, a constant reminder that the mighty Porkers were trying for their 23rd straight victory in the Cotton Bowl.

Arkansas, ranked No. 2 in both major polls, constantly threatened during the game but were able to get but one touchdown, a 19-yard aerial, from Jon Brittenum to Bobby Crockett.

The score came in the first period to give the Porkers a 7-0 lead.

The Bengals struck back the hard way early in the second period when they drove 80 yards, sticking on the ground and overcoming a costly 15-yard roughing penalty.

Nelson Stokely, the Tiger sophomore quarterback who has been sidelined with injuries, got the drive under way and moved the Bengals from their 20 to the Porkers' 43 where he

1966: LSU vs. Arkansas

reinjured his knee and had to leave the game.

On the drive, Stokely hit Schwab with an 18-yard pass for a first down and turned in two runs of four and seven yards.

On this drive, LSU got a first down at the Porkers' 9 and in three carries Labruzzo punched the ball over for the first score and Doug Moreau added the point-after kick to tie the score.

The Bengals moved into the lead a few minutes later when Ronnie South and Nix fumbled on an attempted handoff and Bill Bass recovered for LSU at the Hogs' 34.

LSU moved on in to score in seven plays. Labruzzo got the Bengals a first down at the Porkers' 16, carried to the five on a fine 11-yard gallop and then bulled over left tackle behind blocks by McCormick in three plays. Moreau's extra-point boot was good and LSU led, 14-7, at intermission.

Although they remained behind, the Porkers continued to threaten. Early in the third period they moved to the Bengals' 15 where Ernest Magoire pulled probably the weirdest defensive stunt of the season to halt the drive.

Lindsey, on a counter, got behind Magoire, who desperately swung his leg out and Lindsey tripped over it for a seven-yard loss. This drive finally ended with South missing on an attempted 46-yard field goal try.

LSU failed to make a single first down in the third period but they came back at the start of the final period to stage a 54-yard drive to the Porkers' 2-yard line, where Moreau missed an easy 19-yard try for a field goal, which at the time looked like a costly mistake.

Arkansas took to the air and drove from their 20 to the Tiger 36 with Brittenum tossing strikes to Crockett for eight, 16, and 18 yards before Jerry Joseph broke up the threat at the Tiger 20 when he made a fine interception of a Brittenum pass.

With less than three minutes left in the game, Brittenum again mounted a drive that carried to the Tiger 24 before the final whistle caught the Porkers. The unhappy Hogs were a disappointed group marching off the field.

Arkansas' 22-game win streak was the longest of the current season.

The victory kept the Bengals' Cotton Bowl record intact — the Tigers having never lost a Cotton Bowl fray. In their first one — 1947, they tied the Arkansas Porkers, and in 1963 they bested Texas, 13-0.

Today's win was a sweet one for Coach McClendon, who was highly criticized midway during the regular season when he lost his No. 1 quarterback, Stokely, and quickly dropped resounding games to Ole Miss and Alabama.

However, McClendon pulled Pat Screen back into action and the plucky New Orleans youth played his first game of the year against the Porkers.

Screen called a fine game, keeping possession of the ball and risking passes only when he had to gain a first down.

Labruzzo's great clutch running was a potent factor as was the all-around defensive play.

LSU did just what Coach McClendon predicted they would — not stop the potent Arkansas offense but blunt it enough to

go on and win.

Labruzzo's running gained for him the outstanding back award. Others who received votes were Screen 10, and Arkansas' Harry Jones four.

Dave McCormick, the LSU tackle, gained the outstanding lineman award over Hog end Bobby Crockett in a close vote, 22-18.

Labruzzo carried the ball 21 times and netted 69 yards. Jim Dousay had a fine afternoon with 14 carries and a net 38.

Jones, one of the quickest backs in America, proved the toughest Hog for the Bengals to handle. The fleet back ran 10 times and netted 79 yards for a 7.9 average. The Porkers hard running Bobby Burnett, picked up 44 yards on 12 carries.

For LSU big George Rice, Mike Robichaux, John Garlington, Mike Duhon and David Strange played outstanding ball.

LSU's linebacking duo of Mike Vincent and Bill Bass turned in their finest effort of the season.

The Bengals rushed for a net of 166 yards and passed for 100

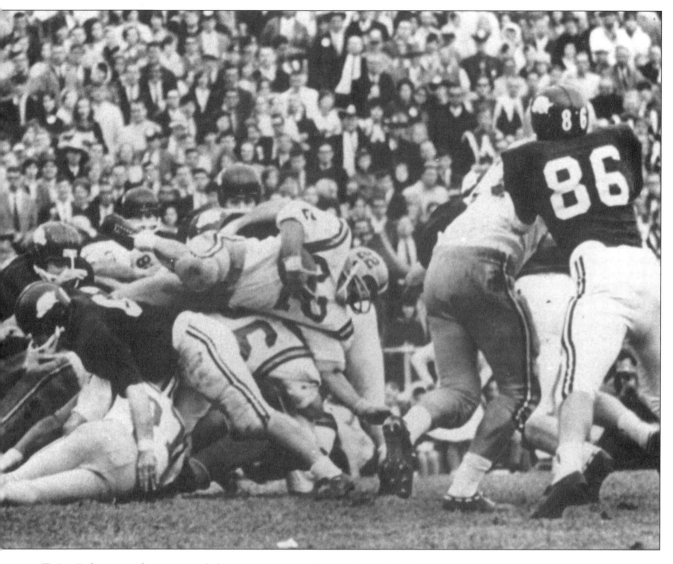

■ Joe Labruzzo, who was voted the game's outstanding back, rushed for 69 yards on 21 carries.

yards for a total offensive effort of 266 yards. Arkansas rushed for 129 yards but passed for 177 in the air for a total of 306.

The Porkers' Crockett caught 10 passes to set a new Cotton Bowl record for receptions.

LSU was the victim of several costly penalties that threatened to stymie them.

In the first period, when the Bengals were trying to get back in the game after the Porker score, Screen scrambled all over the field and finally tossed a 47-yard pass to Moreau at the Porkers' 20 but the Bengals had an ineligible receiver downfield.

Coming back with their tying touchdown, the Tigers had to overcome a 15-yard penalty that set them back.

Screen hit on seven of 10 pass attempts while rival Brittenum hit on 15 of 24.

Masters was the top LSU receiver with four receptions for 45 yards. Arkansas' Crockett caught 10 for 129 yards and a touchdown.

■ LSU outrushed the Hogs, 166 yards to 129.

...

MAC: 'Made 'Em Play Our Way'

By The Associated Press
The Advocate

Dallas, Tex.— *Jan. 1, 1966*

"We slowed them down and made them play our type of game," explained Tigers coach Charlie McClendon, after Louisiana State snapped Arkansas' 22-game winning streak with a 14-7 Cotton Bowl triumph.

"I told you writers before the game that we couldn't match their speed, and we couldn't. But we played control ball and came up with the big play.

"Our kids followed instructions right to the end."

McClendon called the upset on this gloomy New Year's Day his greatest thrill since his playing days with Kentucky and the Wildcats' Sugar Bowl victory over Oklahoma.

That triumph severed a 32-game Oklahoma winning streak.

McClendon said he didn't think his Tigers made a single wrong decision and "We didn't have a fumble or single pass interception."

"There were times when it looked like we should pass," he continued. "But we weren't going to put the ball into the air and give them the chance for that interception. They'll kill you."

McClendon had promised that his thrice-beaten Bengals would have a couple of surprises for the second-ranked Razorbacks.

However, this generally was restricted to fluctuating offensive formations and defensive plays."

"I just told Pat Screen (LSU quarterback) before the game, 'Let's go after them with everything we've got.' He said, 'Coach, I think I'm ready.' "

McClendon said he could not pinpoint a single play as the turning point in the game, although the fourth-period interception by Jerry Joseph was a chiller.

The junior halfback said LSU shifted from a man-to-man pass defense to a half man-to-man and half zone to contain Arkansas Bobby Crockett.

"He'd been going wide on me," Joseph said. "I decided the next time he came down wide, I was going to cut in front of him. He did, and I cut in front and got it."

The interception came at the LSU 20 and punctured a spirited Arkansas scoring threat.

Doug Moreau, who missed what could have been a critical 19-yard field goal attempt in the final period, said he had no excuses.

"I just missed it," he said. "Nervousness didn't have anything to do with it."

McClendon had noted that a successful kick by Moreau would have iced the game for LSU.

■ **The Tigers' solid defense was the key in LSU's upset win.**

1966 Cotton Bowl Remembered

BY SAM KING
The Advocate

Baton Rouge, La. — *Nov. 18, 1995*

Today's Southeastern Conference "no-contest" between LSU and Arkansas couldn't have been more fitting for the 30-year reunion of the 1965 LSU football team.

Heavy underdogs, outmanned and lightly regarded, coach Charles McClendon's team defied all odds and upset Arkansas, 14-7, in the fabled Jan. 1, 1966, Cotton Bowl.

The victory cost the undefeated Razorbacks, who had won 22 straight games, a possible national championship.

More importantly, however, McClendon says the upset created an unbelievable bond among members of the Tigers, who have reunions virtually every year.

Forty-seven players and coaches from that '65 team gathered this weekend and relived their memories, prior to, during and after the present Tigers' 28-0 rout of No. 14 Arkansas.

In fact, they made their entrance into Tiger Stadium, walked beneath the goal post and formed lines for the Tigers to run through onto the field. It was quite a salute for a deserving group.

"This group is the tightest football team I've ever known," McClendon said. "This is what winning a tough game like that does.

"It is amazing how it affected all of these players," McClendon said. "I don't know what the word for it is, but it really brought them together. They were together all year, but the way they came together for that game was unbelievable."

McClendon repeated one of his favorite stories about the game. Because LSU's record was 7-3 and the Razorbacks were hogging the national spotlight, McClendon said Arkansas and Texas fans and the media felt LSU shouldn't even be playing in the Cotton Bowl.

"We had a situation where some Arkansas fans, the night before the game, poked fun at the Tigers as we walked up some stairs," McClendon said. "I can still see these ladies all dressed in red looking at them and one of them exclaimed, 'Well, they

■ **Charlie McClendon and LSU athletic director Jim Corbett celebrate the Tigers' win.**

did show up.'

"You don't embarrass an injured Tiger," McClendon said. "You don't play games with them."

Then came game day.

"They came out and they were dedicated to doing their jobs," he said. "They really had fire in their eyes. They were ready to take on King Kong. It's amazing how it brought everybody together.

"I knew, somewhere down the line, something good was really going to come out of what happened to that team," McClendon said. "It's amazing how they feel this way. They'll feel the same way 20 years from now.

"They'll still be getting together. I wish I could say I'd be around, but I can't.

"I told them one thing, though," he said. "I may not be here at your next reunion, but you can count on one thing, I'm going to be looking over your shoulders to hear what you have to say about me."

Tigers Foil Dietzel's Return

By Bud Montet
The Advocate

Baton Rouge, La. — *Sept. 17, 1966*

oach Charlie McClendon stepped out of the shadows tonight at Tiger Stadium as his gridders presented him with a 28-12 victory over his old boss Paul Dietzel and his South Carolina Gamecocks, before 67,512 rabid Bengal fans.

LSU's partisan rooters also gave Dietzel a personal setback when the Dietzel-inspired "longest boo in history ... " failed to materialize when the former Tiger coach brought his eleven on the field.

The Bengals scored the second time they got their hands on the ball with brilliant little Nelson Stokley going eleven yards around right end and Steve Daniels' placement gave the Bengals a 7-0 lead which they never lost.

South Carolina came right back to go 76 yards for their long sustained drive of the night with their Jimmy Killen going over from the Gamecock 1. Mike Robichaux blocked the try for the extra point.

LSU soon moved ahead as they sustained an 80-yard drive that was climaxed by Gawain DiBetta's two-yard punch early in the second period.

This trio of long drives ended the sustained effort by both teams who then turned to weird football to pile up the rest of

Score by Periods

South Carolina	6	0	6	0 —	12
LSU	7	7	7	7 —	28

■ Paul Dietzel coached LSU to the 1958 national title.

the points on the scoreboard.

Midway in the third period LSU got their third score when Carolina's Jeff Jowers attempted to punt and fumbled the pass from center, ran to the sidelines where he tried a running punt, only to have big Jack Dyer of LSU block the effort and knock the ball over the goal line where George Bevan, LSU's sophomore linebacker, fell on it for the touchdown.

Trailing, 21-6, South Carolina got back into the game when their Bobby Bryant took a 46-yard Mitch Worley punt on his 23 and raced for a 77-yard touchdown jaunt as the clock expired for the third period, the first of the touchdowns to be scored as time ran out.

In an odd fourth period South Carolina was held deep in its own territory and on three occasions tried to run out of trouble on fourth down.

The first time their desperate gamble failed, LSU took over on the Gamecock 27 but after making a first down at the 15 Stokley tossed an interception.

Late in the game with 1:06 left in the fray, Carolina gambled and lost with big Mike Robichaux tossing Mike Fair for a six-yard loss and the Bengals taking over on the Gamecock 18.

This time little Freddie Haynes dove over the goal line as the game expired. Ronnie Manton's boot for the extra point gave LSU its 28-12 victory. The Bengals dominated the erratic contest that was heralded as one of the top games of the opening day of the 1966 season.

LSU gained 283 yards on the ground but completed only one pass in seven attempts.

The usually cautious Dietzel let his quarterback, Fair, toss 17 passes and the junior star hit on six for 71 yards.

South Carolina gained a net of 101 on the ground.

Dietzel, who built the game up as a vendetta on the part of the Tiger coaches and gridders, surprised all of his old Baton Rouge followers when he gambled constantly on fourth down in the opening minutes.

The blond mentor, who was making his debut with Carolina, also pulled out his "shotgun" offense early in the fray with his star, Fair, moving back and taking direct passes from the center.

It was a sweet victory for Coach McClendon who has coached LSU to four straight bowl appearances, but has been under the shadow of his former boss at LSU.

Dietzel, who built the game up as a vendetta on the part of the Tiger coaches and gridders, surprised all of his old Baton Rouge followers when he gambled constantly on fourth down in the opening minutes. The blond mentor, who was making his debut with Carolina, also pulled out his "shotgun" offense early in the fray with his star, Fair, moving back and taking direct passes from the center.

The Bengal mentors uncovered some fine bright young prospects in Tommy (Trigger) Allen and Maurice LeBlanc. Allen carried 12 times and piled up 40 yards while LeBlanc, still slowed down from a pulled muscle, stepped through for 63 net yards in 12 tires.

However, it remained for the plucky little Stokley to lead the squad's rushing attack with a net 78 yards in 15 carries.

Fullback Gawain DiBetta piled up 53 yards on 12 carries.

Defensively, the Bengals of LSU showed flashes of their vaulted form that has made them feared in southern grid circles, but they broke down badly on kickoff and punt return coverage.

South Carolina's Bryant returned three punts for 89 yards with his long one, the 77-yard touchdown jaunt, coming after he picked up a fine block at midfield from teammate Wally Orrel.

Only one Tiger had a shot at Bryant and DiBetta was too far out of the play to make a stop although he desperately dove at the flying Gamecock safety at the goal line.

Bryant returned two kickoffs for 67 yards and South Carolina's Benny Galloway returned a pair of kickoffs for 48 yards.

LSU's first sustained drive, the second time they got their hands on the ball, was sparked by the fine running of Allen, DiBetta and then Stokley, who took over at the 25 and lugged the ball over the goal line in two tries. Stokley and DiBetta started the second sustained scoring drive and LeBlanc, making his debut as a Bengal, came in to contribute runs of eight, six and eight yards again.

Only in their first quarter drive did the Gamecocks show consistency, although they hung on throughout the game and took advantage of Tigers mistakes to halt threatening drives.

Defensively, after their first lapse in the first period, the Bengals showed a stiffened attitude and flankmen John Garlington and Robichaux constantly harried Fair and his teammates and Mike Pharis made key tackles as well as blocking one of the two blocked Carolina punts.

Big John Demarie, the defensive tackle, made several key tackles to halt Carolina in Tiger territory. Tommy Fussell, always a ball hawk for the Tigers, recovered a fumble to halt a Carolina threat.

The game ends the current series between the Carolina Gamecocks and the Tigers.

■ Nelson Stokely (14) eludes a Wyoming tackler in the Cowboys' secondary.

Tigers Rally to Lasso Wyoming, 20-13

BY BUD MONTET
The Advocate

New Orleans, La. — *Jan. 1, 1968*

The "Comeback" LSU Tigers did it again today as they spotted the Wyoming Cowboys a 13-point first half lead before storming back to grab a 20-13 victory in their eighth Sugar Bowl Classic appearance.

The Cowboys' stubborn defense completely halted the Tigers in the first half as the Bengals were able to make just one first down, only 33 yards on the ground, and five yards in the air.

The victory was the third time a Charlie McClendon-led Bengal eleven has humbled an unbeaten eleven in a bowl appearance.

Wyoming, ranked sixth by one major wire service, were riding a 14-game win streak.

Tiger elevens halted a long Texas Longhorns streak in the Cotton Bowl and three years ago handed the Arkansas Porkers a Cotton Bowl defeat to halt a Frank Broyles' streak of 22 games.

The game was McClendon's fifth appearance in a bowl in his six-year tenure as head grid mentor.

LSU got two scoring opportunities in the first period but the Cowboys held them at bay with jarring tackles and alert defensive play.

Jim Kiick, Wyoming's co-captain, opened the second quarter when he broke away from a host of Tigers to score from one yard out and Jerry Depoyster's boot put the Cowboys out in front, 7-0.

Depoyster then got field goals of 24 and 49 yards — the 49-yarder a new Sugar Bowl record. Depoyster set another record when he kicked four times for an average 49.0 yards per boot.

After LSU went in front, 20-13, with but 4 minutes and 32 seconds left, the Cowboys fought back and threatened as the result of a freak 54-yard pass play.

With less than a minute to play, Paul Toscano, the Cowboy quarterback, tossed a long pass to the Tiger 35 where a pair of Bengals batted the ball forward and the Cowboys' George Anderson grabbed the ball and headed for the Tiger goal. But, he was hauled down on the Bengal 17-yard line by Barton Frye. On the final play of the game, Toscano hit his favorite receiver, Gene Huey, who was pulled down on the Tiger five by Kent, who was injured on the play.

LSU's Glenn Smith, a sophomore tailback, who put new life in the Tiger attack in the second half with some fine running, was chosen as the game's Most Valuable Player.

Smith carried 16 times and netted 74 yards for a 4.7 average.

LSU's senior linebacker, Benny Griffin, intercepted two Toscano aerials and was a standout for the Bengals on defense.

It was Griffin's second interception and his 17-yard run back to the Wyoming 31 set-up the winning score for the Tigers.

Another Tiger standout was Tommy Morel, the fleet Tiger end, who grabbed two touchdown passes — his second the winning score, a 16-yard grab between a pair of Wyoming defenders.

The Bengals managed to finish the game with a net 151 yards running and net 91 in the air, while the Cowboys picked up 167 yards on the ground and 239 in the air.

Stokley hit on only six passes in 20 attempts while Toscano hit on 14 of 23.

Score by Periods

LSU	0	0	7	13	— 20
Wyoming	0	13	0	0	— 13

However, the little Bengal pitched a pair of scoring aerials and climaxed his first full-time season with a creditable performance.

Coach Charlie McClendon reached deep into his reserve crew today and had a half dozen reserves in the lineup when the Tigers marched 80 yards for their first score with Smith going over from the 1-yard line.

On this drive, it was Smith's clutch running and Stokley's pitching that kept the drive alive.

A few minutes later, LSU drove 52 yards for the deadlocking score with Stokley pitching to Morel for eight yards and the score.

Roy Hurd, who booted the first Tiger extra point, missed the second and left the game tied at 13-all with 11:39 left in the game.

LSU had a chance in the final seven minutes when Tommy Youngblood intercepted Kiick's halfback pass at the Tiger 35, but the Bengals couldn't move.

Then came the Griffin interception, the second of the day for the Tiger linebacker, and LSU moved in for the victory after Griffin's runback to the Cowboy 31 set up the drive.

Smith hit off right end for 16 yards and a first down at the Wyoming 15 and then made two yards before Stokley found Morel in the end zone and hit him with a fine pitch. Hurd's boot gave the Bengals a 20-13 lead with 4:32 left but the Cowboys never quit and came back to end the game with the ball on the Tiger 5.

Before the Cowboys made their desperate last-second drive to tie the game or win, LSU's Youngblood hit Toscano hard on a driving tackle, forcing a fumble, and Tiger defensive end Johnny Garlington recovered for LSU at the Cowboy 43.

The Bengals attempted to run out the clock but Wyoming used their remaining timeouts to stop the ticking clock and LSU was forced to punt with 45 seconds left to play.

Then came the fluke pass that almost cost LSU a victory when Tiger defenders batted the ball into Anderson's hands and the play was a 54-yard aerial after Frye bumped the big end on the Tiger 17.

Depoyster lived up to his great kicking reputation, despite having his first field goal blocked by Tiger Fred Michaelson.

Depoyster's 49-yard field goal broke the old Sugar Bowl mark of 48 yards set by Alabama's Tim Davis' old mark of 48-plus set in 1964.

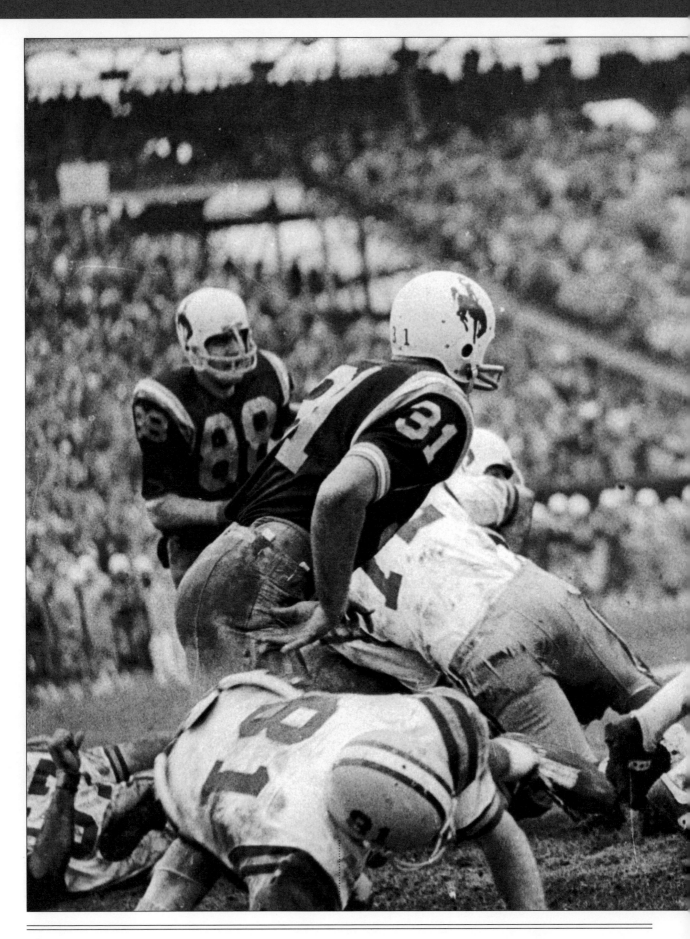

Glenn Smith (26)
dives through the
Wyoming defense for
LSU's first touchdown.

1934: LSU vs. Oregon

Tigers Come From Behind to Defeat Oregon, 13-14

The Advocate

Baton Rouge, La. — *Dec. 14, 1934*

Snapping back with flashy scoring thrusts after being out-classed for nearly half the game and with defeat staring starkly at them, LSU's gridmen overcame a two-touchdown lead today to defeat Oregon, 14-13.

The accurate extra-point kicking toe of Ernie Seago, the brilliant Abe Mickal's understudy kicker, and Oregon derision, that put misjudged faith in a pass instead of a kick for the extra point, directly accounted for LSU's triumph.

Oregon's emerald-jerseyed warriors, playing smart, fast football, and led by the dashing backs, Frank Michek and Maurice Van Vilet, hammered and passed two touchdowns in the first and second periods to lead LSU, 13-0.

Early in the second period, Van Vilet, as if to make up for the missed extra point, broke through left guard from the Tiger 26-yard line and dodged LSU tacklers to the Tiger goal line.

Score by Periods

LSU	0	7	0	7 — 14
Oregon	6	7	0	0 — 13

This time V. Walker, a substitute end, kicked the extra point.

Then LSU coach Biff Jones, after sending in his reserves, who fought viciously, kept the Oregonians at bay for a while, thus allowing his first stringers to get a new strategy and shot them back in. From then on it was a different game.

Mickal began zipping passes to Jeff Barrett, the LSU end and crack receiver, and drove to the Oregon 4-yard line. From there, Mickal slipped a flat one to Barrett over the goal line. Seago kicked the extra point.

With the end of the game nearing, and with Mickal out, Jesse Fatheree, the race-horse of the Tiger squad, tore around left end for 39 yards and a touchdown. Seago's point-after kick sealed the win.

64

Jones & Huey at Odds, LSU Coach Rumored to Resign

The Advocate

Baton Rouge, La. — *Dec. 14, 1934*

Lawrence (Biff) Jones, the LSU football coach said tonight he had "nothing to say" about reports that he had resigned after today's game with the University of Oregon.

Reports were rampant in Baton Rouge tonight that Jones, an army captain and former football coach at West Point, had resigned after an argument with Senator Huey P. Long.

"Have you resigned because of any difficulty with Senator Long?" he was asked.

"I have nothing to say," was his only reply.

Senator Long this year has been an exuberant booster of the LSU grid team and at one time financed a trip for almost the entire LSU student body to the game with Vanderbilt at Nashville, Tenn.

Last month, he masterminded the holding of a mock election on the university campus in which Abe Mickal, the star

LSU halfback, was named a "state senator."

Long had made all the plans for Mickal to take a "seat" in the senate during the last special session but Coach Jones conferred with Long and the elaborate "induction" ceremony was called off.

When efforts were made by telephone to reach Senator Long at his hotel for comment, attendants at his suite announced he had retired for the night and could not be disturbed until morning.

Jones appeared angry as he received questions regarding his reported resignation.

"It's too late to talk," he asserted. "I have nothing to say. I've had a hard season and I'm tired."

Athletic Director T.F. Heard of LSU said he knew nothing of the reported resignation. "I've very sorry, but I don't know anything about it," he declared.

Jones refused to talk to newsmen who sought to interview him at his home, other than to repeat he had "nothing to say."

■ LSU coach Biff Jones lectures his team at practice.

The Kingfish, Biff & the Golden Thirties

BY SCOTT RABALAIS
The Advocate

A benevolent dictator. A demagogue. A consummate politician. And the most ardent and powerful LSU football fan of all time.

Huey Pierce Long was all those things. And from the late 1920's until his assassination in 1935, Louisiana was his state, LSU was his university, and the Tigers were his football team.

When it came to LSU, nothing was too audacious for Long. He recruited players then invited them to live in the governor's mansion. He even once tried to make one of his favorite Tigers a state senator. He transformed the school's band from a small military outfit to a marching musical army. He railroaded the railroads into providing low-cost transportation for LSU students to away games, and bluffed a circus into altering its schedule so it wouldn't draw fans away from a crucial home game.

Huey Long could do it all because he had all the power. His power came from the common people, the ones in later years to whom he preached "Share our wealth," and the people loved football. It is, and was even in Long's day, one of the few spectacles that can draw tens of thousands of people to one place at one time, and the game's popularity, energy and excitement captivated Long.

Though a one-time Tulane law student, Long became a devoted LSU fan. He immersed himself in football and in the Tigers, ecstatic in their victories and laid low by their defeats.

Huey became, as former LSU All-American and later coach Gus Tinsley once recalled, quite well versed in the intricacies of the game. Once in a chance meeting with Tinsley on the state capitol steps following the 1934 season, Long began drawing plays on the slabs of stone with a pencil. His ideas were, Tinsley remembered, very good for someone without a coach or player's knowledge of the game.

In 1928, Long was a newly elected governor and Russ Cohen was LSU's new head football coach, having succeeded Mike Donahue. Cohen's Tigers got off to a superb 4-0 start and were preparing for their then annual battle with Arkansas in Shreveport when Long arrived at the practice fields.

■ **Huey Long enjoys his favorite pastime, leading the LSU band.**

Long came to explain to Cohen the importance of the game in terms of how it affected the Kingfish. He hated everyone in Shreveport, Long told Cohen, and everyone in Shreveport hated him. Therefore, to Long's way of thinking, the Tigers simply had to win.

■ **LSU legendary halfback Abe Mickal led the Tigers to a 23-3-3 record from 1933-1935.**

They didn't, falling 7-0, but Long wasn't in a mood to call for Cohen's head. He was at this stage of his political life not entirely caught up in calling the shots at LSU, but would grow into that role soon enough.

Long did quickly become a recruiter for the Tigers. Shortly after Huey came to power, Cohen told him that he was interested in a hot prep prospect named Joe Almokary. According to Dan Hardesty's book, *The Louisiana Tigers*, this was the gist of Huey's recruiting pitch:

Long: "Are you going to come to LSU?"

Almokary: "I don't know. I think maybe I'll go to Centenary (which had a strong football program at the time)."

Long: "What in the world would you want to go to Centenary for? They can't teach you anything but the Bible, and I know more about the Bible than they do. If you come to LSU you can get any kind of education you want. What do you want to be when you finish college?"

Almokary: "I would like to be a lawyer."

Long: "You want to be a lawyer. I don't think you would be a good lawyer. You look to me like you would make a good engineer. They can't teach you engineering at Centenary. You're good at mathematics, aren't you?"

Almokary: "Yes, sir."

Long: "You're good at algebra?"

Almokary: "Yes, sir."

Long: "Geometry?"

Almokary: "Yes, sir."

Long: "Good in calculus?"

Almokary: "Yes, sir."

Long: "You see, I told you that you would make a good engineer. You certainly should come to LSU."

Almokary admitted afterward he didn't have much idea what Long was talking about, but was scared to say so. He lettered at LSU for three years.

Late in 1930, Long's growing grip on LSU football and the state was becoming quite evident. That fall he was elected to the U.S. Senate, although he served out his term as governor and did not officially take his senate seat until 1932.

Meanwhile, the Tigers had slipped to an indifferent 6-3 record with a 33-0 thrashing by Alabama, and the LSU Board of Supervisors voted to move Cohen from the job of football coach to the athletic director's office. However, the new coach had to be approved by the school's newly appointed president, James Monroe Smith, and Governor Long.

LSU's 1930 finale was a narrow 12-7 loss to a strong Tulane team. But instead of sealing Cohen's demise, the game gave him new life. The Monday following the Tulane game, Cohen signed a new three-year contract in the Governor's Mansion. Cohen was the only man in Louisiana, Long informed him, that had his name on a contract without first providing Huey with his undated resignation.

Long delighted in providing LSU with players, and with providing certain favored players with all the comforts the mansion had to offer.

One such player was Art Foley, a brilliant halfback from Oklahoma. Foley's stay in Baton Rouge was brief — he played just one game before a lung ailment forced him to leave Louisiana's humid climate — but while he was with the team he was Huey's house guest.

So were Tigers Ed Khoury, LSU's team captain in 1931, Billy Butler and Sid Bowman. They feasted on steak, corn-bread, turnip greens and pineapple upside down cake twice a day and washed it down with soured milk (for some reason, Huey believed milk was best if it had been allowed to sit out until it turned sour).

But all of Huey's efforts as a cheerleader, power broker and training table expert turned out to be in vain. Cohen's Tigers struggled through a 5-4 campaign, culminating with a 34-7 pounding by Rose Bowl-bound Tulane. Cohen was out, and Huey was on the search for a new coach.

Finding quality candidates for the job wasn't easy because of one thing: Huey's intrusive presence. They had reason to worry, given Lewis Gottlieb's description of the coaching search in *The Louisiana Tigers*, a search that resulted in the hiring of Lawrence (Biff) Jones:

"I was on the athletic council at the time, but I had absolutely no part in his selection," Gottlieb said. "Nobody really did but Huey. We didn't know anything about it until we were told that Jones was going to be the new coach. He had a good record and nobody complained about the choice, but I'm not sure that it would have done any good if anybody had complained."

Jones had been head coach at Army from 1927-29 and was at the time assistant athletic director at West Point. It took some convincing and a personal request to General Douglas MacArthur, then the Army chief of staff, but Jones finally became LSU's head coach. So that he didn't have to resign from the Army to take the job, the new coach was detailed to LSU as a military science instructor.

■ **Gaynell (Gus) Tinsley was a two-time All-American in 1935 and 1936.**

One of Jones' first acts as head coach was to convince Long to stay out of the pep talk business. For once, Huey listened to someone else's wishes and kept any desires to make emotional pleas to the team to a minimum — for the time being.

Satisfied that he had a good coach capable of building him a winner, Huey began to turn his attention toward improving the LSU marching band — and becoming its bandleader. For the Tigers first road game of 1932, an Oct. 1 trip to Houston, Long led a 150-cadet formation through the downtown streets. Sometimes he was drum major, other times cheerleader, always in control.

"Huey loved the band, LSU and the football team," said Lew Williams, LSU's real drum major from 1929 to 1934. "He did everything he could to help us."

LSU's record in 1932 was a modest 6-3-1, though it did include a 14-0 victory over its most despised rival, Tulane. Among Tiger fans, including Long, optimism reigned as LSU became one of 13 schools to form the Southeastern Conference in 1933.

That year the Tigers enjoyed their most successful season since the perfect 10-0 campaign of 1908. LSU posted the odd-looking record of 7-0-3 and 3-0-2 in the SEC, finishing percentage points behind 5-0-1 Alabama for the league's first title. Expectations rose even high for 1934.

The schedule would prove to be too tough for LSU to post

■ George (Pinky) Rohm was a stellar halfback for the Tigers from 1935-37.

a brilliant record, though the Tigers went 7-2-2. However, Huey was in unprecedented form, his antics the equivalent of an undefeated season in their own right.

From the outset, Long had Jones squirming with boasts to sportswriters that LSU had the best team in the country, and could back up his claim by taking on national contenders Alabama and Minnesota on the same day. The statement may have been laughable, but the Kingfish wasn't joking when, according to T. Harry Williams definitive biography, *Huey Long*, the senator looked into the eyes of an assistant coach and said: "LSU can't have a losing team because that'll mean I'm associated with a loser."

After a season-opening 9-9 tie at Rice, the Tigers prepared for their Oct. 6 home opener against Southern Methodist. Despite LSU's successes ticket sales were sluggish. This was a particularly sticky problem, since athletic director T.P. Heard had to offer SMU a large $10,000 guarantee to make the trip from Dallas.

Long asked Heard what he thought the problem was.

Heard replied that the famous Barnum & Bailey Circus was making an appearance in Baton Rouge that night and was apparently making a big dent in the advance ticket sales. Huey sprang to action like a circus tiger. Before Barnum & Bailey could move its production from Texas to Baton Rouge, Long and an assisting law student looked through Louisiana's sanitary code to find something useful. They did: an obscure cattle dipping law which Huey seized upon to use to his advantage.

Long asked for a meeting with Barnum & Bailey's advance man. To the visitor's astonishment, Huey informed him of the dipping law and Long's intention to enforce it. For vivid effect, Long asked the man if his circus had ever dipped one of its tigers, much less an elephant. All Barnum & Bailey had to do was cancel the Saturday night show.

The circus decided it unwise to call Huey's bluff on so important a matter as LSU football. The performance was canceled, ticket sales surged and Heard made more than enough profit to cover the guarantee to SMU, which battled LSU to a 14-14 tie.

Huey's circus act was just a warmup to bigger stunts in the weeks ahead. As LSU's Oct. 27 game at Vanderbilt approached, the Kingfish decided that he should bring LSU to Nashville, or at least as much of it as could be arranged.

"No student should miss this trip because of a lack of funds," Huey announced, and then set about the task of transporting most of LSU's student body to Tennessee.

The first hurdle was to talk the Illinois Central into providing those students with an affordable fare. Naturally, the railroad balked at slashing the price of what was then a $19 round trip ticket. So Huey responded by suggesting to railroad officials that it would be sad indeed for them if the Louisiana legislature — Huey's legislature — should raise the tax assessment on the railroad's bridges across the state from their current level of $100,000 to their rightful value of $4 million.

Like so many others who squared off against Huey, the Illinois Central backed down. The fare was slashed to $6.

This was still a considerable sum for many students. So Long emptied his wallet in a visit to the campus and later doled out thousands from his suite at the old Heidelberg Hotel. All they had to do was provide their name — or any name as the case might be — and add it to the list headed "I. O. Huey." Many of them borrowed the train fare and $1 for meals.

"I'm expecting most of this money back within a year," Huey said. Months later, he remarked that indeed most of the loans had been repaid, although retired Advocate sports editor Bud Montet didn't remember it that way. "I don't recall anyone who did," said Montet, who was a junior at LSU when he made the trip. "It wasn't like Huey was standing on the street corner."

By Friday afternoon some 5,000 people were ready to make the trip, including a 125-piece band and 1,500 ROTC students. Five trains of 14-cars each pulled out of Baton Rouge, each with a color designation: Red for cadets; white for players, the band and coaches (Huey and his party had their own car on this train); blue for non-military students and co-eds; green and orange for more regular students and fans.

While money was tight enough that many of them needed to borrow money from Huey, there was still enough discretionary income on board to keep craps games going in virtually every car.

"You had nickel, quarter, four bits and dollar games," Montet said. "It was the middle of the depression in '34, so the craps limits were pretty low. It was all quite a show, one not lost upon the media of the day, as told in Harnett Kane's book *Louisiana Hayride*:

"Huey's football shows could not be kept out of the newspapers, no matter how much the newspapers hated Huey. They were spectacles in the Billy Rose-Roxy tradition: 2,000 cadets, 200 musicians, 50 'purple jackets' — co-eds in white pleats, blazers and 50 smiles — octets of dancing boy and girl cheerleaders and 50 sponsors in a row. And the star of the troupe, Huey, swinging, roaring, hightailing it at the head of the march. He led his boys and girls down the main streets of the invaded towns,

razzled-dazzled over the field between halves and, remained, as usual, perilously close to the players during the game."

He had hardly slept when the train arrived in Nashville at 9 a.m. Saturday. Nonetheless the Kingfish, accompanied by bodyguards who had hastily been deputized as Tennessee game wardens so they could carry weapons, jumped from the train ready to lead his cadets on a two-mile march through downtown Nashville. The townsfolk responded with wild cheers and the headline across the front page of The Nashville Banner summed up the moment quite appropriately: "Nashville Surrenders to Huey Long.

A few hours later, Vanderbilt surrendered to LSU, 29-0. About the only disappointment the day may have held for some was that Huey did not announce his candidacy for president as had been rumored.

While Huey was not yet ready to run for the White House, he returned home ready to make LSU's star quarterback a state senator. During one of many special legislative sessions he called during his reign, Long arranged to honor quarterback Abe Mickal as a "de facto" state senator.

The fact Mickal was underage to hold office, wasn't even a Louisiana resident (he was from McComb, Miss.) and that the whole business infuriated Biff Jones because of what he feared it would do to team morale didn't faze Huey. When T.P. Heard relayed Jones' feelings to Long, the Kingfish offered to make all the Tigers state senators. At last, when it was pointed out that the $10 a day paid to senators might jeopardize a player's amateur status, Long finally relented, and "Senator" Mickal was removed from office. By season's end, it was Biff Jones who was removing himself from office.

A bitter 13-12 loss to Tulane left the Kingfish declaring that Jones might not be the worst coach around, "but he sure ain't the best." Apparently, Huey had forgotten the 18-game unbeaten streak LSU had enjoyed under Jones going into the Tulane game.

A 19-13 loss at Tennessee a week later didn't improve the senator's mood, especially when Jones played a battered Mickal against Huey's wishes. It set the scene for cold relations on a cold December day when Oregon visited LSU in the season finale.

LSU played listlessly in the first half and trailed, 13-0, at halftime. As Jones was about to address his players, Long appeared at the dressing room door asking to talk to the team. According to Peter Finney's *The Fighting Tigers*, this was the exchange between coach and senator:

Long: "Can I talk to the team?"

Jones: "No."

Long: "Who's going to stop me?"

Jones: "Well, you're not going to talk."

Long: "Well, I'm sick of losing and tying games. You'd better win this one."

Jones: "Well, Senator, get this: win, lose or draw, I quit."

Long: "That's a bargain."

For the first time as LSU's coach, Jones then asked his Tigers to win one for him. They did, 14-13, but it did little to soothe the situation, especially once word of Jones' resignation reached

■ **Ken Kavanaugh, an All-American end in 1939.**

But as the days passed, Huey became converted by recommendations that he hire Bernie Moore, a long-time assistant of Jones and Cohen who also coached LSU to the 1933 NCAA track and field championship. Long had dispatched Heard to Southern California to keep tabs on Thomas, but when Heard arrived in Los Angeles he picked up a paper which told him: "Kingfish Appoints Moore Head Coach."

Some felt Moore was a political choice, and Moore suffered the loss of some of his friends by way of the association.

Huey kept quiet publicly after Moore's hiring. At the time he was also deeply involved in the LSU band, having "kidnapped" Castro Carazo from his job as orchestra leader at New Orleans' Roosevelt Hotel to become leader of the school's marching band. It was Carazo who helped the Kingfish write the song that would become his anthem, *Every Man a King*, as well as one of LSU's fight songs, *Touchdown for LSU*.

Not long after he appointed Moore, Huey consulted retired Vanderbilt coach Dan McGugin for a can't miss play. McGugin gave Long a play he called "Number 88," which Long passed on to his new coach. LSU may have been working on "Number 88" the last time Huey ever saw his beloved Tigers.

It was Sept. 3, and Long had stopped to watch practice after a cross-country speaking tour that was a prelude to a likely third-party presidential campaign in 1936. The senator had returned to Baton Rouge to preside over yet another special session whose sole purpose was to rubber stamp whatever legislation the Kingfish wanted passed.

Five days later, during a late-night session at the state capitol, Dr. Carl Austin Weiss stepped from the shadows and pointed a .32 automatic pistol at Long. Whether Weiss actually fired the bullet that struck Long or whether it came from one of Long's bodyguards when they saw the young doctor draw his weapon will always remain the subject of conjecture.

Whatever happened, the facts were Weiss was shot to death on the spot and Long was mortally wounded. He would die early on the morning of Sept. 10 at the age of 42. Two days later, with drums muffled, Carazo's LSU band played "Every Man a King" in dirge-like fashion as Long was laid to rest in the gardens fronting the capitol.

"Number 88" went to the grave with Huey, as Moore never felt obliged to call it with the Kingfish no longer patrolling the sidelines. But even if Moore hadn't used the play, Long would have loved what he would have seen from the Tigers in 1935. LSU won the first of two straight Southeastern Conference titles and made the first of three consecutive trips to the Sugar Bowl.

So ended the Huey Long era of LSU football. The Tigers would go on to greater glories in years to come and in the 1960's and 70's became the darlings of another governor's eye, a governor named John McKeithen.

But never again would one governor be able to politically afford to lavish the money and attention on LSU and its football program that Huey Long directed toward them. If Long wanted to make every man a king, the LSU Tigers were the jewels in the crown.

the press. Both men thought badly of their encounter but neither one wanted to back down publicly. In the end, Jones and Long reached an amicable parting, but the fact remained that once again LSU was in the market for a football coach.

After his row with Jones, Huey boasted of bringing in a big-name coach, so big that he would make everyone forget Biff Jones. Indeed it was a big name, Alabama's Frank Thomas, whom the Kingfish set his sights on, and in late 1934 the two hammered out a secret deal that would have paid Thomas $15,000 a year. Thomas' only stipulation was that their agreement stay out of the press he prepared the Crimson Tide for a trip to the Rose Bowl.

LSU Breaks Aggie Win-Streak

By Bud Montet
The Advocate

Baton Rouge, La. — *Sept. 21, 1968*

The LSU Tigers had to come from behind a 12-point deficit to continue their jinx over the Texas A&M Aggies at Tiger Stadium tonight as they staged a fourth-quarter comeback and grabbed a 13-12 thriller that wasn't decided until the final two seconds before 68,000 hysterical fans.

The victory once again proved the Tigers are fast becoming the best "streak" stoppers in collegiate football.

The Aggies entered the game with a seven-game win streak only to see the Bengals stop it. Less than nine months ago the Tigers beat the Wyoming Cowboys in the Sugar Bowl and ended their 1967 undefeated streak.

Coach Charlie McClendon and his Tigers also halted the Arkansas Razorbacks' 22-game win streak in the 1966 Cotton Bowl and in his first effort as head coach of the Bengals, McClendon halted a long Texas Longhorns' streak.

Texas A&M grabbed the first nine points in a minute and 36 seconds when a booming Steve O'Neal boot of 46 yards bounced out of bounds on the Tiger one-foot line.

The Aggies got their first two points when Mickey Christian, a defensive end turned snapper, tossed the ball over Eddie Ray's head in the end zone on an attempted kick.

The safety gave the Aggies a two-point lead with 4:09 left in the first period.

In less than two minutes, the Aggies picked up their lone touchdown when they drove 46 yards in four plays. A Tiger roughing penalty against an Aggie punt returner set up the drive. The Aggies' Edd Hargett pitched 19 yards to Barney

■ **LSU coach Charlie McClendon on the sidelines in Tiger Stadium.**

Harris at the Tiger 32, and came back to hit Bob Long with a 25-yard pass for another first down at the LSU 3.

After Larry Stegent was held for no gain, Hargett pitched to Long in the Tiger end zone for the touchdown and Riggs' extra-point boot gave the Aggies a 9-0 lead.

A poor 17-yard punt by Eddie Ray of the Tigers in the fading minutes of the second quarter gave the Aggies a chance to add a field goal.

The Aggies took over on the LSU 35 and moved to the nine where a penalty caught them and they had to be satisfied with a 31-yard field goal by Riggs.

LSU stormed back to go 80 yards in nine plays with Haynes leading the charge to the Aggie 34 where Jimmy Gilbert, playing his first game at quarterback for LSU, moved the Bengals on in.

Gilbert pitched to Bob Hamlett for 16 yards and a first down at the Aggie 18 and after Kenny Newfield drove for eight yards, Gilbert came back to sweep seven yards around right end for a first own at the A&M 3.

Frank Matte, the Tiger "utility" man, then drove over right guard for a touchdown but Mark Lumpkin missed the point after and LSU had to be satisfied with a 12-6 score at the intermission.

The fourth quarter was one of the wildest ever seen in Tiger Stadium. The Aggies started it off when Riggs missed an attempted 43-yard field goal.

Maurice LeBlanc set up the Tigers' winning march when he returned a 51-yard O'Neal punt 16 yards to the LSU 46.

Haynes then took over and drove the Bengals downfield to score in 10 plays. The winning touchdown came on a pitchout from Haynes to West around left end with the fleet West getting a great block from Tommy (Trigger) Allen to spring him over the goal line.

This time Lumpkin booted the extra-point kick and LSU held a slim 13-12 lead with 7:47 left in the game. The Aggies roared back with Hargett pitching to Stegent and the Aggies gaining the ball at their 48 when Gerry Kent, the Tiger defensive back, was ruled interfering with the receiver.

A 15-yard penalty pushed the Aggies back to their 34 and Hargett was tossed for a nine-yard loss back to the Aggie 25. Hargett then hit Jimmy Adams with a 47-yard aerial for a first down at the LSU 28.

Hargett came right back to hit Long with a 23-yarder and a first down at the LSU 5. After LSU stopped Stegent for no gain, Hargett pitched out to Long who fumbled over the goal line. The play was ruled a touchback and LSU gained possession at their 20.

Haynes put the clincher on the game by keeping a drive

Score by Periods

LSU	0	6	0	7	— 13
Texas A&M	9	3	0	0	— 12

going to the Aggie 37, making the drive eat up the clock time by staying on the ground.

Three times Haynes picked up crucial first down yardage to keep the drive going. However, with less than a minute left, Haynes fumbled at the Aggie 36 and Bill Hobbs recovered for the Aggies with seconds left.

Hargett hit Long with a pass to the Tiger 46 for a first down and, with ten seconds left, Hargett killed the clock with an out of bounds pass.

Hargett then pitched a long pass out of bounds. With two seconds left, Long attempted a 61-yard field goal that fell short and was fielded by LSU as the game ended.

The defeat was a heart-rending one for Coach Gene Stallings and his Aggies. The Aggies haven't downed the Bengals in Tiger Stadium since 1956 and Stalling has yet to post a victory over the Tigers since taking over the head job at Aggieland.

The Tigers' Haynes sparked the Bengals' touchdown drives, getting the first underway before turning the job over to Gilbert and engineering the second and winning scoring push. Haynes also teamed with Allen to slowly drive downfield in the waning minutes to wipe time off the clock and put the Aggies in the hole although a fumble gave them a last second desperate chance to pull the game from a loss to a victory.

Haynes pitched 11 times and hit on five passes for 64 yards and teamed with Allen as the workhorses of the Tiger offense.

Allen accounted for 56 yards on 20 carries.

The Aggies' touted Hargett passed 28 times and hit on 13 passes for 220 yards and one touchdown. His longest pass play was a 47-yarder in the fading seconds.

However, the Aggies' best weapon was the great kicking of O'Neal who punted nine times for a sensational 47.4 average which bettered LSU's Eddie Ray, who turned in a 39.6 average effort.

Not only did O'Neal keep the Tigers in the hole much of the first half, it was his booming boot out of bounds on the Tiger one-foot line that shook the Bengals and allowed the Aggies to get nine points in less than two minutes.

The Bengals edged the Aggies in total offense with 283 yards to 225 for the visitors. LSU gained 203 yards on the ground and 80 in the air while the Aggies netted but 46 yards on the ground and 220 in the air.

The defeat was a heart-rending one for Coach Gene Stallings and his Aggies. The Aggies haven't downed the Bengals in Tiger Stadium since 1956 and Stalling has yet to post a victory over the Tigers since taking over the head job at Aggieland.

■ LSU's Craig Burns (30) returns a Florida State interception for a touchdown.

LSU Scalps Seminoles, 31-27

By Bud Montet

The Advocate

Atlanta, Ga. — *Dec. 30, 1968*

The LSU Tigers spent the night trying to find the handle on the football and Florida State's Bill Cappleman spent three quarters trying to find his ace receiver, Ron Sellers, and when the searches were over LSU won, 31-27, in the inaugural Peach Bowl victory.

The game was played in a steady shower that started an hour before the game. Some 35,545 fans braved the 40 degree weather to watch an exciting see-saw battle.

Score by Periods

LSU	0	10	14	7 —	31
Florida State	7	6	0	14 —	27

Tonight's victory was Coach Charlie McClendon's fifth bowl win in six tries. It was also doubly sweet as McClendon led the Tigers' win over former LSU assistant, Bill Peterson of Florida State.

LSU lost the football on fumbles three times in the opening quarter, opening the game with a fumble by Mark Lumpkin on the initial kickoff.

Florida State scored on their first scrimmage play with the Seminoles' Tom Bailey going 36 yards for the touchdown.

The Bengals then spent the rest of the first period march-

■ **Maurice Leblanc (34) scored LSU's winning touchdown on a 3-yard dive.**

ing on the Seminoles unable to reach the Florida State goal line due to fumbles and interceptions.

The Tigers managed to get over their fumbles after the first period though they had a relapse in the final period when Glenn Smith fumbled on a kickoff to give Cappleman and FSU a chance to go ahead, 27-24.

But the fumbling Bengals failed to give up and marched 61 yards in the fading minutes to score the winning touchdown with Maurice Leblanc going over from the FSU 3 to give LSU its 31-27 victory.

Florida State's Cappleman had trouble finding his ace receiver, the nation's top receiver, Sellers, who caught but one pass for 18 yards in the first half.

However, Cappleman found Sellers in the second half and hit him seven times in the final half. Sellers grabbed eight aerials for 76 yards and two went for touchdowns.

LSU's Mike Hillman, who outpitched

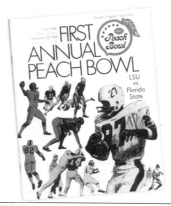

Cappleman, hit 16 receivers in 29 tries for 229 yards and two scores.

The hard working lefty also set up the winning touchdown when he staged a beautiful fake and raced around right end for 11 yards to the Seminoles' 3. Hillman had but one pass intercepted.

His great work gained him the Clint Castleberry Trophy as the outstanding offensive player.

Buddy Millican, a late starter for the Bengals, turned in a superb defensive end performance and this gained him the Smiley Johnson Award as the outstanding defensive player.

Millican constantly harassed Cappleman and tossed him for big losses a number of times.

Cappleman hit on 21 of 41 aerials for 221 yards and three scores.

The Tigers dominated the game, rolling up 22 first downs to 19 for the Seminoles. LSU netted 151 yards on the ground to 92 for the Seminoles.

In passing the Bengals netted 233 yards to 221 for Florida State.

■ Andy Hamilton (80) scored his 62-yard touchdown on the first play of the game.

Bevan Blocks Auburn Kick in Tigers' 21-20 Win

By Bud Montet

The Advocate

Baton Rouge, La. — *Oct. 25, 1969*

The LSU Tigers managed to stay undefeated by the "foot" as Mark Lumpkin's three points after touchdown and Eddie Ray's booming punts in the second half gave the Bengals a 21-20 victory over the bruising and hard-hitting Auburn Tigers.

LSU scored on the first scrimmage play of the game when quarterback Mike Hillman pitched to tailback Jimmy Gilbert who hurled a pass to Andy Hamilton in the open and the fleet wide receiver raced over for the 62-yard touchdown.

For the next 62 minutes Auburn throttled the LSU offense and the Bengals didn't make another first down for the next 26 minutes.

Auburn came right back to tie the score when Pat Sullivan pitched a 12-yard scoring pass to Micky Zofko and John Riley tied the game with his point-after kick.

For the first time this season LSU slipped behind when Auburn's Buddy McClinton recovered an Eddie Ray fumble and moved 39 yards in five plays with a Sullivan to Connie Frederick aerial play for 33 yards — the key play in the drive. Wallace Clark went over from the LSU 2 and Riley added the extra point.

It was the only time this year the Bengals found their side of the scoreboard with a smaller figure than the opposition. Auburn protected their 14-7 lead until 23 seconds of the first half when LSU scored with Hillman pitching to Jim West.

West made a fine catch and Hillman, hotly badgered by a host of visiting Tigers, made a great effort to get the ball off.

Again Lumpkin came through with the point-after kick to tie the game at 14-all.

It was Gilbert's 29- and 15-yard gallops, back to back, that got the Tigers in scoring position.

LSU moved 75 yards in 11 plays the first time they got the football at the start of the second half. Stumpy Allen Shorey sliced through left guard for the touchdown and this time Lumpkin booted his third straight extra point — the one that later proved the difference.

Auburn got back in the game at the start of the fourth period when Sullivan hit Zofko with a 14-yard scoring pass.

Riley's extra-point kick to tie the game was blocked by George Bevan. Bill Thomason earlier had blocked a Riley field-goal attempt.

LSU had another chance to score midway in the fourth period when they moved from their 38 to the Auburn 12 but a penalty stopped the scoring drive and Lumpkin missed on an attempted 28-yard field goal.

In the fading seconds, Auburn tried a fourth down pass but Craig Burns batted the ball out of bounds and LSU killed the clock in two plays.

The victory gave the Bengals a 6-0 record and was their second Southeastern Conference victory.

It was Auburn's second loss and their second in conference play.

■ Auburn's Wallace Clark dives over for a touchdown.

The vaunted Auburn sophomore, Pat Sullivan, harried the LSU secondary defenses with his precision-thrown aerials. The slim sophomore hit on 13 of 34 passes for 221 yards. Sullivan had a pair intercepted.

LSU netted 149 yards on the ground and picked up 157 in the air for a total offense effort of 306 yards against the Auburn eleven that was leading the nation in total defense.

The game figures were about equal as Auburn rushed for 76 yards and passed for 221 for a total offense effort of 297 yards.

Big Ray who fumbled twice in the game made up for it with his great punting. Ray booted nine times for a 44-yard average and in the second half he booted one out on the five and kicked one dead on the two.

With the game hanging in the balance and a minute and 20 seconds left, Ray booted to the Auburn goal line — a 54 yard kick, and LSU held the return to 10 yards. Auburn then tried its final flurry of passes in an attempt to get back in front.

The game reminded one of famed past battles as the two Tiger elevens hit with authority all afternoon. Late in the game Mike Demarie of the Bengals had to leave the field of play.

Early in the game, Auburn kept the Bengals backed up against their goal line by some great kicking by Frederick.

LSU had possession at their 15, 12 and eight in the first half.

Hillman hit on five of 15 passes for 91 yards and one a scoring pass. Tight end Bill Strober was the chief target, grabbing four passes. Gilbert, with 61 yards in 10 carries, was the top Bengal ball carrier. Ray picked up 35 tough yards in 14 carries and Shorey got 22 in 12 carries.

Tommy Casanova had 88 kick return yards in three attempts during the afternoon.

The meeting was the first between the two Tiger elevens since 1942 when Auburn won.

Score by Periods

LSU	7	7	7	0	— 21
Auburn	7	7	0	6	— 20

■ LSU's win over Alabama was its first since a 13-3 victory in 1958.

Tigers Break Loose Against Tide For 20-15 Win

By Bud Montet
The Advocate

Baton Rouge, La. — *Nov. 8, 1969*

LSU's erratic Bengals pulled out a 20-15 victory over the Alabama Crimson Tide, their first victory since 1958 and the first that Coach Charlie McClendon has won over his old coach, Paul (Bear) Bryant.

The victory was a hard fought one as LSU was constantly plagued by penalties and several times had ball carriers slopping down to stymie promising drives.

After the first half ended in a 3-3 deadlock, LSU came out at the start of the second half and drove 76 yards to score and take a 10-3 lead. They were never behind, although the Tide constantly threatened on the long bombs tossed by Alabama's Scott Hunter, who set two Tide school records with his great performance against the Bengals.

Alabama's two touchdowns came in the fourth period on long passes by Hunter. After LSU took their 10-3 lead. Hunter fired a 36-yard pass to Hunter Husband, a tight end, for a touchdown to get within four points of the Bengals.

LSU moved well out in front again with a 51-yard drive with Allen Shorey going over from the one — his second one-yard scoring jaunt of the game.

Trailing, 20-9, Alabama came right back with Hunter pitching five completions on the drive. The touchdown pass was a 34-yard shot to David Bailey, a sophomore split end, who beat Tiger James Earley to the end zone.

Mark Lumpkin put the Tigers in front in the second period with a 30-yard field goal but Alabama's Oran Buck tied the game at 3-all with his 26-yarder with 36 seconds left in the first half.

The Bengals blasted the Alabama ground defenses as stocky little Shorey raced for 118 yards in 26 carries and two touchdowns. Big Tiger fullback Eddie Ray gained 102 yards on 16 carries. It was the first time this season that an LSU back has netted more than 100 yards from scrimmage.

Hunter had his greatest night passing since he challenged Ole Miss's Archie Manning several weeks ago. The Alabama junior hit on 18 of 35 passes for 284 yards and two touchdowns.

However, he failed to get help from his rushers as LSU held the Alabama Tide to a net 47 yards on the ground.

LSU moved by rushing with 239 yards on the ground and 138 in the air. In total offense LSU totaled 377 yards and Alabama 331.

Aside from the many penalties, most coming in the first half, and other mistakes, the Bengals dominated the game with only Hunter's scoring bombs giving the Bengals trouble.

Tiger quarterback Mike Hillman used the aerials sparingly and pitched but 18 passes and hit on nine for 113 yards.

Split end Lonnie Myles was the chief Tiger receiver with five catches for 69 yards. Ken Kavanaugh Jr., the son of LSU's famed All-American Ken Kavanaugh, caught two aerials.

But the Bengals victory was achieved by blasting the Tiger lines with Shorey and Ray doing most of the carrying.

LSU threatened early in the game when midway in the first period they drove from their 13 to the Tide 39 where Hillman was tossed for a 13-yard loss and Butch Duhe missed on an attempted 47-yard field goal.

Alabama threatened at the start of the second quarter when they drove to the Tiger 21 where LSU held.

Midway in the second quarter, LSU drove from their four-yard line to the Tide 6 where a five-yard penalty set the Tigers back and LSU had to settle for Lumpkin's 30-yard field goal that put them in front.

Alabama got back into the game when Hunter pitched to George Ranager for 47 yards to the Tiger 24 and Alabama then had to settle for a field goal by Buck, a 26-yarder.

Ray and Shorey teamed at the start of the second half to put LSU in front to stay. It was Shorey's one-yard dive that gave LSU its first touchdown.

LSU got a break after the kickoff when Alabama's Phil Chaffin fumbled on his 35 and Bozeman recovered for LSU. The Bengals failed to score a touchdown when on the Tide 5 quarterback Buddy Lee slipped down on a third down play and LSU had to be satisfied with a 25-yard field goal by Lumpkin.

LSU came right back to threaten again and moved to the Tide 35 where Hillman laid a perfect pass on Andy Hamilton's hands on the Alabama 5-yard line but the fleet Bengal dropped the ball.

Alabama started the fourth period with a great Hunter to Bubba Seay pass for 57 yards. However, the Tide couldn't capitalize on the threat as Ranager, a flanker, fumbled on a reverse and the Bengals' Tommy Casanova recovered for LSU at the Tiger 5.

Alabama then struck with the bomb with Hunter pitching to Husband for 37 yards and a touchdown.

Alabama gambled with an onside kick and LSU took over at their 49 and moved on in to get their second touchdown of the game with Shorey again going over from the one.

Alabama came right back as LSU went into their "prevent" defense but were unable to keep the Tide from crossing their goal line, with the score coming on Hunter's 34-yard pass to Bailey.

Hunter had to settle for new records as the Bengals took the game victory.

The hard-throwing Tide junior set a new mark of 1,592 yards for the season, breaking his old mark of 1,471 yards set last year.

Hunter also set a new Alabama season total offense mark with 1,594 yards which breaks the old mark set by Steve Sloan, now a member of the Alabama coaching staff.

Kicker Mark Lumpkin set a new LSU mark of 52 points by extra-point conversions which broke the old mark of Doug Moreau of 51, set in 1963-64.

For Coach McClendon the game itself must have been as frustrating as his past efforts against his old tutor, Bryant. Time after time it appeared as if the Bengals were going to break the game wide open, only to slip up with a glaring mistake.

The victory gave LSU a 7-1 record to date and it was the third loss for the Crimson Tide.

Alabama hasn't lost three games in a single season since 1958 when they lost four encounters.

Score by Periods

LSU	0	3	10	7 —	20
Alabama	0	3	0	12 —	15

■ **LSU tailback Art Cantrelle (24) dives for a touchdown in the second quarter.**

Tigers Make It Two in a Row Against Tide, 14-9

By Bud Montet
The Advocate

Birmingham, Ala. — *Nov. 7, 1970*

The LSU Tigers put back-to-back victories together over standout Alabama elevens as they humbled the Alabama Crimson Tide, 14-9, here before 70,371 fans to follow their upset win over Auburn two weeks ago.

The win wasn't an easy one as the Bengals had to stave off a last-minute threat by the Tide which was attempting to strike back late in the game.

The victory was the second in successive years for the Bengals over the Tide, a feat they haven't been able to accomplish since the mid-fifties.

It was also the first Tiger win over Alabama in Birmingham since 1909.

After the Tide jumped into a first quarter 3-0 lead on Richard Cieminy's 23-yard field goal, LSU came back to get a touchdown with Art Cantrelle diving over from the two.

LSU scored their second touchdown in the third period on a long 37-yard sustained drive, one of the longest of the season for the Tigers. Buddy Lee pitched a two-yard pass to little Jimmy LeDoux for the score.

Alabama got its lone touchdown of the game in the fourth period when Scott Hunter pitched 10 yards to David Bailey.

LSU's defenses once again held a grid eleven from scoring a touchdown on the rush — their tenth straight performance in that department.

The last time a rusher scored against the Bengals was in last year's Ole Miss game when Archie Manning, now injured and out for the season, tallied on a sprint-out.

The Tigers missed scoring opportunities but their defensive unit made the 14 points stand up for victory.

Once again Coach Charlie McClendon of the Bengals bested his old grid boss, Paul (Bear) Bryant.

At the opening of the game the Tigers, playing their first game on artificial turf, stumbled numerous times before they became accustomed to the footing.

The Bengals' defense was sparked by a brilliant performance by Craig Burns, who intercepted two passes and ran them back ... to put the Bengals within striking distances and the burly safety raced back two punts for a total of 51 yards.

■ **Allen Shorey's touchdown attempt from the Tide 2 failed in the fourth quarter.**

Early in the second quarter, Burns took a Frank Mann punt and raced it back 33 yards to the Tide 23 and LSU moved on in to score in five plays, with Cantrelle getting the touchdown.

A few minutes later, Burns intercepted a Scott Hunter pass and raced it back 17 yards to the Tide 35, but Bert Jones slipped down after two plays and lost 14 yards to stymie the drive.

Early in the third period, Burns grabbed a Hunter pass and raced it back 25 yards to the Tide 12 but Alabama held again.

Burns set up another Tiger threat midway in the fourth period when he ran back a Mann punt 28 yards to the Tide 42 and LSU moved to inside the 2-yard line where they failed on a sweep by Allen Shorey.

The play set up a weird set of situations when Dantin fumbled and the ball was recovered by Ed Hines, who then fumbled when hit hard by several Tigers.

The ball then bounded into the end zone where a Tiger dove on it but the ball squirted from his grasp and was recovered by the Tide's Lanny Norris.

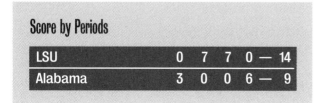

Score by Periods

LSU	0	7	7	0 —	14
Alabama	3	0	0	6 —	9

The officials, after making several signals, finally determined that LSU had given the impetus to the ball over the goal and it was called a touchback and Alabama gained possession at their 20 and moved on in to score their lone touchdown.

Oddly enough with the exception of two technical calls of pass interference, which is labeled a penalty at the spot of infraction, there wasn't any other penalties called in the hard hitting game.

LSU lost the services of Andy Hamilton for most of the game as he was hit on the head and was groggy the rest of the way.

Tommy Casanova missed part of the third and fourth periods when he suffered a knock on the head.

John Sage also was knocked out early in the game but returned to the action.

Up front, the Tiger foursome and trio of linebackers turned in an excellent game in containing the vaunted Johnny Musso. Musso, who had averaged 99 yards a game until today, was held to 44 yards in 18 carries, the best job done against him this season.

While the Bengals allowed Hunter the short passes they managed to keep the receivers within hand, Hunter hit on 19 of 37 passes for 207 yards and one score. LSU intercepted four of his tosses.

Ned Hayden pitched seven passes and hit on four for 42 yards.

Alabama netted but 79 yards on the ground but it picked up 249 in the air for a total offense of 238 yards while LSU netted 107 on the ground and 138 in the air for 245 yards total offense.

The key to the game according to Coach McClendon was the kicking game. Sophomore Wayne Dickinson booted an average of 40.3 yards while the touted Mann booted for 43.8 yards.

But LSU had a total of 155 yards in returns while Alabama was held to only five yards.

Once again, hard working Art Cantrelle was the chief LSU ball carrier with 82 yards in 23 carries and one score. Cantrelle picked up 24 on one jaunt for his longest run. Once the tailback slipped into the open and was seemingly going for long yardage when he stumbled and was nailed down.

Lee hit on seven of eight passes for 49 yards while Jones hit on three of six for 89 yards.

LSU couldn't get out of their own territory in the first period and failed to make a first down and netted but seven yards on the ground and none in the air.

However, the Bengals started to move at the start of the second quarter and drove from their 15 where Bill Norsworthy intercepted a Hunter pass. The Bengals moved to the Tide 8 with Jones tossing a 57-yard pass to fleet Al Coffee. Coffee caught the ball on the Tide 15 but stumbled as he tried to get going which enabled the Tide's Norris to haul him down at the eight.

LSU tried a field goal but Jones fumbled a poor pass from center and Mark Lumpkin tried to run the ball but was nailed at the 10.

Burns' 33-yard punt return gave the Bengals a chance to go ahead and they held a 7-3 halftime lead.

Early in the third quarter, the Bengals drove 87 yards in 12 plays to get their insurance score. On the drive, Cantrelle put the Bengals within reach with a 24-yard gallop to the Tiger 14

and LSU picked up the touchdown on Lee's pass to LeDoux.

On the Alabama touchdown drive Tiger James Earley was judged interfering with receiver George Ranager at the Tiger 22 and LSU drew a 36-yard penalty on the play.

With little over a minute to play Hunter tried to pitch the Tide back in the game but Louis Cascio picked off a pass at mid-

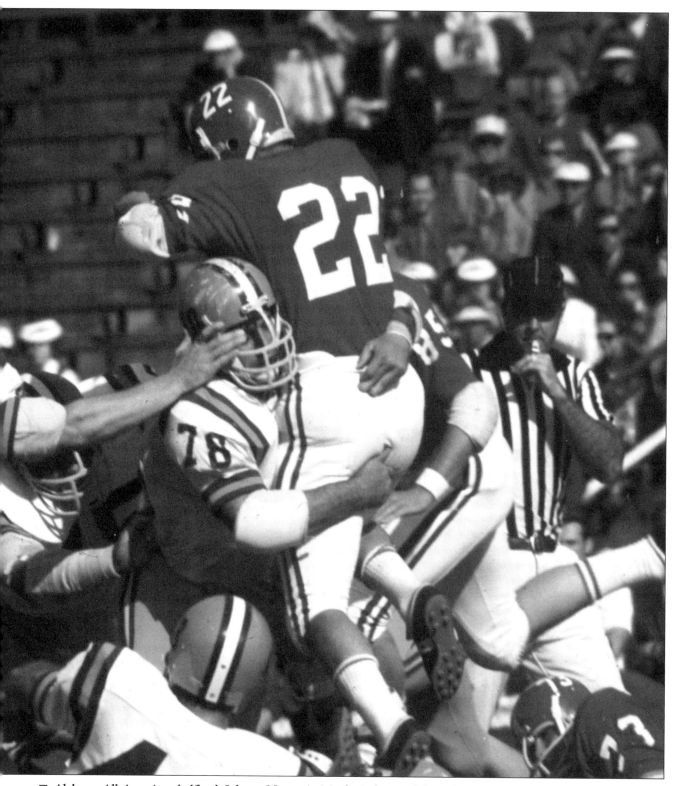

■ **Alabama All-American halfback Johnny Musso (22) is denied a touchdown by LSU's Ron Estay (78).**

field and Lee took two losses to run out the clock.

Up front the Tiger rush was sparked by Ronnie Estay, the junior tackle, who was credited with eight clean tackles. His teammate, John Sage, picked up six tackles and two assists despite missing part of the game.

Burns added to his laurels making six tackles in the secondary. Big Mike Anderson was credited with a half dozen and Cascio got four.

■ Mark Lumpkin's fourth-quarter field goal attempt was blocked by the Irish's Bob Neibart.

Irish Field Goal Defeats Tigers, 3-0

BY BUD MONTET
The Advocate

South Bend, Ind. — *Nov. 21, 1970*

T he "bowling" Notre Dame Fighting Irish had to take advantage of a pass interference and a possible interception in the end zone that was dropped to take a 3-0 victory over the LSU Fighting Tigers in the final two minutes and 54 seconds, keeping their win streak going at nine in a row.

Scott Hempel booted the 24-yard field goal that gave the Irish their slim win over a gallant band of Bayou Bengals who blunted the nation-leading offense all afternoon.

Notre Dame got its chance on a short Wayne Dickinson punt midway the fourth period and the Irish's Mike Crotty returned the ball six yards to the Tiger 36.

On the first play, Ed Gulyas moved to the Tiger 17 where the officials judged James Earley interfered and Notre Dame had its chance.

On the third down, Joe Theismann tried a pass into the end zone and Tommy Casanova got a hand on it but failed to hold the ball, giving the Irish their chance at the field goal.

Earlier, LSU got a chance when the Tigers' Bill Norsworthy grabbed a pass that bounded out of the hands of Bill Barz and Norsworthy was there to grab it at the Irish 34. LSU moved to the 17-yard line of the Irish and after LSU halted them Mark Lumpkin came in to try a 34-yard field goal and Bob Neibart broke through to block the attempt.

A few minutes later the Irish got their chance.

Notre Dame, which led the nation in total offense for a game average of 540.1 yards was held to 227 yards — 78 on the ground (25 of those coming with a 26-yard jaunt by Theismann, the Irish's brilliant quarterback after the Irish went ahead) and 149 in the air.

While the Bengals' offense was spotty, the Tigers rushed for 83 yards, mostly gained by Art Cantrelle, and picked up 82 in the air for a total offense of 165 yards, their lowest of the season.

The game was a hard-fought battle from start to finish and LSU did a fine job of rushing Theismann and dumped him for considerable losses several times.

Theismann was able to connect on 14 of 30 aerials for 149 yards and had one intercepted.

The Bengals contained Theismann on his keeper with the one exception in the fourth period and also halted the running of the Irish running backs.

Notre Dame, which had announced prior to the game, that they wouldn't make the bowl decision until some time Sunday, were almost knocked out of the ranks as the "most desirable" bowl foes for 1970.

In the first half the Tigers held the Irish to 55 yards on the ground and 55 in the air while they picked up 29 yards on the ground and 122 in the air.

However, the bruising first half battle was just a prelude to the fierce encounter in the second half.

Both elevens had several breaks for chances to move into the end zone but were never able to capitalize until the Irish got their chance once too often.

Early in the game LSU got a break when Early grabbed a fumble by Dennis Allan. However, Notre Dame threw

Score by Periods

LSU	0	0	0	0 —	0
Notre Dame	0	0	0	3 —	3

Cantrelle and Buddy Lee for successive nine-yard losses to blunt the chance.

Several minutes later the Irish got a chance when Ralph Stepaniak intercepted a Lee pass and returned 16 yards to midfield.

A 34-yard pass from Theismann to his tight end for 34 yards to the Tiger 13. LSU was backed to their three-yard line when Lloyd Frye hit Darryll Dewan hard, causing a fumble and Richard Picou recovered for LSU at the four.

The Irish moved into Tiger territory several times in the second quarter but the tough Tiger defense held them at bay.

Midway in the period, Lumpkin tried a 49-yard field goal, but was far short of the cross bar. In the third period, Notre Dame got into LSU territory only twice — once to the 44 and once to the 45.

In the fourth period, the Bengals missed their chance on the Norsworthy pass interception and the resulting miss of the short field goal by Lumpkin.

Notre Dame's tremendous rush on the Tiger passers cut down on the effectiveness of Lee and Bert Jones, as both got only three completions.

Once again Cantrelle proved the workhorse of the Tiger backfield, going for a net 94 yards in 23 tries. His longest gain was for 15 yards. Chris Dantin got 42 yards in nine attempts.

Notre Dame's top runner Gulyas was held to a net 25 yards in nine carries.

The Irish's favorite receiver, Tom Gatewood, was held to four receptions for 21 yards. His longest catch was for nine yards. Most of the time, Gatewood was covered by Casanova, who turned in a fine effort in stymieing the fine Irish receiver.

The Tiger front four and linebackers all played superb defensive football, Buddy Millican, John Sage, Ronnie Estay, Art Davis, Mike Anderson, Louis Cascio and Picou.

Davis tossed Theismann for a loss of 18 yards and Bobby Joe King came through for losses of nine and three yards. Estay got to the quarterback for a sack of seven yards.

The Irish, who were held to a 10-7 score last week by Georgia Tech and then had to scramble for their 3-0 win over LSU, are favored to take a Cotton Bowl bid. At the end of the game, LSU was still in doubt whether it would get a major bowl bid or any bowl bid at all.

The close loss was the second of the season for LSU against seven victories. The Bengals meet Tulane and Ole Miss in their next two outings.

TITTLE KELLOW CRASS HARRELL

ROGERS

■ **TCU's defense stopped LSU's Bill Crass at the goal line in the second quarter.**

Manton Kicks No. 1
Frogs to 3-2 Win

By W.I. Spencer
The Advocate

New Orleans, La. — *Jan. 1, 1936*

The low scoring jinx that has hung over two previous football games between Louisiana State and Texas Christian extended through their Sugar Bowl classic here this afternoon with the worst "football weather" of the year, spoiling the New Year's fete for some 35,000 spectators. Taldon Manton's accurate toe booted a field goal late in the second quarter that gave the Horned Frogs a 3-2 victory.

LSU, by fiercely rushing Sammy Baugh, the great TCU quarterback, in the second quarter as he attempted a daring pass behind his own goal line, forced the Frog field general back of his own end line for a safety, as he futilely tried to get rid of the ball.

TCU scored shortly after the safety as the second quarter's minutes were ebbing away.

Willie Walls, the best Horned Frog on the field today, covered Bill Crass' fumble on the LSU 45-yard line. Jimmy Lawrence, a hard-running back and pass receiver for the Texans, crossed up the Tiger defense by hurling a fine pass to this same "thorn in the Tiger side," Walls. The TCU end was cleanly tackled on the LSU 13-yard line by Junior Bowman.

The Tigers threw the Frogs back four yards after three plays. Manton, the big fullback who played a whale of a game backing up the line and was always good for gaining yardage through the line, then dropped back to the LSU 28, where he booted a perfect field goal from a slight angle and into the teeth of a good northern wind.

LSU threatened in the fourth quarter, when Crass led a smashing drive from the TCU 31-yard line, following a Baugh fumble that had been recovered by Bernie Dumas.

The Bengals moved to a first down on the TCU 8-yard line, and after a six-yard swing around right end by Junior Bowman, the touchdown the Tigers wanted so much seemed in sight.

But TCU stiffened, halted Crass on three successive plays and the ball went over.

The Horned Frogs threatened in the closing minutes, when Baugh broke away for 42 yards around left tackle, with Gaynell Tinsley finally bringing the Frog down with a hard, diving tackle on the Tiger 4-yard line, and drew a penalty to the LSU 1-yard line for unnecessary roughness.

But here Marvin Stewart, Ernest Seago, Justin Rukas, Tinsley and the rest of the Tigers showed their greatness, and in four plays smeared the Frogs back on the LSU 10 to take the ball on downs.

Playing what probably was the greatest game of this career, Baugh was an All-American back in every sense of the word. His passing was good — what he did of it. But his punting was masterly, his blocking and ball-carrying brilliant and better than anything else he did, his defensive work was superb. On more than one occasion, Baugh stopped what looked like a sure LSU touchdown. And intercepting a couple of Tiger passes deep in TCU territory, he saved nobody knows what else for his team.

Jimmy Lawrence, Drew Ellis, Wison Groseclose, Bob Harrell, Darrell Lester, Walter Roach, Willie Walls and L.D. Meyer also contributed to the great Frog defense — one of the gamest and most durable seen here in a long time.

One of TCU's "threshold" stands against LSU cost the services of the great Lester, twice an All-American center. He was hurt stopping a plunge over center by Bill Crass in the second period — stopping Crass' charge on the one-foot line.

You might say the "breaks" went against first one side and then the other to cause the points.

But there really was nothing lucky about the 32-yard return of a punt by Bowman from midfield to TCU's 18-yard line. Nor had there been anything lucky about the fine punt Bill Crass had put out of bounds on TCU's 6-yard line on a previous play to force this danger zone punt.

No luck either, attached to the fine pass from Bill Crass to Jeff Barrett to put the ball on the TCU 2-yard line. Though you might have called it bad luck for LSU that the Frogs had Sam Baugh playing safety instead of somebody else. Because when Baugh tackled a

Score by Periods

LSU	0	2	0	0	— 2
TCU	0	3	0	0	— 3

man, that man stayed tackled.

The Tigers fought themselves to a standstill trying to find a way through the TCU line. But they couldn't. And they finally lost the ball on downs at the TCU 6-yard line

Sam Baugh, backed up to the crowd in the end zone, faked a punt and then shot a pass which slipped out of his fingers and fell incomplete in the end zone. Gaynell Tinsley had crowded Baugh and had made him dodge and that probably accounted for the poor pass.

Anyhow, it put the ball out on the 20-yard line and the Tigers had a two-point margin. But not for long.

A bad break against them came a few minutes later. Bowman had run the kickoff back 15 yards to the LSU 45-yard line but on the first play Crass fumbled and Willie Walls carved a niche for himself in TCU's hall of fame by recovering the ball.

A few seconds later, Walls turned the niche into an alcove when he gathered in a fine pass from Jimmy Lawrence for a gain of 23 yards to put the ball on LSU's 17-yard line.

There the Old Gold and Purple held as it never had before. It pushed the Frogs back on three plays.

With one shell left in their gun, the Frogs decided to gamble on Manton and when that young man dropped back to the LSU 26-yard line and booted a "liner" through the goal posts even the LSU rooters cheered him.

It was a "money" kick — one that Manton probably never will forget.

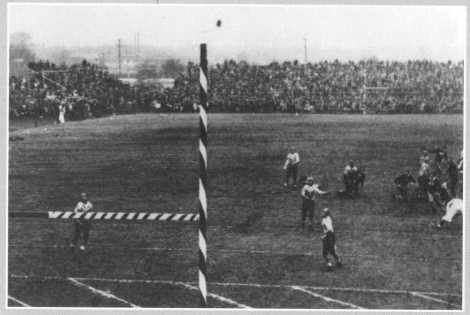

■ **Taldon Manton's field goal ensured the Horned Frogs' victory.**

LSU Romps Over Rebs, Wins SEC Title

By Ted Castillo

The Advocate

Baton Rouge, La. — *Dec. 5, 1970*

LSU's student body pelted the field with oranges and the Tiger football team belted Ole Miss, 61-17, tonight at Tiger Stadium before 67,590 keyed-up mostly Tiger fans. The surprisingly one-sided victory not only sends the Bengals on to a New Year's night Orange Bowl date with Big 8 champion Nebraska but also made LSU the Southeastern Conference champion for the first time since 1961.

Coming against an arch rival and one LSU had not beaten since 1964, the sweeter-than-sugar victory gave Tiger coach Charlie McClendon's team a 5-0 SEC slate and a 9-2 season record.

The loss left Ole Miss with a 4-2 record in the SEC and 7-3 overall for its Gator Bowl date with Auburn on Jan. 2.

A crippled Archie Manning, who wore a protective covering on his left arm, was unable to rally the Rebels as he had done for two previous years against LSU.

Manning left the game midway in the third period. A report later indicated that his right arm was injured. The protective gear of the Reb whiz was okayed by umpire Cliff Norvell, prior to the 8:30 kickoff of the regionally telecast game.

Manning threw a 9-yard pass to Jim Poole for the game's first score, set up by one of LSU's three first-period fumbles, all of which the Rebels recovered. But after that the hampered Manning was practically stymied.

LSU scored so many touchdowns it was hard to keep count. The Tigers erased an early Ole Miss 7-0 lead on a 20-yard pass from soph quarterback Bert Jones to Jimmy LeDoux.

After Poole's 21-yard field goal tipped the balance back in the Rebels favor, 10-7, the Tigers went to work and scored again on Buddy Lee's 46-yard bomb to Andy Hamilton.

Tommy Casanova's first dazzling punt return, for 61 yards, accounted for the next Tiger TD and Ronnie Estay's dumping of Manning in the end zone left the Bengals with a 23-10 halftime lead.

Mark Lumpkin's 21st LSU field goal, a new career record, followed and then Craig Burns scampered 61 yards with a punt.

Score by Periods

	1	2	3	4	Final
Ole Miss	7	3	7	0	17
LSU	7	16	10	28	61

Shug Chumbler directed Ole Miss to its second touchdown and the third quarter closed with LSU showing a 33-17 margin.

But the dam really broke in the final quarter. Tailback Art Cantrelle stepped 55 yards for one score; Casanova returned another punt all the way for 74 yards and a touchdown; Jones' pass to Ken Kavanaugh Jr. for 13 yards added another; and LeDoux streaked nine yards around the left side for the final marker.

LSU's total was the highest ever collected by either team in the series while the setback was the most one-sided in the heated rivalry since a 52-7 Tiger victory in 1917.

Individually and collectively, LSU set a number of records. The three punt returns for touchdowns tied an all-time NCAA record.

In the individual departments, Cantrelle, who jetted 117 yards on 25 carries, broke Steve Van Buren's 1943 rushing record of 847 yards with a total of 892 on the season. Hamilton caught three passes for 98 yards and smashed Ken Kavanaugh's most yards gained on receptions mark of 1,075, set in 1937-39. With another year left, Hamilton has 1,141 career reception yards.

Lumpkin broke the field goal mark of 20 set by Doug Moreau in 1963-65 and Lee, with 177 yards on passes, moved into third place on LSU's all-time passing list behind Y.A. Tittle and Mike Hillman. Lee has 1,641 yards passing in his career.

The courageous Manning was limited to 82 yards and 12 completions in 27 attempts by one of the best Tiger pass rushes in years, and some excellent secondary defense as well. Manning was intercepted twice and dumped four times for losses of 28 yards.

Manning finished with a minus 25 yards rushing. Chumbler connected on 6 of 17 passes for 50 yards and was intercepted three times.

The Rebs managed only 2 yards rushing against the nation's top rushing defense while the Tigers had 214 yards rushing plus 291 yards passing. Lee missed only three of 10 passes and Jones connected on 7 of 14 passes for 114 yards. Jones threw the only Tiger interception and it set up an Ole Miss field goal.

LSU crammed 28 points into the final quarter and scored every way a team can in the game, including eight touchdowns, a like number of conversions, Lumpkin's 24-yard field goal, and a safety.

Tigers Stun Ole Miss, Orange Bowl Brass

By Bernell Ballard

The Advocate

Baton Rouge, La. — *Dec. 5, 1970*

There never was an LSU victory like this one.

Orange Bowl officials looked stunned as LSU chalked up a record 61-17 win over Ole Miss before a capacity crowd at Tiger Stadium and a regional television audience.

"It was one of the most tremendous football games I have ever seen," stated W. Keith Phillips Jr., the president of the Orange Bowl. "It was unbelievable and certainly a great individual victory for Coach McClendon. And it assures the Orange Bowl the best bowl game ever, not only of those bowls this New Year's but ever. With Nebraska, the fine offensive team, and LSU's great defense and all-around team, we should have it made."

And oranges, hundreds of them, sailed onto the field all night as fantastically fired-up LSU fans tossed them from the stands until finally warned to stop by the public address announcer or LSU would suffer a penalty.

Still, after LSU's touchdowns mounted and mounted, more oranges came until one Ole Miss player, in utter frustration, finally jumped up from his stance, picked up an orange, and tossed it back toward the LSU stands.

After Jimmy LeDoux streaked nine yards for LSU's final touchdown with only 42 seconds remaining, the Tigers got another chance when Bill Norsworthy intercepted Shug Chumbler's pass and returned it 30 yards to the Ole Miss 16-yard line with 14 seconds still remaining.

But 10,000 LSU fans stormed onto the field in wild jubilation, preventing any possible attempt for the Tigers to add any more points to the staggering victory total.

Police had to assist the LSU players from the field as fans mobbed the Tiger gridders en masse.

It was the biggest LSU win over Ole Miss since 1917 when the Tigers beat the Rebels, 52-7.

And it's pretty certain it was like hell for Ole Miss, who was greeted with "Go to hell, Ole Miss, go to hell," from start to finish by screaming Bengal fans.

"This is the greatest thing I ever envisioned could happen," said an overwhelmed LSU coach Charles McClendon, "I've been to bowl games before, but that was the most important victory of my life."

All will agree, McClendon can rest assured, it was a big one.

"Our kids played a football game which compliments our entire coaching staff. Togetherness is the name of the game. You can't imagine how I feel. Our kids are probably able to live with this better than I ever will," McClendon said.

Not only did the victory establish an all-time scoring mark against Ole Miss, but it also added to the ever-growing list of records on the LSU record books.

Tommy Casanova's two punt returns for touchdowns, a 61-yarder and a 74-yarder, made him the first SEC player ever to accomplish the feat. And Casanova became only the third college player in NCAA history to run back two punts for touchdowns in a game.

The other, a 61-yard punt return for touchdown by Craig Burns, coupled with Casanova's two, gave LSU a new SEC punt return yardage record of 205 yards for a single game, wiping out the old conference mark of 203 by Vanderbilt in 1948.

Those three punt returns for scores also tied another NCAA mark of most touchdowns by a team by punt returns in one game.

■ **All-American linebacker Mike Anderson and Charlie McClendon enjoy recounting a big play in the Tigers' 61-17 win over Ole Miss.**

Bengals Blast Irish, 28-8, in Tigerland

By Bud Montet
The Advocate

Baton Rouge — *Nov. 20, 1971*

Score by Periods

Notre Dame	0	0	0	8 —	8
LSU	7	7	7	7 —	28

The Sun Bowl-bound LSU Fighting Tigers gained sweet revenge when they took a 28-8 victory over the Fighting Irish of Notre Dame before 68,000 rabid-Cajun fans at Tiger Stadium tonight.

After building a 14-0 first-half lead, the Tigers went to work on the Irish records. They picked up touchdowns in the third and fourth periods, breaking the Irish streak of holding its 1971 foes scoreless in second-half play and the string of 20 games in which the Irish have held their foes scoreless in the final quarter of play.

The Bengals added the final crushing blow to the mighty Irish when, following the lone Notre Dame score, they took over at midfield and moved in for the final score of the game, a Paul Lyons to Andy Hamilton 12-yard pass play.

With a second left on the clock some LSU fans swarmed through the field fence to surround the players. The final second was never played.

The victory gave the Bengals a 7-3 record for the season and was the second setback for the Irish. LSU has only Tulane left on its 1971 regular season schedule

LSU will later clash with Iowa State in the Sun Bowl on Dec. 18. The Irish voted earlier in the week to skip any bowl appearance this season.

Surprise starter Bert Jones of the Bengals pitched to his cousin, Andy Hamilton, for the first two LSU scores, with one aerial going 36 yards, the first touchdown, and the second traveling 32 yards. Jones scored the third period touchdown with a five-yard keeper. Lyons' 12-yard pitch to Hamilton accounted for the final Tiger score.

The lone Notre Dame touchdown came in the fourth quarter with Cliff Brown pitching to Tom Gatewood for seven yards.

Although they held a 14-0 advantage at halftime, the Bengals spent most of the half defending their goal line with tactics that reminded of the Chinese Bandits of the 1958 National Championship eleven.

LSU, despite giving away a tremendous weight advantage, managed to rush for 143 yards and pitch for 156 for a total offense of 299 yards. The Irish rushed for 172 yards against the stubborn Tiger defense and passed for 151 for a total offense of 323 yards.

Jones hit on seven of nine aerials for 143 yards and his chief target, Hamilton, caught seven for 153 yards and three touchdowns.

Art Cantrelle figured in the only other Tiger pass completion, a three yarder.

The Irish's Brown put the ball in the air 29 times and hit on 13 for 151 yards. Gatewood was his chief target with seven catches for 75 yards.

The Bengals' fierce defense honors had to be shared by all. Ronnie Estay picked up 13 individual tackles and four assists.

Richard Picou and John Weed picked up seven individual tackles.

Warren Capone picked off two Brown passes, one halting a Notre Dame drive and the other setting up the second LSU score in the second period.

In the third period, the Irish were on the Tiger 32 when Capone wrestled a Brown pass from the Irish receiver, halting the threat.

LSU scored the first time they got their hands on the football in the first period, moving 77 yards with Jones pitching to Hamilton for 36 yards and the score.

LSU was moving again when they ran into trouble of their own making with Jones fumbling and giving up the ball at the Tiger 37.

Notre Dame marched to the Tiger 1-foot line where the Bengals stopped Andy Huff short of the goal and the first down.

Early in the second period, the Irish moved to the Tiger 1-yard line where Norman Hodgins pulled down Brown on a keeper play and forced the Irish to turn over the ball.

A few minutes later the Irish drove to the Tiger 3 where a fourth down Brown pass failed.

LSU took command in the second half but early in the fourth period Casanova's interception in the end zone stifled one Irish threat but midway in the period the Irish put together the long scoring strike.

While the Bengals were spoiling some Notre Dame streaks, their own gridders were setting new Tiger standards.

Paul Lyons, who served as the backup quarterback, set a new season mark of 16 touchdowns scored, which broke the old mark of 15 which Lyons shared with Y.A. Tittle.

■ **The LSU defense stopped Notre Dame's Andy Huff (20) at the goal line in the first quarter.**

Lyons has scored six touchdowns and passed for 10.

Andy Hamilton's three touchdown grabs tied the LSU record of touchdown receptions in a game. The old mark is held by Ken Kavanaugh Sr., set against Holy Cross in 1939. Kavanaugh's son is a Tiger tight end.

Hamilton also tied another old record held by Kavanaugh — seven touchdown passes in a single season. Kavanaugh set his mark in 1939.

Hamilton's 16 career touchdowns record ties the old mark held by Kavanaugh.

The fleet Tiger wide receiver has the Tulane game left in which to break Kavanaugh's old records.

Tonight's game wound up the brief two-game series. Notre Dame won, 3-0, last year at South Bend.

For most of the game it appeared that LSU would hold the Irish scoreless, a feat none have accomplished since Miami blanked the Irish in 1965.

LSU put together two drives for two scores and took advantage of breaks to get their other two scores. Capone's intercep-

tion and 32-yard runback gave the Tigers the impetus for their second touchdown.

Norman Hodgins' recovery of a Brown fumble at the Irish 33 gave LSU its chance for the third touchdown.

LSU's Cantrelle was the workhorse on the ground with 18 carries for a net 53 yards.

Dantin carried nine times for 36 yards and Allen Shorey six times for 25.

Huff was the top ball carrier for the Irish with 13 carries for 42 yards. Ed Gulyas carried 15 for 39 yards.

The Bengals who have been plagued all season with costly mistakes on offense seemed destined to have to live through it all over again.

After fighting off a trio of Irish threats in the first half LSU took the second half kickoff and marched from their 41 to the Irish 31 when Cantrelle fumbled and the Irish took over.

From that point, the Bengals took command of the game, until the Notre Dame scoring drive early in the fourth period.

■ LSU quarterback Bert Jones dives for a first-quarter touchdown.

LSU Wins Wild Thriller Over Rebs, 17-16

BY JOE PLANAS
The Advocate

Baton Rouge, La. — *Nov. 4, 1972*

A teenage blonde cried in the end zone, an elderly gentleman asked for some nitroglycerin pills, and Heisman Trophy candidate Bert Jones compressed football history into a mere second tonight.

About 70,502 fans — some of them not able to believe the spectacle — watched as soph Brad Davis hugged deliriously a Bert Jones pass tossed to him after the final gun in LSU's unbelievable 17-16 triumph over Ole Miss.

Jones, who had set a few records in total offense and number of touchdowns responsible for, had started to march LSU the necessary 80 yards with 3:02 left in the game after a determined LSU defense forced the Rebs to punt after three offensive plays. With last-down-and-everything facing him, Jones threw to Davis in the flat and the former Hammond High sparkler sparkled by making the grab that was reminiscent of Doug Moreau's two-point catch in the end zone in LSU's 11-10 win over the Rebels in 1964. There was one second left on

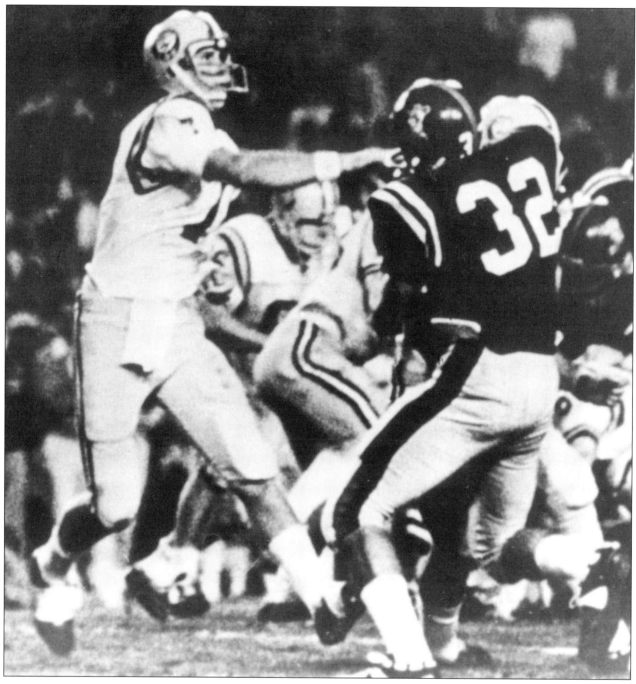

■ **Bert Jones unleashed his touchdown pass with no time left on the scoreboard clock.**

the clock when Jones got the snap and the horn sounded before Jones pumped his arm. If there was ever a finer finish in a football game, it had to have happened in Utopia, or somewhere like that.

A pass interference call against the Rebs after LSU had taken its last timeout with 10 seconds left had elevated Tiger hearts and advanced the ball from the Reb 20 to their 10. But, with four seconds left, those same hearts went down deeper into chest cavities when little Jimmy LeDoux watched Reb Mickey Fratesi bat away a Jones aerial. Then came the one-sec-

Score by Periods

Ole Miss	3	3	7	3 —	16
LSU	7	3	0	7 —	17

ond confrontation, Jones' response to it, and the still hard-to-believe final outcome. The pass was really a two-point play but LSU got 300 percent out of it.

■ Rusty Jackson's extra-point kick gave LSU a 17-16 win over the Rebels.

■ **In the end zone, the official signaled the results of Brad Davis' catch.**

For 59 minutes and 59 seconds, Ole Miss had been the superior football club. But, it only takes a second — they say. Jones had started LSU on the 13-play, 80-yard caper with 3:02 left in the game. He didn't waste a minute, or, for that matter, even a second. Rusty Jackson's kick was a formality the fans expected.

"I just fell over the flag," offered a wet Davis who still had shaving lather on his face and was trying to be polite by not letting water from his shower spill on a sports writer's coat. "The pass was meant for me and I just grabbed it. I think I've caught only two others this season." The 10-yard reception was the only catch Davis made all night. The other two he had caught prior to the Ole Miss game were good for minus-one yard.

Davis, who brilliantly led Oscar Lofton's Hammond Tors to many football victories, also looked good running the ball. He finished the evening with 56 yards in 15 carries — his longest run being for 15 yards. Chris Dantin, whose longest gainer was for 16 stripes, was LSU's leading rusher with 60 yards in a dozen trips.

"We only had one second left and only one play left," Jones said. "I knew I had to get rid of the ball quickly to let somebody get a chance at catching it. I thought Brad lost it somewhere up

there in the lights but I guess he found it. Yes, I do think we're ready for Alabama."

Jones was on target 14 of the 21 times (167 yards.) He threw for 67 percent and had one intercepted. The completion total gave him a career mark of 181 completions, breaking Mike Hillman's total of 171. Though utilized for losses of 20 yards in all, Jones upped his total offense figures to 2,726 yards, cracking Tittle's total of 2,694. He also eased past Tittle's touchdowns-responsible-for mark of 30 by shoving his own to 31. Not bad for a country boy from Ruston.

"In all my years here I don't think I remember an LSU team winning with no time on the clock," a joyous Charley McClendon said. "Can you imagine what we did? Our defense stopped 'em from getting their first down with under five minutes left to go, and then we go and take it right to 'em and win. I'd rather fight any football team in America than that clock. That clock, fellows, just doesn't give you any consideration."

McClendon was happily interrupted by former LSU gridders R.B. Nunnery and O.J. Ferguson, who patted him on the back and said how great the win was. "You're part of it, you know, R.B. and O.K. You fellows are all part of it."

■ **Wasting no time, Bert Jones joins his teammates in the end zone celebration.**

McClendon turned his praise on Jones and Davis and rugged, play-for-forever Warren Capone. "When you work under adversities, that's what Heisman trophy winners are drawn from," Mac noted. "And you'd have to say Bert was working under adversity in those last seconds. It was a great game for Jones and should raise his stock in the Heisman voting."

Did Mac call the play:

"That was coach 'Charlie Pevy's play,' " McClendon noted. "He deserves credit for calling that one. Yes, Davis was the primary receiver on that one, but we send three receivers out just in case. Brad was a splitback and just went out in the flat. He's a dutch player you know, sorta has a star on his forehead."

Then McClendon started thinking defense. "You know Warren Capone had a fantastic game for us." Jolly Cholly remarked. "Someone told me he had 13 individual tackles and seven assists, but fellows, I knew he had played a whale of a football game before I heard those statistics."

How much of a thrill was it in beating Ole Miss?

"You'd have to call this one victory one of the all-time thrills in Tiger football history," Mac opined. "Ole Miss played excellent, smart football. I guess you could say the only mistakes they made were missing that field goal and getting that costly pass-interference call. You know as a coach you preach to kids that as long as there's a second left you've got hope. We had hope and it came through for us."

Mac had more praise for Ole Miss. "They played excellent football and seem to bring out the best in the Tigers," Mac said. "They controlled the football — lot more than we wanted them to and that Norris Weese from Chalmette is one fine football player. But then, he always plays well against us."

In the shower room, other LSU players chanted "Go to Hell, Ole Miss." Earlier, Dantin and Paul Lyons had embraced and following that, someone kissed Davis on the flank. "You deserve to be kissed after a catch like that," the donator said.

Coach Dave McCarty said he didn't believe the win. He was that excited.

An aging sports writer admitted his ticker couldn't stand "many more like this baby."

"It was beautiful," said an old lady who lingered with the crowd outside the LSU dressing room. "Simply beautiful," she added.

Now all Mac has to do is beat Ole Miss every year through 1976 to play .500 ball against the Rebs.

■ Trojans quarterback Paul McDonald connected on 14 passes for 145 yards against LSU.

No. 1 Trojans Stage Late Comeback to Defeat LSU

BY BUD MONTET
The Advocate

Baton Rouge, La. — *Sept. 29, 1979*

Hailed as THE football team of the final quarter century, the Southern California Trojans had to stage a desperate 79-yard march in the fading minutes to overtake the LSU Tigers and win, 17-12 before the second largest turnout at Tiger Stadium today before 78,322 fans.

■ Tigers coach Charlie McClendon congratulates USC tailback Charles White after the game.

LSU grabbed a 9-3 halftime lead and added three points in the third period to grab a 12-3 lead but the mighty Trojans scored twice in the fourth period to grab the victory and keep their string going at four games and protect their No. 1 ranking in the nation.

Heavily favored prior to the contest, the visitors, meeting LSU for the first time, were hard put in the early stages.

LSU's stubborn defenses, led by middle guard George Atiyeh, harassed the Trojans throughout, although Heisman Trophy candidate Charlie White netted 185 yards in 31 carries.

LSU held White from the goal line until late in the fourth period when the All-American plunged over from the four-yard line and put the Trojans within striking distance.

Southern Cal put points on the board first when Eric Hipp booted a 32-yard field goal in the first quarter with 4:58 left.

In the second quarter, LSU drove 60 yards in eight plays to

Score by Periods

Southern Cal	3	0	0	14	—	17
LSU	0	9	3	0	—	12

move in front with Steve Ensminger pitching to LeRoid Jones for 14 yards and a touchdown.

With only 2:16 left in the half, Tiger walk-on kicker Don Barthel booted a 32-yard field goal to give LSU a 9-3 lead at the intermission.

Near the end of the third period the Bengals missed a chance to widen the margin with a touchdown when they moved to the Trojan 2-yard line and four downs to make the score.

■ **Charles White (12), who rushed for 185 yards on 31 carries, shakes loose of a LSU defender before turning upfield.**

An attempted end around with Tracy Porter carrying the ball backfired and lost nine yards. Carlos Carson dropped a pass in the end zone and LSU had to settle for a 28-yard field goal by Barthel that gave them a 12-3 lead.

The fourth period belonged to the Trojans as they drove 56 yards in a half dozen plays to score their first touchdown with White going over from the four.

LSU missed a chance to put the game away midway the fourth period when freshman Alvin Thomas recovered a Marcus Allen fumble at the Trojan 17. On their first play, LSU tried a double reverse pass play and drew a 15-yard penalty that stymied the threat.

The Trojans got the ball at their 21 and with 4:16 left in the game moved to the Tiger 8-yard line. From there, Paul McDonald pitched to Kevin Williams for the winning score.

LSU kept coming after the kickoff with only 32 seconds left in the game. A 15-yard penalty gave LSU possession at their 42 and an Ensminger pass to Robert DeLee to the Trojan 30 set up two desperation passes by Ensminger into the Trojan end zone and both failed.

The vaunted Trojan offense didn't eclipse the Bengals by any great margin. Coach John Robinson's team piled up 396 yards while LSU totaled 272 yards.

Southern Cal netted 251 yards on the ground with White getting 185 yards of that total. In the air, the Trojans picked up 145 yards as McDonald connected on 14 aerials.

The Tigers picked up a net 169 yards on the ground and 103 in the air.

LSU suffered a crippling blow in the first half when their starting tailback, Hokie Gajan, was injured and missed the entire second half. Gajan carried the ball 10 times in the first half before he was injured.

LeRoid Jones came in for Gajan at the tailback slot and picked up 67 yards in nine attempts to lead the Tiger rushers. Fullback Jude Hernandez was also injured in the first half but came back to play in the second half and netted 40 yards in five carries.

Atiyeh with superb play in the middle forced the Trojans to move White. Atiyeh got seven solo tackles and four assists.

■ **LeRoid Jones' 14-yard touchdown in the second quarter gave LSU a 7-0 lead.**

Linebacker Jerry Hill brought back memories of former linebacking greats at LSU when he netted nine solos and five assists for his outstanding performance of the season.

Marcus Quinn, who was injured during the week played a standout defensive game, getting six solo tackles and seven assists.

USC's speedy defense slowed down the Tiger passing game which probably was the key to the contest. David Woodley and Ensminger had trouble getting away from the Trojans' pass rush. Woodley was tossed for 20 yards in losses while trying to throw.

Swift Chris Williams kept the Trojans at bay in the first period when he made a grab of a McDonald pass on the 2-yard line, bobbled it and then gained possession in the end zone.

A Tiger mistake gave the Trojans their chance to get on the board. First, when Jeff Fisher intercepted Woodley's pass at the Tiger 33 and USC went on to get their field goal.

It was Ensminger who came off the bench to get the Tigers rolling, leading them on their 6-yard scoring drive. On the drive, Ensminger connected on three passes.

Williams' pass interception in the first period was his 13th career interception and set a new Tiger record. The interception was the first thrown by McDonald this season.

After two victories over non conference foes and their loss to the Trojans, LSU swings into SEC play next Saturday when they entertain the Florida Gators at Tiger Stadium.

LSU Sends Mac Out A Winner, 34-10

By John Adams
The Advocate

Orlando, Fla. — *Dec. 22, 1979*

The end was much like the beginning for LSU coach Charles McClendon here tonight as his LSU Tigers — his last LSU Tigers — rolled up 24 points in the first half and charged to a 34-10 victory over the Wake Forest Deacons in the 31st Tangerine Bowl.

McClendon, the winningest coach in LSU history, was riding high-on the shoulders of his players after posting his 137th career victory. His first victory came 17 years ago against Texas A&M in the 1962 season opener.

His assistant coaches, most of whom were also coaching their final game at LSU, were given free rides, too, after the Tigers had erased the "Miracle" from Wake Forest's "Miracle" Deacons.

Wake Forest, which went from 1-10 to 8-3 in one year, matched up more to those 1-10 days against a Tiger team that played perhaps it best game of the year.

Of all the Tigers, senior quarterback David Woodley was the one who played the best. He ran for two touchdowns and passed for another — all in the first half — as LSU boosted its record to 7-5.

Woodley, who completed 11 of 19 passes for 199 yards, was named the game's Most Valuable Player. Jerry Murphree who caught five passes for 60 yards and one touchdown, was the offensive player of the game while Tiger tackle Benjy Thibodeaux was selected as the game's best defensive player.

"We broke a bunch of jinxes tonight," said Tiger center John Ed Bradley, one of 17 LSU seniors playing his final game. "People said we couldn't win on the road and we couldn't beat a good team. We did that tonight. I'm proud to end my career

■ David Woodley completed 11 of 19 passes for 199 yards and was named the game's MVP.

Score by Periods

LSU	14	10	0	10 —	34
Wake Forest	0	3	7	0 —	10

■ **A pair of LSU defenders scramble to recover a Wake Forest fumble.**

like that. We're going out winners. It's time to go out and tie one on."

Wake Forest, now 8-4, was just tied up. Quarterback Jay Venuto, the Atlantic Coast Conference player of the year, was intercepted three times, and was repeatedly harried by the Tigers' strong pass rush, led by Thibodeaux and defensive end Lyman White.

"LSU played well throughout the game," said Wake Forest coach John Mackovic. "Their offense did a good job controlling the game and their pass rush was tremendous.

"We dropped some passes in the first half and that hurt us. They just outmanned us in spots. They came to win, there's no question about that."

After Woodley directed LSU to three first-half touchdowns and a field goal by Don Barthel, the Deacons finally scored on the last play of the half on a 43-yard field goal by Phil Denfeld.

That seemed to spark the Deacons in the second half. Wake

Forest, which overcame an 18-point first-half deficit in a regular-season victory over Auburn, moved for a touchdown on its first possession of the second half.

Venuto, who completed 10 of 20 passes for 165 yards, drove the Deacons 80 yards, with the final 34 yards coming on a pass to split end Wayne Baumgardner.

However, the Deacons lost their momentum when they failed to take advantage of a Hokie Gajan fumble — one of three Tiger turnovers — on the Deacon 38.

They had another opportunity moments later when Venuto teamed up with Baumgardner for a 16-yard completion to the LSU 38. Fullback Bob Ventresca followed with a 15-yard run to the Tiger 17.

Then, Venuto — pressured by defensive end John Adams — attempted to throw the ball away before he was sacked near the sideline. His throw away landed in Thibodeaux's lap, and the Tigers had the football on their own 29.

"When the Venuto pass was intercepted we had a great opportunity to score and they sort of stopped us on that play," said Mackovic. "At the half, we determined that we had to come out and play with more intensity and I thought we did a good job early in the second half. We lost a great deal of momentum on that one play."

Woodley then passed 48 yards to Tracy Porter on the second play of the fourth quarter. After the Tiger quarterback was sacked twice and LSU lost another five yards for delay of game, Barthel kicked a 41-yard field goal.

On LSU's next possession, Steve Ensminger completed three straight passes in leading the Tigers on a 43-yard touchdown march. Ensminger got the final score of the evening on a 4-yard run with 8:32 to play.

"I really don't feel anything right now," said McClendon, who is being replaced by Bo Rein after 18 years as LSU's head coach. "We came out at the beginning of the game certainly ready to play. I believe that had to be the best first half we've had all season."

The Deacons wouldn't argue that point.

After the first half, the 12,000 Wake Forest fans that followed their team to Orlando, must have been asking one another, "We waited for this?"

The Deacons, who hadn't been to a bowl game in 31 years, spent the first 30 minutes of the game assisting LSU in adding lots of footage to its 1979 highlight film.

Not until Phil Denfeld booted his 43-yard field goal with no time showing on the scoreboard clock did Wake Forest have any reason to think a bowl game was supposed to be fun. If the Deacons had been bowling for dollars, they would have owed money at the end of the first half.

With Woodley having the best half of his three-year career at LSU, the Tigers amassed 17 first downs and 306 yards in total offense in rolling to a 24-3 lead. Another drive was blunted by a Jesse Myles fumble at the Deacon goal line and a second was cut short when the Tigers were stopped on a fourth-and-one situation at the Deacon 31.

In the first quarter, there was no stopping Woodley or the Tigers. On LSU's first possession, Woodley completed four of five passes — one was dropped — for 44 yards, and then ran 13 yards for a touchdown in the 80-yard, 12-play march.

Jerry Murphree had two catches, the first on third-and-2 at the LSU 28, to add more fuel to the drive. His second reception — for 13 yards — gave LSU a first down at the Deacon 21.

Fullback Jude Hernandez then broke through the middle for 8 yards to the Deacon 13, setting up Woodley's scoring run. Guard John Watson contributed a key block on Woodley's TD.

Moments later, the Tigers were in scoring position again. After McDonald had gained 19 yards on a third-down draw play, Tiger safety Marcus Quinn intercepted Venuto's pass on the Deacon 35.

Woodley struck quickly hitting Orlando McDaniel for a 15-

■ **Charlie McClendon argues with an official about the scoreboard clock.**

yard gain to the 20. Then facing a third-and-8 at the Deacon 12, Woodley — who was unaffected by noseguard James Parker pulling on his leg — lobbed a 6-yard completion to Carlos Carson.

On fourth-and-2, Woodley — aided by a Hernandez block — scampered 9 yards around the right side for a first down. On the next play, he rolled left, then cut between two would-be tacklers at the goal line for the second Tiger score.

With Steve Ensminger taking over at quarterback on the next possession, LSU again appeared on its way to a touchdown.

The Tigers' offensive line continued to control the line of scrimmage, as Ensminger, freshman Jesse Myles and Danny Soileau took turns riddling the Deacon defense.

After a pass interference call against Deacon defensive back Derek Crocker, who was covering Murphree in the end zone,

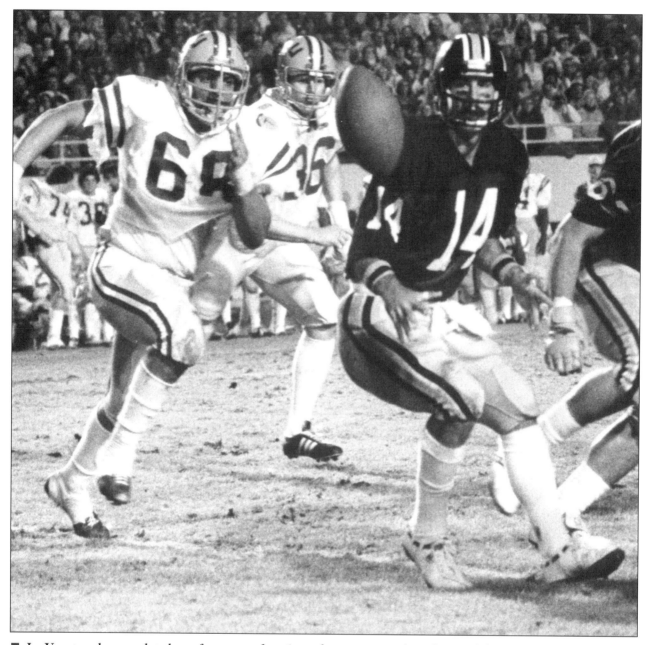

■ Jay Venuto, who completed 10 of 20 passes for 165 yards, was constantly under attack by the LSU defense.

the Tigers had a first down at the Deacon 1. However, on second down, Myles fumbled as he was hit at the goal line and Wake Forest's Eddie Green recovered.

Another Tiger drive was halted at the Wake Forest 31 before Woodley returned to engineer a 90-yard scoring drive. A 30-yard completion to Carson, open on the sideline when defender Lewis Owens fell down, accounted for most of the yardage. Two plays later, Woodley passed 19 yards to Murphree, who made a diving catch in the end zone for LSU's third TD of the evening.

The Tigers missed another scoring opportunity when Albert Richardson recovered an Albert Kirby fumble on the Wake Forest 20. After a 9-yard Woodley-to-Lionel Wallis

completion, LSU was pushed back 5 yards on an illegal procedure penalty. Two passes fell incomplete before the Tigers turned to Don Barthel, who responded with a 31-yard field goal.

Wake Forest came to life in the final minute of the first half after Landon King intercepted a Woodley pass on the Wake Forest 34.

Sophomore David Webber then replaced Venuto at quarterback and completed a 15-yard pass to tight end Mike Mullen. A 16-yard completion to Baumgardner seconds later gave the Deacons a first down on LSU's 27.

On the final play of the half, Denfeld put the Deacons on the scoreboard with his 43-yard field goal.

In A Difficult Hour, the Torch Is Passed

BY MARVIN WEST
Special to The Advocate

It is a strange, strange story, a chilling mystery, a haunting twist of fate ... one man's heart was broken, another man died. Another, after dreaming 15 years and being denied, saw his dream come true.

This is the stunning story of how Jerry Lane Stovall became head football coach at Louisiana State University.

Stovall, a Tiger halfback two decades ago, wanted to be the coach where he had played. He prepared properly, touched all the bases, knew the time was near.

On a day when the date could just as easily have been set, Jerry Stovall got the coldest message of his life. Paul Dietzel, back in Baton Rouge as athletic director of LSU, was playing with a different deck of cards. The game had changed. Jerry didn't fit the criteria imposed on Dietzel by the school's Board of Supervisors.

Stovall is smart. He learns quickly. In a matter of minutes, some twenty years ago, he realized he'd never be the boss of the Bengals. Oh, how that hurt!

About the same time, Charles Y. McClendon was twisting in the wind. After all those good years in Tigertown, between the time Dietzel left and returned Cholly Mac was told to go, that he was finished, that his time had expired.

Well, he could stay as head coach through 1979.

Stovall, forced to choose between an apprenticeship in athletic administration, a far more lucrative business offer or dying on the vine as a McClendon assistant on the field, made a wise decision. He went on down the road with Dietzel.

After all, it was Dietzel who first put him on the path, played him as running back, receiver and safety, gave his such a chance, Jerry fell only a few votes short of the Heisman Trophy.

Dietzel training helped Stovall play as pro. When his fun and games ended in the NFL, it was Dietzel who took Stovall into coaching, as an aide at South Carolina, and told him some day he'd be a head coach.

That was good but Columbia, SC., wasn't home and when Jerry got a chance, he rushed back to Baton Rouge, to assist McClendon, to give back some of the things he had learned as a Tiger, to further prepare for the time when the top job would be his.

■ Jerry Stovall, a 1962 All-American halfback for the Tigers, became LSU's coach after Bo Rein's death.

■ Charlie McClendon served as an assistant to Paul Dietzel and later coached the Tigers for 18 seasons.

■ Bo Rein took the job to succeed McClendon, but died in a plane crash while on a recruiting trip 42 days later.

Then, the whole dream was gone ... but Dietzel was still there.

Dietzel lashed unfairly by some for allegedly undercutting Cholly Mac, only did what the LSU administration had dictated when he returned. McClendon was to be phased out, as gracefully as possible, and an established head coach be found to replace him.

That requirement knocked out the bridge for Stovall. He had never been a head coach. It didn't matter that he was Dietzel's down-deep choice, that they had a father-son relationship, that Paul was sure Jerry would be an inspiring leader.

Dietzel spent more than a year in a serious search. LSU faithful split into factions. Some wanted new life for McClendon. Some wanted Ara Parseghian, Lou Holtz or Bobby Bowden. Some thought Dietzel should attempt a comeback, try to again catch lightning in a jar, as he did with the national championship Tigers of 1958 the time of Billy Cannon.

Dietzel is too smart for that. He hired Bo Rein, 34, a former Ohio State wingback, and four years the head coach at North Carolina State, with a record of 27-17-1, two bowl teams and one Atlantic Coast Conference championship.

Yes, Bo Rein was the man. He had no Tiger ties. He could unify the family. He was enthusiastic, energetic, a tireless recruiter. Rein brought seven helpers from his Raleigh staff, came to town while the McClendon team was still milling around the office, and hit the road to round up prep talent.

"This man has the look of an eagle," Dietzel said of Rein. "I liked him when I saw him, and, of course, when I hired him. Now that I have seen him at work, I like him even better."

Rein logged thousands of miles for LSU in 42 days. That's how long he was head coach of the Tigers.

On a Thursday night, Jan. 9, 1980, with pilot Lewis Benscotter, in a sophisticated corporate plane, on loan to LSU football, the coach was flying to home base from a recruiting trip in Shreveport, La.

A storm line near Alexandria may have forced the pilot to change his course, but that should not have been a problem. The almost new Cessna Conquest, owned by Nichols Construction Company, was a twin turbo prop, pressurized to be safe at 33,000 feet, and equipped with a radar transponder that automatically

■ **Charlie McClendon took his teams to 13 bowl games in 18 seasons.**

returned it to a charter course after any pilot adjustment.

But for some strange reason, still unexplained, the Rein plane didn't follow its "mind." The pilot had requested clearance of Fort Worth air control to 25,000 feet but controllers, watching the blip on their screen, saw it ease on up to 29,000 and turn northeast toward Memphis instead of southeast to Baton Rouge.

An FAA report says the Forth Worth tracking crew tried to establish radio contact but failed.

The Air Force Rescue Center near St. Louis dispatched two F-4 fighter planes from Seymour-Johnson Air Force Base, near Raleigh to seek information — standard procedure when an event so puzzling is in progress. The jet pilots spotted the Cessna, but saw no cabin lights, no sign of life aboard. Again, radio contact efforts failed.

Many find it ironic, if not spooky, that the Rein plane flew near Raleigh, where he had worked three years for Holtz and four on his own, where the family home hadn't been sold, where the Rein daughters, nine and 13, were still staying with relatives.

Why Raleigh?

Another Air Force jet, an F-106, went up from Langley AFB near Norfolk, Va., to see what it could see. This pilot reported "close fly-bys," said he blinked landing lights and fired an afterburner in a bid to attract the Cessna's attention. Nothing happened.

Something finally did. The Rein ride went on, as high as 41,000 feet and more than 1,000 miles in the wrong direction, until it crashed, apparently out of fuel, about 120 miles off the Virginia coast, into the Atlantic Ocean. The Coast Guard reported the plane hit, with great impact in an area past the continental shelf, where water is up to 6,000 feet deep.

The tragedy rocked LSU to the foundations. What would happen to the young family? How about the assistant coaches who had followed Rein to Tigertown and now had no leader? What about the LSU football program, so long struggling with instability? The recruiting race was about to peak.

Dietzel, up through a night of anxiety, into a morning of shock, started home from the office at 5:45 a.m. Something had to be done in a hurry.

"I remember my prayer ... 'Lord, what do we do now? Please guide my decision. It is in Your hands now.' "

After two hours rest, Dietzel rushed to the office of Chancellor Paul W. Murrill. They agreed the loss was terrible, that Rein's staff was devastated, that chaos was near. There was not time for another search. The school had an obligation to McClendon's assistants until June and to Rein's for a year. It could not, with any logic, hire another established coach with another staff and pay three!

Yes, Dietzel said, he could have a recommendation for a Saturday Board of Supervisor's meeting.

Stovall was the only solution, the only man who would stick his finger into the dike with a chance to stop the leak.

"Jerry Stovall was absolutely and completely qualified in every way," says Dietzel, looking back. "He is young, tough, aggressive, articulate, a great recruiter, the best I ever had.

"He is highly intelligent, professionally trained, with superior integrity. He knew LSU through and through and, of all the people I could think of, he knew Bo's staff best."

Stovall, working as LSU fund-raiser out of Dietzel's office, knew the assistants far better than did the athletic director. Stovall had seen them come into the state, meet people they had never seen, go to towns with names they couldn't pro-

■ Jerry Stovall
served as an assistant
to Paul Dietzel at
South Carolina
before joining
McClendon's staff at
LSU.

■ **Jerry Stovall was a runner-up for the Heisman Trophy in 1962.**

nounce and do a job for LSU. He had escorted them, individually, to booster club meetings in their new recruiting territories.

Stovall would take the head coaching responsibility and keep all the assistants that wanted to stay.

Why the haste? Did it have to be Saturday, one day and a few hours after the ill-fated flight?

"We were already getting calls with suggestions on who we ought to hire this time," recalls Dietzel. "The division was beginning again. For the sake of LSU, it had to be stopped. Jerry Stovall was the obvious solution."

And so, Dietzel advanced the name he would have liked in the first place, had the supervisors not demanded a coach with a name already in lights.

Jerry Stovall, the only choice in a time of great crisis, got the job he couldn't get when there was a year to evaluate. It's like asking a man to leave the mansion when dinner is about to be served and then calling his name in desperation when the roof is on fire.

Stovall responded with sadness ... and perfectly normal delight.

"I would gladly surrender this job, and any other, and my

right arm if Bo Rein could still be here," said Stovall, a sincere man, a Christian.

"Yes, this is a dream come true," he would say later. "I am so happy to have the opportunity but I regret deeply the circumstances that gave me the job. It involved tragedy in others' lives. I am keenly aware of the hurt Sue Rein and her family are going through. I wouldn't wish than on anyone.

"But there's no way on God's Earth I am going to hang my head and say I backed into this job. I am the head coach at LSU and I am proud to have been chosen. I would like to think I was the person who could plug the dike. I don't know how many others could. I do know Paul Dietzel could have done it."

Stovall started dreaming this dream in 1964.

"That's when Judy and I started dreaming it. I say 'we' because we are a team. And it is Judy and Jerry, if anybody asks. We are not Mr. And Mrs. Stovall, we are Mrs. and Mr. I couldn't do anything that requires the time and energy of coaching by myself. It takes both of us to do the job."

"Both of us" resigned from dental school in St. Louis in 1964 and made the commitment to coaching. "Both of us" wanted to come back to Baton Rouge when Coach Mac had an opening.

"Both of us" were broken-hearted when they discovered

there was no end to the rainbow, that Judy and Jerry couldn't be head coach when Coach McClendon was through.

"We talked about it, decided the Good Lord does not close one door to you without opening another. A good friend in Birmingham, Ala., offered us a job in Denver at a lot more money.

"I was very, very disappointed by what happened at LSU but I didn't really want to leave. We had to face that 'Never be head coach' and live with it. We cried. We wanted it so badly, you don't get over such a trauma in a week."

When Judy and Jerry decided they'd stay, they put the hurt behind them and went back to work, just as hard for LSU. Such is the character of the new head coach.

Can Stovall compete?

"I believe in Jerry Stovall," said Jerry. "I've stolen enough good ideas from Coach Dietzel and others to be good.

"You want to go to the blackboard with chalk in hand and do X's and O's? Let's go.

"You want to hit the road and recruit? I'll do it against anybody.

"You want to talk about motivation? Hey, I'll go head-to-head."

Stovall says the experience of not getting the LSU job in the beginning may have better prepared him when it came.

"I had to accept the facts. I found out that part of my prayer — Your will be done, Lord — was very real. I had been living life pretty much my way, the way I wanted it to go. When it headed off in the other direction, I wondered, for a minute, if the old ship would sink. But, there was that old verse about all things working for good for those who love the Lord."

What was a Stovall way back then, that we might get a clue to what is a Stovall today?

"LSU signed 52 the year I came in. I was No. 51. I came with minimal talent, marginal skills. My best 100 (-yard dash time) was 10.2, in living color. One sportswriter, generous to a fault, called me a 'slender youngster from West Monroe.' I was a skinny runt.

"The only real asset I had was the fact that I would try. Then and now, you may whip me but you better bring a big stick and a sack lunch to the fight ... because it's going to last a while!

"I'm not very fast or quick or strong or big ... but I will try."

Can a coach be so religious?

"I've been mixing faith and football a long time, now. I can keep doing it. I will not compromise my principles to get through this jungle. I can win without cheating.

"There are still too many good people working very hard at raising children in the right way, so they'll be quality people, positive people, with genuine values when they grow up.

"We just need 30."

Stovall, after being selected as the new coach, attended a memorial service in Raleigh for Bo Rein on Sunday, Jan. 12. He met with Rein's coaches, told them he wanted them, told them they were better qualified, by six weeks, to help LSU through the crisis than anyone else in America.

"I told them I am a Christian, that they needed to understand that. They needed to know what I stand for, why I want to do what is right. I told them if they didn't agree with that basic concept, they should not consider returning to LSU.

"I saw some questions on some faces. They wondered what the words meant. Will he let me coach hard? Is he tough enough to win? What will he do if others cheat on the player I am recruiting? Does he have enough guts to get on the phone and do something about it?

"This is a place where you can not only win, you can dominate! I'm not interested in winning 10 of 11. I want to win 'em all. I don't want to go out there and whip you a little. I want to stop your will to compete against me.

"It's not a question of whether we'll win or lose. It's how badly we are going to whip you, on the scoreboard and physically. We're gonna stick those yellow headgears in some ears."

This article was originally published in Fall 1980.

■ Alan Risher completed 13 of 16 first-half passes against the Crimson Tide.

Risher & Tigers Upset Alabama, 20-10

By Jimmy Hyams
The Advocate

Birmingham, Ala. — *Nov. 6, 1982*

After 12 years of bondage, the LSU Tigers finally freed themselves. The cage was opened. The chains were unbuckled. No longer are they "owned" by Bama and the Bear.

Their Moses was a feeble-looking, yet heady player named Alan Risher, who orchestrated miracle after miracle with his right arm and wiggly feet to end more than a decade of frustration.

■ **Dalton Hilliard (21) only rushed for 30 first-half yards, but turned in a dazzling 33-yard pass reception.**

LSU's senior quarterback parted the Crimson Tide with 20 completions and scrambled for numerous crucial first downs to lead the No. 10 Tigers to one of their most brilliant victories in LSU football history, a 20-10 upset over No.7-ranked Alabama before 77,230 fans in Legion Field this afternoon

So dominant was LSU's performance, it had Alabama coach Bear Bryant, the winningest coach in college history, talking retirement.

"I think this is the biggest win for anyone associated with LSU in the last 12 years," said Risher, who threw for 182 yards and one touchdown. "This ends 12 years of suffering as a fan and player."

The usually reserved Risher even did a little "victory dance" on the field after he'd picked up a first down with four minutes

Score by Periods

LSU	0	17	0	3 —	20
Alabama	0	0	10	0 —	10

to go. "I was just real happy," He said.

So was LSU coach Jerry Stovall, who had downplayed LSU's earlier victory over then No. 4-ranked Florida.

"Without a doubt, this is the biggest victory I've ever had as a coach," said Stovall, who gave the game ball to his wife, Judy. "It's been a long, long time. You can't understand what it's like to get hit in the mouth 11 years in a row."

It was LSU delivering the knockout punch today, though, using a wide open offense and a stingy defense as its 1-2 punch. The Tigers erupted for 17 second-quarter points on Dalton Hilliard's 16-yard run, Risher's 3-yard pass to Malcolm Scott and Juan Carlos Betanzos' 23-yard field goal. And the defense held on in the second half after the Tide had cut the margin to 17-10.

LSU is now 7-0-1 on the season and second in the Southeastern Conference with a 4-0-1 mark. The Tigers had hoped to move into the SEC lead, but first place Georgia (5-0) bombed Florida, 44-0. However, the Tigers are still in the thick of the race for the Sugar Bowl, which automatically goes to the conference champion.

Georgia plays its final conference game at Auburn next Saturday while LSU visits Mississippi State in Starkville, Miss. Also its league finale.

Alabama which has won or tied for the SEC title nine of the last 11 years in now 7-2 and 3-2.

"I think that's the best beating we've had since the 1960's," said Bryant, whose team was outgained 321 yards to 119. "LSU had the superior team and I know that they had the best coach. They were better prepared."

It appeared that way from the beginning.

Using a more simplistic scheme than in the last two years to stop the wishbone, LSU's Bandit defense held the Crimson Tide without a first down and only 32 total yards in the first half. The Bandits contained Alabama quarterback Walter Lewis so well, he was benched in favor of Ken Coley in the last five minutes of the first half.

Lewis, who is second on Alabama's all-time single-season total yardage list was held to 21 yards rushing and 74 yards passing. The Tide managed only 45 yards rushing against the nation's No. 1-rated defense.

"I think our game plan was just super," said LSU senior linebacker Albert Richardson, explaining that LSU had at least two men assigned to the fullback, quarterback and pitch man on each play.

So frustrated was the Tide offense, Bryant had them running plays before the start of the third quarter. The Tide did show more spunk in the second half, but it wasn't enough.

"Lewis has beaten everybody they've played this year," said LSU linebackers coach Buddy Nix, who served as a graduate assistant at Alabama in 1961-62. "We had different ways to take him (the quarterback) out of plays if we needed them — and we did. Alabama discovers what you're doing on the first series and they hone in on it. We just rotated which man had who on their option."

But even Nix, who calls LSU's defensive signals, was surprised at LSU's first half success, which included holding Alabama to 10 yards on 15 carries. The Tide was averaging more than 300 yards rushing per game.

"If somebody had told me we'd hold them without a first down in the first half, I'd have said they were crazy," admitted Nix, who lost to Alabama five straight years while he was a defensive assistant at Auburn (1976-80).

"I've been coaching a long time (21 years) and that's the

sweetest (win) I've ever been around," he said.

Not only was LSU's defensive game plan a marvel, the offense showed a series of different sets and new plays which kept Alabama off balance for all but the first quarter. LSU dominated time of possession, holding the ball for 39 minutes and 30 seconds against a team noted for its ball control. The Tigers also converted 14 of 26 third downs while Alabama was 0-for-11.

"The game plan worked probably exactly like we wanted it to," said LSU quarterbacks coach Mack Brown, who also calls the plays. "We felt like we had to break all of our tendencies and throw about 50 percent of the time on first down — Alabama has done such a great job coaching against tendencies."

Brown also had high praise for Risher, who hit 13 of 16 first half passes and had 218 total yards in the game.

"Alan has come 10,000 miles since the first of the year," said Brown, who has added flare to the Tiger offense in his first season at LSU. "He's as good a quarterback mentally as any in the country."

Risher, however, lost his smarts for a few moments during a brutal defensive struggle in the first quarter. He sat out two plays and one series before re-entering in the second quarter.

"I just got my bell rung." Said Risher, who holds 15 LSU records. "I got hit in the head by one of their linebackers. I just wanted to come out and get my head together."

During the series Risher missed, LSU missed an excellent scoring opportunity. Cornerback Eugene Daniel recovered a Lewis fumble at the Alabama 24 with 6:03 left in the first period. But reserve quarterback Timmy Byrd was sacked on consecutive plays for minus-20 yards and the Tigers ended up punting from the 43.

Alabama, the SEC's No. 1 scoring team, couldn't take advantage of two first-half breaks. The second low punt-snap from center Curt Gore of Fairhope, Ala., gave the Crimson Tide possession on the Tiger 40. And Eddie Lowe recovered a Garry James fumble at the Tide 46 five minutes later. On both occasions, Alabama was stifled by the hard-charging Bandits.

LSU drew first blood with 8:14 left in the second period when Hilliard used blocks by Mike Montz and Malcolm Scott to dash around left end 16 yards for a touchdown. He dragged two Alabama players with him across the goal line to cap an 11-play, 90-yard drive. Betanzos' PAT made it 7-0.

"I felt I had to get in the end zone," said Hilliard, who rushed for 30 first-half yards before sitting out all but one series in the second half with a bruised thigh and calf. "Against Alabama, you have to make each play a big one."

Hilliard made another big play in the drive, catching a swing pass from Risher and turning it into a 33-yard gain by running through three potential Tide tacklers. Only a shoestring stop at the 29 by Rocky Colburn kept Hilliard from going 62 yards and a score. Risher said it was a new play — a tailback delay pass in the flats.

LSU then got 10 quick points thanks to Alabama's uncharacteristic generosity. On Coley's first play from scrimmage, halfback Joe Carter fumbled and Liffort Hobley recovered at the Tide 27 with 5:37 left before intermission. Nine plays later,

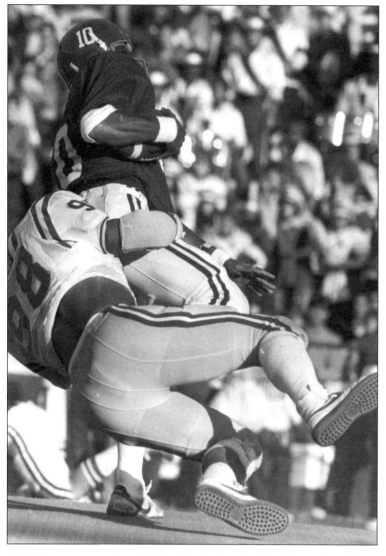

■ **Alabama quarterback Walter Lewis is sacked by Ramsey Dardar.**

Obviously embarrassed by its first half showing, Alabama came out with fire.

After Parker's 33-yard punt on another low snap, the Tide marched to the LSU 5. But on third-and-four, Lewis was hit by linebacker Lawrence Williams and fumbled out of bounds at the 14. Peter Kim was called on to kick a 31-yard field goal with 8:08 left in the third period to cut the gap to 17-3.

On LSU's next possession, Hilliard fumbled a pass from Risher and Al Blue recovered at the LSU 28. On the next play, Lewis then fired a 28-yard scoring pass to Joey Jones, whose post-corner route had cornerback James Britt beaten by a step. Kim's PAT made it 17-10 and gave the Tide its second score in 26 seconds.

It had all the makings of a typical Alabama comeback.

"Yes, there was little bit of fear," said LSU outside linebacker Tim Joiner. "They scored 10 quick points and I started to wonder."

"I was thinking we'd have to play a little bit harder," said defensive tackle Leonard Marshall. "And that's what we did."

LSU answered with a 9-play, 37-yard drive. Although it didn't produce any points, it cut off the Tide's wave of momentum.

When the Tigers got the ball back, they went 63 yards in 13 plays to set up Betanzos' ninth field goal of the year — a 20-yarder with 10:41 left to play to make it 10-10. The drive consumed 5:55 and was highlighted by Risher completions of 13, 6, 5 and 11 yards.

The Tigers finally put the game away when tackle Bill Elko sacked Lewis, forcing a fumble which linebacker Gregg Dubroc recovered at the Tide 48 with 4:57 remaining.

Risher fired a 3-yard bullet to Scott on a third down play-action pass with 58 seconds showing.

Betanzos' ensuing sky-kickoff was fumbled by Craig Turner — one of four Tide turnovers — and Alvin Thomas recovered at the Alabama 30. Risher's 12-yard rollout moved the ball to the 11, and two plays later Betanzos kicked a 23-yard field goal with five seconds left. His boot came after consecutive timeouts by LSU, then Alabama. It sent LSU into the dressing room with a 17-0 cushion to the delight of some 12,000 Tiger fans who made the trip.

Unlike the second half against Florida last month, when LSU became conservative in an effort to protect a 24-5 lead, Brown continued with a wide open attack.

"We felt like we could not sit on the ball," said Brown. "We told our kids at the half to play like it was 0-0. We knew Alabama, with their tradition and athletes, had a chance to score every time they had the football."

It looked that way at the beginning of the third quarter.

"I was just thinking, 'Please don't throw that damn ball,'" Elko said of his rush on Lewis. "I was hoping he wouldn't. I got a good clean hit and the ball popped out."

And when Dubroc pounced on it, he had more than just the football. He had a piece of LSU history. When the Tigers proceeded to run out the clock by marching to the 9, it snapped a dozen years of sometimes bitter frustration.

"This is the highlight of my football career," said Elko, a transfer from Arizona State who was plagued by injury last season. "Hopefully, it won't be the last."

Nose guard Ramsey Dardar hopes Elko is correct.

"Right now we are tasting Sugar," said Dardar. But he knows LSU must not only beat Mississippi State next week to gain a Sugar Bowl berth. He knows Auburn must beat Georgia for LSU to win the SEC.

That, of course, hasn't happened in 11 years. Which leaves Risher with a few more chains to unbuckle and another cage to open.

The Tigers' Domination was Total

■ The relentless pressure of LSU's defense shut down Alabama's wishbone attack.

By John Adams
The Advocate

Birmingham, Ala. — *Nov. 6, 1982*

There was a twin killing here this afternoon. Two long-time LSU tormentors bit the artificial turf at Legion Field.

The wishbone was the first to go. It was buried somewhere between the 20s.

And don't tell Alabama quarterback Walter Lewis about the wishbone's triple options. He'll tell you there are no options at the bottom of a pile, which is where he found himself too many times today.

Having broken — make that shattered — the wishbone, the rest was easy.

Let quarterback Alan Risher go to work on a Tide secondary that didn't include its best player — injured strong safety Tommy Wilcox. Then give them a little fancy footwork —

Dalton Hilliard — and watch the Tide defense look as befuddled as Oregon State, Florida and all the others that have tried to bring Hilliard to his knees.

That's how it was when it mattered today as LSU remained unbeaten with a 20-10 victory.

"They made the big plays," said Alabama defensive end Mike Pitts. "That's what college football is all about."

Risher has been making big plays all season. But he's never made so many big plays in a game that was so big.

He completed 20 of 26 passes for 182 yards. And when he wasn't shooting holes in the Tide secondary, he was outsmarting the folks up front with scrambles and bootlegs.

Although Hilliard only gained 30 yards rushing, he dazzled the Tide in LSU's 90-yard touchdown drive in the second quarter. Go back to the 40-yard line near the north end of the field, and you'll probably find two defenders kneeling in wonderment over a three-way collision that grounded everybody but Hilliard on a 33-yard pass-run play.

But this game was won by LSU's defense. Because to beat Alabama, you need to stop the wishbone. The Tigers did more than stop it. They shook it until it rattled.

Ask Lewis what the Tigers took away from the wishbone, and you'll draw a pause. His look said, "Everything."

"Let me think," he said. "I'm too tired to think. Oh, I'm tired ... They gave us very little."

That's a little as in no first downs in the first half, 45 yards rushing for the game, 119 yards total offense. And this was no pop-gun outfit. This was an Alabama offense that had been cranking out 300 yards per game rushing this season. In fact, the Tide has been producing outrageous rushing statistics ever since Bryant borrowed Texas' wishbone in the spring of 1971.

LSU hasn't beaten Alabama since then. From Terry Davis to Ken Coley, it seems like LSU has been forever chasing the wishbone into the end zone.

This time, it didn't have to catch the wishbone. There was never a take-off, just a few occasional gasps and sputters.

When Lewis took a snap, his whole offensive line seemed to collapse under the weight of Bill Elko, Ramsey Dardar, Leonard Marshall, Albert Richardson and Lawrence Williams. It happened so many times, it looked choreographed.

After that, Lewis was running naked, calling on his athletic talents — which are considerable — for survival. In other games — such as against Penn State — Lewis has turned such odds topsy-turvy.

But Lewis couldn't run clear of outside linebackers Rydell Malancon and Tim Joiner. They were too fast for him and his blockers, who were often nothing more than embarrassed spectators.

"They're so quick," Alabama center Danny Holcombe said of the Tigers' front seven. "You go to block them over there, and when you get there, they're gone. Yes, they're definitely the quickest defense we've played."

Even down 17-0 at halftime, there's a reluctance to dismiss Alabama as a threat. You think about all that tradition and all those comebacks. Just three years ago, Tennessee had the same lead at halftime. Final score: 27-17, Alabama.

But LSU was playing with too much confidence to let this one slip away. You can almost imagine Lawrence Williams, rather than an official, rapping on the Tide's dressing room door at halftime: "Time to come out, boys."

Alabama cut the lead to 17-10 because its defense hit hard enough to knock the ball loose from Hilliard and because Lewis had just enough time to hurl a marvelous pass to a speeding Joey Jones, a step ahead of James Britt in the LSU end zone.

But neither could turn the game Alabama's way. After the Tide cut the lead to 17-10, LSU converted on four of eight third-down conversions — and another time on fourth — in subtracting vital minutes from the clock and adding three precious points to the scoreboard.

Throughout the game, LSU made the plays that Alabama usually makes. It forced seven fumbles and recovered four, two of which set up scores.

Conversely, Alabama appeared stupefied at times. When the ball squirted free from halfback Joe Carter in the second quar-

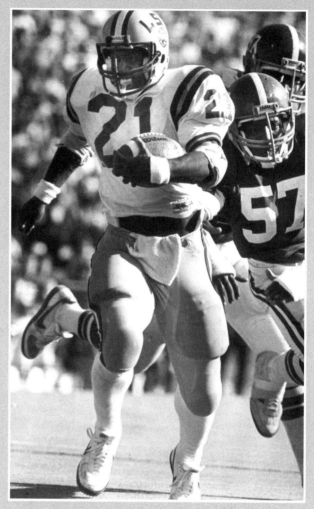

■ **Dalton Hilliard scoots 16 yards for a touchdown in the second quarter.**

ter, offensive guard Mike Adcock never left his feet as the ball bounced and bounced until it found the welcome arms of Liffort Hobley. His recovery set up LSU's second TD.

Midway in the fourth quarter Lewis broke from the pocket and began running wide in hopes of converting a third-and-13. He all but begged fullback Ricky Moore to scrap the pass play and pick up an oncoming defender. Moore never responded to Lewis' signal, and the deserted quarterback was dropped 9 yards short of a first.

"I think that's the best beating we've had since the 1960's," said Bryant, who talked as though the Alabama football program was in the hands of an incompetent leader.

While Bryant was hinting at retirement, the slower moving fans were in for another shock as they filed out of Legion Field. A whiskey bottle came sailing over the top of the stadium and crashed in the middle of five fans.

Seconds later, another bottle hit the pavement. Then a third. There were no victims, just scattered glass in the parking lot.

But inside the stadium, Alabama football had just been victimized. And if you didn't mind digging for evidence, there were pieces of a wishbone buried beneath Legion Field.

LSU Mauls Seminoles, 55-21

By John Adams
The Advocate

Baton Rouge, La. — *Nov. 20, 1982*

When you have Dalton Hilliard and Alan Risher pointing the way, Baton Rouge to Miami is an easy trip. Just make sure you don't trip over the oranges or get lost in the fog.

The Tigers avoided the hazards with ease as they roared to a 55-21 victory over the Florida State Seminoles tonight before 76,637 fans in Tiger Stadium. The victory earned the Tigers, 8-1-1, a berth in the Orange Bowl, and put Florida State, 8-2, in the Gator Bowl.

While today was the first day for officially extending bowl bids, LSU and Florida State entered the game knowing the winner would meet the Big Eight champion in the Orange Bowl New Year's night in Miami, and the loser would be paired against West Virginia in Jacksonville, Fla., Dec. 30.

There was no doubt which bowl the Tiger fans preferred. While no one threw an alligator onto the field, the sidelines were littered with oranges before the game ever began.

More were soon to fall as LSU broke open a 14-14 game with two touchdowns in the final 38 seconds of the first half. The 12th-ranked Tigers then overwhelmed the seventh-ranked Seminoles, 27-7, in the second half.

"I haven't seen any better team than LSU this year," Charles Kimbrell, the president of the Orange Bowl's team selection committee, said of the Tigers' performance. "And I think

Score by Periods

Florida State	7	7	0	7 —	21
LSU	7	21	14	13 —	55

■ LSU quarterback Alan Risher threw for three touchdowns against Florida State.

■ **Alan Risher (7) had an incredible game against the Seminoles, completing 8 of 12 passes for 212 yards.**

Hilliard is a Heisman Trophy candidate in the years ahead."

Speaking of the Heisman, Hilliard produced Herschel Walker-like figures tonight. He gained 183 yards on 36 carries and scored four touchdowns to break the NCAA touchdown record for freshmen.

The record of 15 was shared by Georgia's Walker (1980) and Lou Kusserow of Columbia (1945). The Tigers' freshman tailback has scored 16 touchdowns with one regular-season game remaining, next week against Tulane.

Hilliard said that kind of production was nothing more than his older teammates deserved. "We came into the season respecting our upperclassmen," he said. "And I felt we owed

them a lot. It wasn't easy.

"We had to establish our running game tonight. We were motivated both by last week's loss and thoughts of the Orange Bowl."

Hilliard rushed for three touchdowns and also caught a 40-yard TD pass from Risher, who completed eight of 12 passes for 212 yards and three touchdowns. Risher's other scoring passes went to Eric Martin and covered 34 and 70 yards.

That gave Risher 17 TD passes this season and 31 for his career. Bert Jones held the records of 14 and 28.

While the passing of Kelly Lowrey and Blair Williams helped the Seminoles pile up 425 yards against the Tigers' No. 2-ranked defense, Florida State couldn't keep pace with the

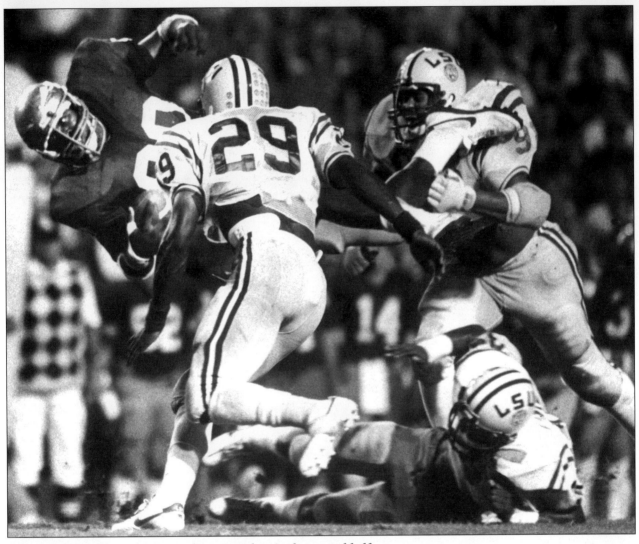

■ **LSU's defense kept the Seminoles wrapped up in the second half.**

Tigers in the final minutes of the first half.

The Tigers, who gained 20 yards total offense, broke the 14-14 tie on a 2-yard run by Hilliard. They added another TD on a 34-yard Risher to Martin pass after Sean Moore recovered a fumble by Tony Smith on the ensuing kickoff.

That left the Seminoles staggering, and they never regained their balance in the second half.

The victory means LSU will play the winner of this week's game between fourth-ranked Nebraska and Oklahoma. But at this point, head coach Jerry Stovall wasn't interested in the opposition.

"It doesn't matter," he said when asked about Nebraska-Oklahoma. "These little ragamuffins are looking forward to going to Miami and playing.

"Our team was prepared emotionally to play. A great deal of credit should be give to the young men who worked last spring and this year in preparation for a good year.

"I can't say enough about what our coaches and young men have done. The staff gave them a lot of confidence. Before the season, nobody wanted the young men so they gave them back to me. Tonight they made us — not only the coaches, but the state of Louisiana — extremely proud."

Tonight's victory highlighted LSU's turn-around from 3-7-1 a year ago. Not since 1973 has LSU won as many as nine games in a season, a feat the Tigers can accomplish with a triumph over Tulane next Saturday.

"We knew what was at stake," said senior offensive guard Mike Turner, who missed last season with a broken leg. "At 3-7-1, nobody loved us. It's been a dogfight to overcome that."

The oranges came first tonight. Then the

■ **It was a long night for FSU coach Bobby Bowden.**

■ **Dalton Hilliard scored four touchdowns — 3 rushing and one receiving.**

On a third-and-five, Risher ignited the Tigers' first scoring drive with a 12-yard completion to tight end Malcolm Scott against an inside blitz.

After another completion to Scott, Risher spotted Hilliard behind linebacker Tommy Young and pitched a strike to the Seminoles' 26. Hilliard then eluded Gary Henry and Brian McCrary and raced into the end zone to complete the 46-yard play with 3:31 left in the quarter.

Florida State responded with a 56-yard drive in seven plays. The Seminoles lost one touchdown when Jessie Hester, a step ahead of Eugene Daniel, dropped a pass deep in the end zone.

Following the long miss, Lowrey went short to Tony Smith in the right flat and he rambled 25 yards to the Tigers' 5-yard line. After a timeout, Lowrey faked to Greg Allen, who executed a high dive over the middle without the ball. With the ball on his hip, Lowrey rolled around left end for the touchdown with 2:05 left in the quarter.

Florida State, which ranks second in the country in total offense, came roaring back from its 21 to the Tigers' 33. But Lowrey was called for intentional grounding when pressured by Leonard Marshall on second down, and tight end Zeke Mowatt fumbled after receiving a Lowrey pass on third down. Richardson made the hit and Daniel recovered.

Risher countered quickly with a pass to Martin over the middle for 17 yards to the Seminoles' 44. Two runs by Garry James gained one first down and helped set up the Tigers' second TD.

On a second-and-1 at the Seminoles' 23, James took a Risher pitch, rolled right and hurled a touchdown pass to Herman Fontenot deep in the end zone behind Henry and McCrary. Juan Betanzos' extra-point kick put LSU on top, 14-7, with 9:43 left in the half.

passes. It was enough to keep the cheerleaders and the defenses ducking for cover in the first half.

"I didn't think a whole lot about it," center Mike Gambrell said of the flying fruit, which cost LSU two 15-yard penalties for unsportsmanlike conduct. "I didn't want anything to keep me from going to Miami."

On the field, LSU's throwing paid off first, but only after the Tigers had turned back a Florida State threat on the 17-yard line midway through the first half. Lowrey fumbled when he was sacked by Jeffery Dale, and Albert Richardson recovered on the Tigers' 23.

Then came the oranges. And more oranges. Fifteen yards worth, in fact. The penalty for unsportsmanlike conduct came after the LSU fans had been warned repeatedly by the public-address announcer.

Kicking off from his 25-yard line, Betanzos booted the ball out on the 9, and tried again from his 20. Billy Allen, who returned a kickoff 97 yards for a TD against LSU last year returned the kick 47 yards to the LSU 30.

After a 4-yard loss on first down, Lowrey caught the defense off guard with a short pass in the right flat to Smith, who made

■ **FSU tailback Greg Allen was sent soaring by a pair of LSU defenders.**

the reception on the 28, dodged Lawrence Williams, and sprinted for the right corner of the end zone. Phillip Hall's extra-point kick evened the count at 14-all.

The last 9:16 of the half belonged to the Tigers, however. And it began to go their way after Scott Watson downed Clay Parker's punt on the Seminoles' 6-yard line.

Beginning their next series from the 50, the Tigers moved for the go-ahead score in 11 plays. With LSU's front six taking control at the line, Hilliard carried eight times for 46 yards in the drive.

"We started running our basic offense, that's all," Turner said of the drive. "We knew we had to score some points. As many times as the defense has pulled us through this year, we knew we had to come through tonight."

On second down-and-2, Hilliard came through, diving into the end zone as he was hit by Harry Clayton at the goal line with 38 seconds left. The Tigers then got two breaks. First, the fans didn't throw oranges. Second, Smith fumbled the kick over to the Tigers' Moore on the Florida State 34.

One play and six seconds later, LSU had a two touchdown lead. Risher passed to Martin, who beat Clayton across the middle, and dashed 34 yards for a touchdown.

"The two touchdowns they scored right before the half threw the whole game out of whack," said Florida State coach Bobby Bowden, whose team had beaten LSU the last three years in Tiger Stadium. "They were able to come out in the second half and beat us by keeping the ball on the ground."

The last minute of the first half was the beginning of the end

■ Eric Martin had touchdown receptions of 34 and 70 yards.

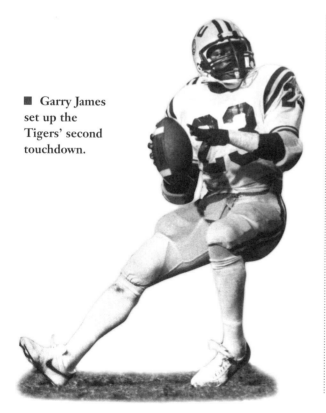

■ Garry James set up the Tigers' second touchdown.

for the Seminoles, who found themselves in a fog before the natural haze settled over Tiger Stadium late in the third quarter.

A massive dose of Hilliard dimmed the lights on the Seminoles. He carried 14 times in a 16-play, 80-yard scoring drive to open the second half. Hilliard, who accounted for all but 15 yards in the drive, scored on a 1-yard run with 6:16 left in the period.

Four minutes later, it was Risher's turn. He scrambled away from Alphonso Carreker behind the line and unleashed a 69-yard scoring pass to Martin.

A dazed Seminole defense was subjected to more Hilliard early in the fourth quarter as Stovall stuck with his first unit despite the 42-14 lead.

Following a 16-yard completion from Risher to Scott and a 14-yard gain by Mike Montz, Hilliard broke free around right end for a 28-yard scoring run.

The second team didn't fare badly either. Freshman quarterback Jeff Wickersham directed a 75-yard, 13-play drive after Florida State had scored on a 21-yard pass from Blair Williams to Hester. Wickersham capped the scoring with a 12-yard run around left end.

But that didn't end the throwing. Fans showered the field with oranges at the end of the game. In fact, the oranges were so thick, you almost couldn't see the fog.

Nebraska Rallies to Defeat Tigers, 21-20

■ Nebraska's defense kept pressure on Alan Risher all evening in the Orange Bowl.

By John Adams
The Advocate

Miami, Fla. — *Jan. 1, 1983*

The No. 3-ranked Nebraska Cornhuskers, who couldn't hold on to the football for two and a half quarters, never let go of it in the final five minutes to nail down a 21-20 come-from-behind victory over the LSU Tigers in the 49th annual Orange Bowl here tonight.

Trailing, 7-7, midway through the third quarter, Nebraska cranked out touchdown drives in the third and fourth period, and then controlled the ball for the last 5:05 after Juan Betanzos' 49-yard field goal had pulled the Tigers to within a point.

Before Nebraska's late surge, it appeared the 10-point under-dog Tigers were about to pull off the biggest upset of the new year before a disappointing crowd of 54,407 — the Orange Bowl's smallest in 36 years. LSU slowed down a Nebraska offense that averages 41.1 points and 518 yards per game with an alert defense that claimed five turnovers — four fumbles and an interception. Three turnovers in the first half and a pair of 1-yard TD runs by freshman tailback Dalton Hilliard had given the Tigers a 14-7 halftime lead. Betanzos upped the advantage to 17-7 with a 28-yard field goal with 6:04 left in the third quarter.

But Nebraska, which outscored its opponents 169-28 in the fourth period, began to roll. Quarterback Turner Gill and tailback Mike Rozier teamed up to spark scoring drives of 80 and 47 yards as Nebraska claimed its 12th victory in 13 games.

Gill, who completed 13 of 22 passes for 184 yards, tossed an 11-yard TD pass to Rozier to cap the first march, then scored on a 1-yard dive to put Nebraska on top with 11:14 left.

LSU, 8-3-1, had one more chance at winning the game, following a 20-yard interception by Lawrence Williams. Beginning at the Nebraska 37, LSU gained 9 yards in three plays — a 5-yard pass reception by Hilliard and two short runs.

On a fourth-and-one, Hilliard was stopped for no gain. But the play was negated by a delay-of-game penalty — flagged before the snap — against LSU. Betanzos then booted a 49-yard field goal to cut the lead to one with 5:05 left.

Nebraska never let go of the ball afterwards.

On its possession, Nebraska showed no signs of the frustrations to come in the first half. The nation's No. 1-ranked offense proved that. It advanced from its 20 to the LSU 37 on nine straight running plays before Gill completed a 13-yard pass to Irving Fryar on third-and-10. Nebraska then needed only two more plays to run out the clock.

"I told my players all week we were going to win the football game with 30 seconds left on a field goal," said LSU coach Jerry Stovall. "We would have to beat those suckers if we had got the ball back."

Asked about not going for the TD on fourth-and-6, Stovall said, "We kick a field goal and we still have five minutes to get the ball back. We get it back, Juan was kicking well, and it would have been 23-21.

"I wouldn't trade this football team for any other one in America tonight. They showed more strength and more character than any team I've ever been associated with."

The Nebraska offense was as good as advertised on a six-play, 51-yard touchdown drive.

Following a 25-yard Clay Parker punt, quarterback Turner Gill opened up with a 22-yard pass to wingback Irving Fryar, who was run out of bounds on the LSU 29. Nebraska then followed Gill's quick feet to inside the Tigers' 10-yard line.

Gill broke runs of 6- and 14-yard options around left end, then kept over left guard for 3 yards to the 5. A crushing block by All-America center Dave Rimington cleared the way for reserve fullback Mark Schellen's 5-yard scoring run on the next play with 10:57 left in the first quarter.

LSU responded quickly, moving from its 38 to the Nebraska 29 on two pass receptions by tight end Malcolm Scott and an alert play by Dalton Hilliard. After Scott caught a

■ LSU held a 14-7 halftime lead, then Nebraska caught fire in the second half and won, 21-20.

21-yard pass from Alan Risher, he fumbled when hit by Bill Weber. Hilliard dove on the loose ball to keep the drive alive.

After an illegal-procedure penalty, Hilliard left a pair of Nebraska defenders spinning following a short pass from Risher, Hilliard gained 18 yards to the Cornhuskers' 16.

When the defense stiffened, LSU turned to Juan Betanzos, who kicked a 35-yard field goal. Coach Jerry Stovall decided he wanted more, however, after Allen Lyday was flagged for a late hit on Betanzos.

A 10-yard penalty gave LSU a first down on the 9, but the Tigers came up empty handed two plays later when tackle Toby Williams deflected a Risher pass and caught the ball on Nebraska's 10.

Then the Nebraska turnovers began to fall LSU's way. Rozier fumbled when he was rocked by Ramsey Dardar, and Liffort Hobley recovered on Nebraska's 11. After Hilliard sliced over left tackle for 8 yards, it took three plays — the last a 1-yard sneak by Risher — to produce a first down at the 1.

From there, Hilliard took two shots wide right. He scored the second time following a lead block by fullback Mike Montz.

Nebraska looked as though it would have little trouble breaking the deadlock. Gill completed three passes — two to Todd Brown — and Fryar gained 9 yards on an inside reverse as the Cornhuskers rolled from their 30 to the LSU 13.

On the first play of the second quarter, an LSU defense that recovered 23 fumbles during the regular season came up with

Score by Periods

LSU	7	7	3	3 —	20
Nebraska	7	0	7	7 —	21

its second of the game. Schellen lost the ball in the middle of the line and Rydell Malancon fell on it at the Tigers' 15.

Nebraska got its hands on the ball four plays later, but once again it couldn't hold on. Fryar fumbled before he was ever hit on a punt return and Gene Lang recovered at Nebraska's 45.

The Tigers' scoring drive was Hilliard and more Hilliard. He handled the ball by running or passing on all nine plays in a 45-yard scoring drive.

Twice, he turned short passes into big gainers with those darting moves that bedeviled so many defenders during the regular season. One gained 24 yards to the Nebraska 21. The second was on third-and-six from the 17. He made the catch on the 12 and raced to the 3-yard line.

He needed four plays to cover the next 3 yards. On fourth down, he received a pitch from Risher and swept wide left for one yard and the go-ahead touchdown. Betanzos' extra point gave the Tigers a 14-7 lead with 9:32 left in the half.

On its next try, Nebraska failed by an inch converting on a fourth-down fake punt at midfield. But after fullback Doug Wilkening was tackled short of the first down, LSU moved no further than the Cornhuskers' 39.

Nebraska had a chance to tie the game before halftime after a 33-yard Parker punt to the Tigers' 42. Gill connected with Fryar for a 17-yard completion on first down, but on third-and-five Malancon intercepted Gill's pass at the LSU 13. Gill was pressured on the play by strong safety Jeffrey Dale.

Nebraska was also frustrated on its first possession of the second half. A 20-yard kick return by Jeff Smith set the Cornhuskers on their 49.

Rozier gained 7, then broke three tackles on a 12-yard run to the 30. Facing a fourth-and-three at the 22, Kevin Seibel was four-for-four before the 39-yard field goal try.

Nebraska's fifth turnover in the game enabled LSU to up its lead to 10 points. Gill pitched wildly when hit by Dale and Lawrence Williams recovered on the Nebraska 41 with 8:17 to play in the third quarter.

On second down, Risher completed a 15-yard pass to Hilliard. Eric Martin then made a spectacular one-handed diving-catch on the Nebraska 7.

Montz carried to the Cornhusker 1 on the next play, but an illegal procedure penalty pushed LSU back to the 12. After Risher threw three straight incompletions, Betanzos kicked a 28-yard field goal with 6:40 left in the quarter.

Before the quarter ended, Nebraska showed what it can do when it doesn't drop the football. The Cornhuskers, who averaged 41.1 points per game during the season, marched 80 yards in 12 plays for their second TD.

The Tigers helped Nebraska along with a late hit that was worth 15 penalty yards to the Cornhuskers' 35. Gill gained 14 yards on an option to the LSU 44. And on fourth-and-one, Gill faked a handoff into the middle before completing an 18-yard pass to Brown on the LSU 17.

Three plays later, Rozier caught a swing pass from Gill in the right flat and ran down the sidelines untouched until he

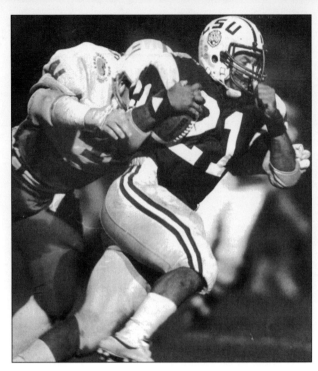

■ **Dalton Hilliard scored both of LSU's touchdowns in the first half.**

reached the end zone. Seibel's extra-point kick trimmed LSU's lead to 17-14, with 1:25 left in the half.

Nebraska's offensive momentum proved contagious. The Cornhuskers sacked Risher twice on LSU's next series to set up a fourth-and-19. When Parker was rushed on fourth down, he elected to run. Running with one foot bare, he went to the LSU 47, but was 8 yards short of a first down.

Once again, an LSU penalty got the Cornhuskers started. James Britt was flagged for pass interference on Brown at the 36. Two plays later, Gill hit Fryar cutting over the middle at the 25. He dashed to the LSU 5 before he was knocked off his feet.

Rozier slammed through the middle for 4 yards to the 1. Then Gill leaped over center for the go-ahead touchdown.

Nebraska almost added to its margin on its next possession. Fryar, who ranks third in the country in punt returns, eluded three LSU tackles on a 42-yard return to the Tigers' 25.

On a fourth-and-two at the 17, Nebraska, which is famous for trick plays, caught LSU off guard with a fake field goal but botched the execution. Tim Brungardt appeared to be running off the field before the ball was snapped. But when Gill took the snap and stood up from his holder's position, Brungardt cut down the left sidelines. Gill's pass was on target, but Brungardt dropped the ball at the 5.

LSU narrowed the gap to 21-20 following an interception by Williams, who returned the ball to the Nebraska 37. On a fourth-and-one, LSU was called for delay of game. Stovall then elected to go for a field goal, and Betanzos had room to spare on a 49-yard kick with 5:05 remaining.

Gill's Ball Control Spoils Stovall's Dream

BY JIMMY HYAMS
The Advocate

Miami, Fla. — *Jan. 1, 1983*

Jerry Stovall had a premonition earlier this week, but Nebraska quarterback Turner Gill foiled his dreams.

"I told the team all week we'd win the ballgame in the last 30 seconds with a field goal," said LSU's head coach. "It was set up perfectly . . . ."

Except for Gill.

After LSU had pulled to within 21-20 on Juan Betanzos' 49-yard field goal with 5:05 left in the fourth period, Gill faced a third-and-10 from his own 37 with 1:23 to play. The junior then hit Irving Fryar for a 13-yard gain allowing Nebraska to hold on for a 21-20 victory over the Tigers in the Orange Bowl tonight.

"We'd have beaten those suckers if we'd gotten the ball back," Stovall said.

Betanzos, who also kicked a 28-yard field goal and had a 35-yarder wiped out by a penalty, felt the same way.

"All we needed to do was cross the 50," said the sophomore sidewinder, "because I was kicking real good tonight. But we never got the ball back."

Nebraska, now 12-1, drove from its 20 to the LSU 16 before time expired, dropping the Tigers' record to 8-3-1.

"It was frustrating," Betanzos said of waiting on the sidelines in the final minutes hoping the Bandits would stop the nation's No. 1-ranked offense. "I couldn't do anything about it."

LSU punter Clay Parker tried to do something about it earlier, but his move backfired.

Facing a fourth-and-19 from his 36 one minute into the final quarter, Parker eluded a rusher, looked upfield, and instead of punting took off running. He was stopped eight yards shy of a first down.

Nebraska then marched 47 yards on seven plays, with Gill scoring from the 4 on a quarterback sneak with 11:14 to play. A pass interference call against cornerback James Britt and Gill's 28-yard pass to Fryar which carried the ball to the LSU 5 were the key plays.

"The snap was to the left and pressure was coming from the left," said Parker, a sophomore from Columbia. "I faked the guy coming from the left, and when I looked up field, it was wide open. I knew I had a long way to go for a first down. I just didn't think they would

react that quickly. I realized I was six or seven yards short.

"It was one of those plays where if I get the first down, everybody says what a great play it was. But the way it turned out, I should have punted."

While it was a break which led to the Cornhuskers' winning score, LSU took advantage of breaks to score all 20 of its points. Fumble recoveries at Nebraska's 11 and 45 in the first half led to a pair of 1-yard TD runs by sensational freshman Dalton Hilliard, who played all but a couple of series since Garry James was suffering from a pulled groin.

In the second half, LSU's two field goals resulted from a Lawrence Williams fumble recovery at the Nebraska 41, and a Williams interception which he returned 20 yards to the Nebraska 37.

Following Williams' first fumble recovery, LSU marched to the Cornhusker 7. But fullback Mike Montz's run to the 1-yard line was nullified by illegal procedure, forcing the Tigers to eventually settle for a field goal.

"They said our split end (Eric Ellington) wasn't on the line of scrimmage," said LSU quarterback Alan Risher, who completed 14 of 34 passes for 173 yards. "We had an opportunity to win the game. If we go up, 21-7, we probably would have won."

Risher said the two key plays which went against LSU were the illegal procedure and Parker's failure to get a first down on the run from punt formation.

Risher said he "respected" Stovall's decision to go for the field goal on fourth-and-six in the final five minutes. "Give Nebraska credit," he said, "they held the ball and didn't give it back to us."

Risher said he thought Nebraska's defensive line played "excellent" and he said the Cornhuskers' secondary made it difficult for him to find open receivers, especially during the first half.

Stovall called Nebraska the "best team I've seen in my three years at LSU."

LSU nose guard Ramsey Dardar, who was matched against Nebraska's All-American center Dave Rimington.

Asked about the matchup, Dardar said, "I think I got the best out of the deal. The only thing was on passes, he held his butt off. I was telling the refs, but they just laughed."

But in the final minutes, there was nothing to laugh about on the LSU sidelines.

Stovall's dream on this New Year's Day was shattered when Gill played ball-hog in the final minutes.

■ Garry James (33) meets up with USC's Tim McDonald (6) en route to setting up LSU's second touchdown.

Tigers Trample USC in Coliseum, 23-3

BY BRUCE HUNTER
The Advocate

Los Angeles, Calif. — *Sept. 29, 1984*

The University of Southern California mascot, Travellor III, took his traditional gallop around the Coliseum just before kickoff today, but was never heard from again.

The Trojan horse makes a triumphant trek around the famous Olympic track to celebrate touchdowns and other big plays for Southern Cal. LSU didn't give the Trojans a chance for any such pleasure in a 23-3 victory in front of a crowd of 60,128.

"We gave the game ball to the defense for the shutout," said LSU head coach Bill Arnsparger.

Of course, it wasn't technically a shutout. USC scored a field goal after LSU's only turnover of the game early in the first quarter.

The Tiger defense, however, stole the show for the final 56 minutes of the game. It produced five turnovers and went through a pair of USC quarterbacks.

"I thought it was a great win for the team," said Arnsparger. "I was proud of the defense with the shutout. It's hard to lose when you have a shutout. It was a real tough hitting game and that was the type of game we expected."

LSU remains undefeated, improving its record to 3-0-1 with a three-game winning streak. It has a week off before returning to Southeastern Conference play against Vanderbilt Oct. 13 for homecoming in Tiger Stadium.

The win will certainly boost the Tigers in the rankings. They entered the game ranked 18th by the United Press International and USC was ranked 14th by UPI and 15th in The Associated Press poll.

LSU bounced USC from the unbeaten ranks after it had won its first two games. This was the first time LSU had ever played in the Coliseum and the victory will go down as one of the greatest in school history. LSU was a slight favorite entering the game, but played its finest game of the season to totally devastate the Trojans.

"We knew about the USC tradition," said LSU tackle Lance Smith. "It's great to be in California. It's a great win for us."

Linebacker Ricky Chatman called it the best game the Tigers have played in his five years on the team. It was even more important to Chatman that the Tigers won because he almost went to USC.

"It's a thrill for me to come out here and win," he said. "To come out and win in their backyard makes me feel great.

"Right now it's the biggest win of my career. But hopefully, there will be a bigger win coming up."

Sophomore defensive end Karl Wilson, who had another big game up front, also had a reason to treasure this victory.

"I wasn't an LSU fan the last time LSU played USC," said Wilson. "I had a dream about playing in the Rose Bowl for USC, but I guess this is my Rose Bowl."

■ **LSU's Herman Fontenot is stopped by USC cornerback Darrel Hopper after a 24-yard reception in the first quarter.**

LSU's only other meeting with USC came in 1979 when the Trojans rallied in the closing minutes to win, 17-12.

The Tiger defense never let the Trojans get established and the offense played a near-perfect game, especially in the first half.

It was actually the defense that did the most severe damage in the half.

Trailing, 3-0, LSU set up its first touchdown when linebacker Michael Brooks separated USC quarterback Kevin McLean from the football. Wilson covered the fumble to give the Tigers possession at the USC 15.

"We had the eagle (blitz) on," said Brooks. "I just read the play and made the tackle. Nobody touched me."

Tailback Garry James carried twice, giving the Tigers a first-and-goal at the 2, and Dalton Hilliard went behind Smith at right tackle to score on his feet. Juan Betanzos added the extra point to give LSU a 7-3 lead and all the points it would need.

Early in the second quarter, USC had switched tailbacks and backup Zeph Lee was met head-on by Tiger linebackers Gregg Dubroc and Shawn Burks. The ball was dislodged and

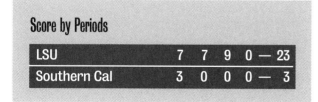

Score by Periods

LSU	7	7	9	0	— 23
Southern Cal	3	0	0	0	— 3

■ **Herman Fontenot (40) and Mitch Andrews celebrate after Fontenot's 2-yard touchdown reception.**

Burks recovered to stop a USC drive, setting the stage for LSU's only sustained scoring drive of the game.

Quarterback Jeff Wickersham marched the Tigers on a 16-play, 79-yard drive with Hilliard scoring on another 2-yard run. He got blocks from flanker Herman Fontenot and tailback Craig Rathjen and scored standing up to put the Tigers ahead, 14-3.

Wickersham, who completed 14-of-27 passes for 171 yards and a touchdown, completed passes to James, Mitch Andrews, Eric Martin and Rogie Magee on the expertly engineered drive.

The Tigers needed a little help, though. On fourth-and-1 from the USC 44, Clay Parker dropped back to punt, grabbed

an errant snap and raced down the left sidelines for 16 yards and a first down.

"No, it wasn't planned that way," said Parker, who had his best game of the season. "It was open and I ran for it."

The Tigers had an excellent scoring opportunity taken away on the next series of downs. Freshman cornerback Kevin Guidry picked off a McLean pass at midfield and raced all the way down to the USC 14. But a clipping penalty on the play set the Tigers back to their own 37.

The LSU defense didn't get any more turnovers in the first half and neither team threatened to score as the half ended with

LSU in front, 14-3.

Tiger lightning struck again in the third quarter when reserve safety Steve Rehage made a diving interception of another pass by McLean, giving LSU the ball at the USC 30.

"I looked up and the tight end was coming across the middle. He tried to get it to him," Rehage said. "It looked like somebody must have hit the ball."

This time, LSU couldn't move the ball after the turnover. Betanzos came in to kick a 46-yard field goal to put the Tigers ahead, 17-3, with 4:39 remaining in the third quarter.

USC head coach Ted Tollner decided McLean, who replaced injured starter Sean Salisbury, wasn't getting the job done. So Tollner called on senior quarterback Tim Green. He wasn't any more effective against a defense which pressured the quarterback all afternoon.

"They (LSU) came in here to win. I think they're a real good football team," said McLean. "Our defense played well, but our offense has to get it together. LSU is going to go to a bowl game."

After Green failed to move the Trojans on his first try, they punted and gave LSU good field position at its own 49. Wickersham didn't need any help from his own defense this time.

The junior quarterback, who had his best game since the opener with Florida, completed his longest pass of the season, a 34-yard touchdown play to freshman receiver Glenn Holt, who fooled the Trojan defense and was wide open at the 10-yard line. It was Holt's first college reception.

"We spread it out and the safety bit on Herman (Fontenot) going across the middle," said Wickersham. "He (Holt) was wide open."

Betanzos missed the extra point, but the Tigers still led, 23-3, with 1:35 left in the game.

The Tigers almost added to their large margin of victory in the fourth quarter when Liffort Hobley made his second interception in two games, collecting a bad throw by Green. Hobley returned the ball 10 yards to the USC 34.

"It was just an overthrown pass," said Hobley, who set up the winning touchdown with an interception last week against Arizona. "I was just in the middle waiting for it and I tried to get as far downfield as I could. I made sure I was deep enough."

The Trojans pressured Wickersham with blitzes and he missed an open James at the goal line. So the Tigers punted from their own 32 after a penalty for delay-of-game. They probably would have kicked a field goal if the game was close. Also, Betanzos was erratic, missing an extra point and a 25-yard field goal on the day.

LSU went conservative in the closing minutes to run down the clock and USC never mounted a serious threat.

After the first few minutes of the second quarter, the Trojans never penetrated beyond the LSU 40.

Their only offense was the running of tailback Fred Crutcher, who gained 97 yards on 22 carries and was the game's leading rusher. Hilliard rushed for 81 yards on 28 carries for LSU.

Crutcher had a long run of 15 yards, but never really hurt LSU. He was stopped in all the critical situations.

"My initial reaction is that the turnovers finally caught up to us," said Tollner, whose team had been bothered by turnovers in its first two games, too. "It's obvious there's more to it than that, but it's critical for us to play our style. That's running the ball and not falling behind."

The Trojans had a chance to take a significant lead early in the game after Martin fumbled the ball over to the Trojans at the LSU 42 on the opening series. Crutcher ran the ball four times as the team moved inside the 10.

But on third down, McLean missed split end Hank Norman in the end zone. Norman beat Guidry on the play and was open. USC settled for a 22-yard field goal by Steve Jordan for its only points of the game.

USC had one more scoring chance in the first half when it moved from its own 43 to LSU's 23 behind the running of Lee. But Dubroc and Burks forced Lee to fumble, ending the threat.

■ Herman Fontenot was a four-year letterman for the Tigers.

Tigers Send the Tide Tumbling

BY BRUCE HUNTER
The Advocate

Birmingham, Ala. — *Nov. 10, 1984*

The Alabama Crimson Tide threw a giant road block in LSU's path to the Southeastern Conference football championship.

But the Tigers used a block of their own to salvage a 16-14 victory in Legion Field on this stormy afternoon.

Sophomore Michael Brooks led a 10-man rush and blocked a punt by Alabama's Terry Sanders to set up the winning touchdown early in the third quarter. The Tide was punting from its own 45 when Brooks broke through for the block and the ball bounded toward the end zone with Kevin Guidry recovering for the Tigers at the Tide 12.

Three plays later, Dalton Hilliard broke through the right side of the line to score a touchdown from 7 yards away and put the Tigers ahead for good, 16-14, with 7:53 left in the third quarter.

"That's the first time that we've worked on the all-out rush in practice," said Brooks, who pressured Alabama quarterback Mike Shula all afternoon on pass rushes. "We felt they had a breakdown in their punt protections and we felt we could get to them."

Brooks lined up on the right side of the line and found an opening between center and guard. "I just went right through and we made the big play," he said.

There were several other Tigers in position to make the critical block if Brooks wasn't able to do so.

"We brought some faster, specialized people up there," said LSU safety Jeffery Dale. "We brought in (Kevin) Guidry and Liffort (Hobley) and they had never been there before."

LSU head coach Bill Arnsparger said the Tigers tried the 10-man punt rush against Ole Miss last week. This was the first time the Tigers have come close to blocking a punt this season.

"It looked like Terry was slow getting the punt away," said

■ **Michael Brooks' block of an Alabama punt in the third quarter set up LSU's winning touchdown.**

Alabama head coach Ray Perkins. "I'd have to look at the films though. It could have been a combination of both."

The blocked punt and several outstanding returns on kick-offs and punts were the only bright spot for the Tigers, who improved to 7-1-1 overall and 4-0-1 in the SEC. With Florida's win over Georgia today, the Tigers can clinch at least a share of the SEC crown and a possible Sugar Bowl berth with a victory at Mississippi State next Saturday.

Dalton Hilliard rushed for 78 yards and became the third LSU back to rush for more than 1,000 yards in a season.

Score by Periods

LSU	7	3	6	0 —	16
Alabama	7	7	0	0 —	14

The Tigers haven't won the SEC title since 1970 and haven't gone to the Sugar Bowl since 1968.

Following the blocked punt, tailback Garry James ran over right guard to get down to the Alabama 10 on first down. Hilliard went over the left side for 3 yards on second down, breaking the 1,000-yard rushing mark for the season and joining Charles Alexander and Terry Robiskie as the only Tigers ever to accomplish the feat.

Hilliard's next carry was even more important. On third-and-five from the Tide 7, the Tigers surprised Alabama with a draw to Hilliard, who slid through the right side and fought his way into the end zone.

"I got a good block from Tommy Campbell at center," said Hilliard, who rushed for 78 yards on 17 carries to bring his season total to 1,055. "I was reading on Campbell's block, and tight end Mitch Andrews got a good block to get me into the end zone."

The Tigers elected to go for two points after the touchdown, but flanker Herman Fontenot dropped Jeff Wickersham's pass in the end zone. LSU didn't want to be left in a position where a field goal would tie the game because a tie would have knocked the Tigers out of title contention.

Alabama fell to 3-6 overall and 1-4 in the SEC, and is assured of it first losing season since 1957. But the Tide, which had won 12 of the previous 13 meetings with LSU, thoroughly dominated every phase of the game except special teams play.

The final statistics read like a horror story for the Tigers. They gained only eight first downs and 161 yards of total offense for their worst offensive showing of the season, while Alabama more than doubled their output with 22 first downs and 332 yards of total offense.

LSU's ball-control philosophy went out the window after its opening drive of the game.

The most telling factors in the game are Alabama's 85-49 advantage in offensive plays and an overwhelming edge in time of possession, 40:49 to 19:11.

The Tigers' longest drive was seven plays and they had to punt eight times.

Alabama had four drives of at least 10 plays, controlling the game from start to finish. The Tide built a 14-10 lead at half-time and had two prime opportunities to win the game in the second half with long marches.

■ **Sammy Martin (23) moved from tailback to wide receiver and caught eight passes for 75 yards.**

LSU Grabs First Win Ever in Irishland

By Bruce Hunter
The Advocate

South Bend, Ind. — *Nov. 23, 1985*

On an afternoon when conference championships and major bowl bids were being decided all over the country, the happenings on the hallowed grounds of Notre Dame Stadium seemed rather insignificant, attracting representatives from only one bowl.

Yet, for traditional powers Notre Dame and LSU, today's game was a collision of a program fighting for its life and another one fighting for its dignity. LSU's struggle for respect prevailed in climactic fashion, 10-7, for the Tigers' first victory ever in the shadows of the Golden Dome.

"It's history," said Garry James, who scored the winning touchdown on a 2-yard run with 3:26 left. "We made history. Put it in the books. I wish we were at home, so we could put it up on the wall. Where's a wall? We'll put it up here."

James couldn't find an appropriate wall in the visitors' locker room on which to display the 10-7 score, but LSU's come-from-behind triumph in a game dominated by defense probably brought the walls down on Gerry Faust's five-year stay here. Faust began his career here at with a 27-9 win over LSU in 1981.

The Fighting Irish, who are more accustomed to playing for national championships in November, fell to 5-5 and must beat fourth-ranked Miami Saturday to salvage a winning season. LSU, ranked 17th, improved to 7-1-1 and kept alive its slim hopes of returning to the Sugar Bowl.

The Tigers' only hopes of going to the Sugar Bowl rest in a Tennessee loss to Vanderbilt in those teams' season final Saturday. However, if the Vols win, LSU is headed for a Liberty Bowl date with Baylor on Dec. 27 in Memphis, Tenn.

Baylor accepted its bid to the Liberty Bowl after losing 17-10 to Texas after falling from Cotton Bowl contention.

"If I am retained, that's fine," said Faust. "If I'm not, that's part of life. I never even thought about this being my last time walking off the field at Notre Dame. And that's the honest to God truth."

Most of the afternoon it appeared the Fighting Irish would extend their six-game winning streak at home and possibly Faust's career at Notre Dame. The Irish scored on their first possession with an impressive, 64-yard drive to go ahead, 7-0, with less than six minutes expired. But that was the end of such offensive prowess for the next three quarters, during which LSU's Henry Thomas blocked two field goals and forced John Carney to miss a third try.

The Irish maintained their 7-0 lead until the last play of the first half when LSU got a field goal by Matt DeFrank, subbing for Ron Lewis. Then the 7-3 advantage lasted until the closing minutes of the game at which time the Tigers rallied for their first victory in three games here.

"I have to compliment my players for hanging in there,"

■ LSU linebacker Ron Sancho wraps up Irish tailback Allen Pinkett.

said LSU coach Bill Arnsparger. "They really worked hard to win this football game. It was one of those games where I don't imagine anyone turned off their TV sets. It was close and kept everybody hanging until the end."

LSU quarterback Jeff Wickersham, who set a record for the most completions (31) ever against a Notre Dame team, directed the Tigers on a pair of fourth-quarter drives. The first one didn't produce any points, but worked to set up the winning drive.

With 11:31 left in the game, LSU started at its own 14 and worked down to the Notre Dame 42. Wickersham completed 5 of 7 passes on the drive, including a couple of 11-yard passes to Dalton Hilliard and Rogie Magee.

Arnsparger gambled early on the drive when the Tigers came up six inches short on a third-down pass from Wickersham to tight end Mitch Andrews. The ball was just inside the LSU 35, but Wickersham sneaked a yard and a half on fourth down to maintain possesion. Several plays later, Wickersham hit tailback James for a first down at the Irish 42, but the drive stalled and DeFrank had to punt.

DeFrank's punt landed around the 15 and rolled to the 6 to pin Notre Dame deep in its territory. Irish tailback Allen

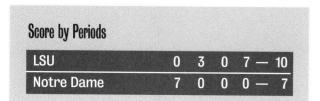

Score by Periods

	1	2	3	4		Total
LSU	0	3	0	7	—	10
Notre Dame	7	0	0	0	—	7

Pinkett, who went over 4,000 yards for his career in the game, could manage only 4 yards on two carries and quarterback Steve Beuerlein threw incomplete on third down, forcing Dan Sorensen to kick from his end zone.

LSU took over at its own 48 with 4:53 remaining in the game and Wickersham went straight to work. He connected with Andrews for a 9-yard gain on second down and found a weak spot in Notre Dame's defense to hit Hilliard for 18 yards on third down, going to the Notre Dame 25.

"It was a blitz read," said Wickersham, who completed 31 of 42 for 244 yards and moved into third place on the all-time Southeastern Conference list for total offense. "They brought their strong safety in, and Dalton and I read it. We were able to hit it for a big gain."

The Tigers came right back with another long gainer when Andrews turned a routine short-yardage pass from Wickersham into a 21-yard pickup, setting up a first-and-goal at the 4.

"I ran inside for an 8-yard hook route," said Andrews. "The linebackers went after our running backs and Jeff made a good read. He hit me and I broke a tackle. I smelled the goal line and I wanted to get in."

Notre Dame linebacker Tony Furjanic wrestled down Andrews before he could break into the end zone, but it only delayed the touchdown. James got half of the necessary yards on first down by powering over the left side for 2 yards.

Then James hit the same hole on second down and dashed through untouched behind the blocks of left tackle Curt Gore and guard Keith Melancon to score the winning touchdown. DeFrank added the extra point for a 10-7 lead with 3:26 left.

"I got excellent blocking by the offensive line," said James. "They wanted it more than anyone. They've been taking a lot of stuff from everyone." James' TD run concluded the scoring in the game, but the action was far from over. Three of the afternoon's four turnovers came in the final two minutes.

Beuerlein tried to rally the Irish for a tying field goal or winning touchdown, but his pass to split end Reggie Ward was tipped and intercepted by LSU linebacker Ron Sancho at the LSU 31 with 1:50 left.

The Tigers tried to run out the clock, but Hilliard's second straight carry ended in a fumble. Notre Dame tackle Eric Dorsey dislodged the ball from Hilliard, then recovered the fumble at the LSU 36 with 1:35 still to play.

"I thought that was going to be it because it aroused so much motivation and at such a critical point in the game," said Dorsey. "It seemed like it could be like one of the famous Notre Dame comeback stories."

The story ended abruptly for the Irish. Beuerlein attempted to pick up a large chunk of territory on first down by going to flanker Tim Brown across the middle, but Brown couldn't handle the hard pass and it was deflected into the hands of LSU safety Steve Rehage.

This time Hilliard held on to the ball and LSU ran out the

clock successfully to clinch the school's second win in five games against Notre Dame.

The fifth game between the two schools was very similar to the inaugural meeting in 1970 when Notre Dame took a 3-0 victory here on a field goal late in the game.

As this contest developed, it seemed Notre Dame's first touchdown might stand as the winning margin. Each team had several long drives that ended in a big defensive play or a missed field goal. LSU was 1 of 4 in field-goal tries and the Irish missed all three, due to Thomas' ability to break through the line.

On the opening series of the second half, Notre Dame staged a beautiful, 18-play march with Pinkett, who rushed for 103 yards on 30 carries, getting the call 10 times.

The senior tailback gained only 25 yards on this circuit, but made a clutch run on fourth-and-2 from the LSU 23. He broke a tackle by cornerback Kevin Guidry and powered down to the 30 for the first down. The rest of the work was done by Beuerlein, who completed two passes to Brown and another one to Ward for a total of 48 yards.

From the 20, Beuerlein connected with fullback Frank Stams for 9 yards and on the next play, Stams rushed 2 yards for a first-and-goal at the 9. The Irish couldn't punch it in, though, as Thomas threw Stams for a loss on second down and linebacker Michael Brooks pressured Beuerlein into throwing an incompletion on third down, setting up a 23-yard field-goal try by Carney that was blocked by Thomas. Guidry picked up the ball in the end zone and returned it 17 yards.

LSU's offense responded with a long drive of its own, going 71 yards in 11 plays. Wickersham was 6 of 6 for 34 yards and Notre Dame helped the Tigers' cause with two 15-yard penalties for a late hit and facemasking.

But a 26-yard run by James to the Notre Dame 2 was nullified by a holding penalty. Notre Dame finally stopped the drive on a tackle by Furjanic that left Wickersham short of a first down at the 12. On fourth down, DeFrank tried a 29-yard field goal, but missed wide to the right, leaving the score at 7-3 with 1:19 left in the third quarter.

Once the Irish got the ball back, Pinkett had runs of 5 and 6 yards to go over the 1,000-yard mark for the third year in a row. Pinkett had several more gains as the fourth quarter opened. Notre Dame's deepest penetration was to the LSU 48, following a 4-yard gain by Pinkett, but Rehage tipped away a third-down pass from Beuerlein to Miller, which left the Irish in a punting situation.

LSU got the ball again and Wickersham engineered the two crucial possessions that led to James' touchdown run.

The Tigers' defense prevented the Irish from mounting any offense, which enabled LSU's offense to get the necessary field position to get on the scoreboard. Linebacker Toby Caston led the Tigers with 10 tackles and four others, Karl Wilson, Shawn Burks, Thomas and Sancho, had nine tackles each. Wilson had the Tigers' only sack.

Thomas, Tigers Got Respect

BY BRUCE HUNTER

The Advocate

South Bend, Ind. — *Nov. 23, 1985*

Henry Thomas tried not think about those painful memories.

A year ago the LSU nose guard was on his way to leading the Tigers to a national championship, as far as he was concerned. Thomas had developed into one of the premier defensive linemen in the Southeastern Conference and LSU had climbed to No. 6 in the nation.

But it all came crashing down on top of him Oct. 27 in Tiger Stadium, where Notre Dame dealt LSU a 30-22 loss and Thomas a season-ending knee injury.

"I wanted to keep my mind off that," said Thomas. "I didn't want it to affect me today."

Obviously it didn't. Thomas led a defensive effort that resulted in LSU beating Notre Dame, 10-7, today in Notre Dame Stadium. He more than made up for last year's disappointment by making numerous key plays to help the Tigers win for the first time here.

Thomas really came through on field-goal rushes, blocking two attempts by Notre Dame's John Carney and forcing him to kick wide into "Never Never Land" on another try. Thomas also had nine tackles, including one behind the line.

"I figured they owed me something," said Thomas, a 6-2, 255-pound junior from Houston. "They owed our team some respect. I think they lost some respect for us after they beat us last year."

The Fighting Irish manhandled LSU's makeshift defense, riddled with injuries on the line, in last year's triumph. It was a completely different story today, however.

Notre Dame scored on its first possession of the afternoon, but couldn't produce anything on its next 11 tries as LSU's defense took control. The closest the Irish got to scoring was the field-goal attempts by Carney, who had made 30 of 36 attempts (.829) for a school record before he ran into Thomas.

Thomas received plenty of assistance from his defensive teammates who felt Notre Dame "took something away from us" last year. Inside linebackers Toby Caston and Shawn Burks combined for 19 tackles, and outside linebacker Ron Sancho and Karl Wilson had nine tackles each. Sancho also had an interception and broken up pass, while Wilson added a sack.

"It just took a lot of determination," said Sancho. "Our defense has been playing with a lot of determination and pride all year. It was gut-check time and we just slugged it out."

Outside linebacker Michael Brooks, a finalist for The Butkus Award for the outstanding linebacker in the country, finished with five tackles and one hit behind the line. He made an important play on Notre Dame quarterback Steve Beuerlein to force him to throw an incompletion on a third-and-goal play.

LSU's defense was ranked second in the nation in points allowed (9.0 average) going into the game. The Tigers had shutouts against Kentucky and Ole Miss, but this may have been an even stronger defensive showing.

"We came out here thinking that we had to earn some respect against Notre Dame," said cornerback Norman Jefferson, who had four tackles. "They were more physical and a lot of people thought they would dominate us. We had to prove today that we're one of the best teams in the country."

Both Thomas and Darrell Phillips had blocked kicks in earlier games this season. It's something that the defensive linemen really work on with Coach Pete Jenkins. Thomas said he learned something on Carney's extra point after the first-quarter touchdown that enabled him to break through on three straight field-goal rushes.

"We had an outside block on for the extra point," said Thomas. "Karl (Wilson) came over to me and said 'I think we can get this guy.' So he ran the outside block and I just went through the line."

Thomas had more than enough time to get in position to block Carney's first try from 52 yards in the second quarter. The kicker seemed to hesitate slightly, which made Thomas' job that much easier.

When Carney went back in to try another 52-yarder before halftime, Thomas was in the backfield, causing Carney to kick way off to the left.

"I came through and it went off the other way," said Thomas. "It went into Never, Never Land."

The final kick by Carney was a 23-yard attempt, coming at the end of an 18-play drive to open the second half. The Irish came away with nothing as Thomas got his hands on the ball again.

LSU had some kicking problems of its own, making only 1 of 4 attempts. Ron Lewis missed from 49 and 26 yards, which brought his season's stats to 4 of 15. So the Tigers went with Matt DeFrank as their kicker for the first time.

DeFrank made a 27-yard field goal at the end of the first half, but missed a 29-yard try in the third quarter.

"What I was trying to do was just punch it through," DeFrank said. "I just got under it too much the first time, but it went through. The second one I hit it good. It was just two feet wide."

Tigers Roll Back the Tide, 14-10

■ Tommy Hodson completed 9 of 21 passes for 68 yards and one touchdown.

By Bruce Hunter
The Advocate

Birmingham, Ala. — *Nov. 8, 1986*

For the third straight time, LSU's defense captured Legion Field.

The determined Tiger defenders stopped Alabama twice in first-down situations inside their own 14 and came away with three fourth-quarter turnovers to hang on for a 14-10 victory tonight before 75,808 in Legion Field and a national television audience on ESPN.

"It doesn't matter how many times you win here. It feels great every time," LSU senior defensive end Roland Barbay said.

The victory was LSU's third straight in Legion Field and each time it's been the Tigers' defense leading the charge against their arch-rivals, who have held the upper hand in their long series.

The 18th-ranked Tigers, 6-2 overall, moved into a first-place tie with Alabama in the Southeastern Conference, both at 4-1, and can assure themselves of at least a share of the conference crown with a victory against Mississippi State next Saturday night in Jackson. The sixth-ranked Crimson Tide fell to 8-2 overall and finishes its SEC season here against Auburn on Nov. 29.

In 1982, the Tigers won, 20-10, here and salvaged a 16-14 decision in 1984. Both games were won by staunch defensive efforts by LSU, as was the case tonight.

"A couple of guys on this team and I are very fortunate to be able to make the statement that we've been able to beat Alabama three times here," said another LSU senior defensive end, Karl Wilson. "I don't think anybody else in SEC history could say that."

LSU scored all its points in the second quarter to build a 14-7 lead at intermission. Then its defense went to work in the second half, limiting Alabama to a 22-yard field goal by Van Tiffen early in the third quarter.

The Crimson Tide was in scoring position throughout the fourth quarter, but the Tigers wouldn't relent. Linebacker Eric Hill stripped the ball from halfback Bobby Humphrey just outside the goal line and cornerback Kevin Guidry recovered in the end zone to halt Alabama's best chance.

"The offense got the points in the first half and it was up to us to do it in the second half," Barbay said. "We almost shut them out in the second half. It was a great team effort by the defense."

In addition to causing a fumble, Hill intercepted a Mike Shula pass late in the fourth quarter to seal the outcome. Strong safety Greg Jackson accounted for the Tigers' other two takeaways with an interception in the third quarter and fumble recovery in the fourth quarter.

The Tigers had scoring drives of 80 and 62 yards in the second quarter to rally from a 7-0 deficit. Reserve quarterback Mickey Guidry scrambled 4 yards for the first touchdown. Later, starter Tommy Hodson, who completed 9 of 21 for 68 yards and two interceptions, threw a 6-yard touchdown pass to Wendell Davis for the other score. Davis had just three catches in the game.

Alabama scored first on a 3-yard touchdown pass from Shula to tight end Angelo Stafford in the first quarter, but that was the Crimson Tide's only touchdown, even though it crossed into LSU territory five more times, including three times in the final period.

"Our guys gave a real fine effort," said Alabama coach Ray Perkins. "They fought hard. We lost to a real fine team in LSU. That was not the same team that played Miami of Ohio and Ole Miss."

The Tigers were coming off a 21-19 upset loss to Ole Miss, but added Alabama to their own list of upset victims, which includes Texas A&M and Florida. They're 3-0 as the underdog this season.

Early in the third quarter, the Tigers gave the Crimson Tide

Score by Periods

LSU	0	14	0	0	— 14
Alabama	7	0	3	0	— 10

a prime scoring opportunity after an offensive pass interference call against Davis forced Matt DeFrank to punt from deep in his own territory. Greg Richardson fielded the punt at the LSU 49 and got down to the 44.

From there, Humphrey had a pair of 13-yard runs, both around right tackle. On first-and-goal from the 9, Humphrey tried going to the left side. He broke a tackle at the 5 and fought his way into the end zone. But a holding call against the Crimson Tide spoiled it and moved the ball back to the 19.

Shula, who completed 16 of 27 for 190 yards, a touchdown and two interceptions, gained a couple yards on first down and threw a screen to fullback Doug Allen that went for 12 yards to the LSU 5. Then Shula's third-down pass to Stafford was thrown out of the end zone, forcing Alabama to settle for a 22-yard field goal by Tiffen that made it 14-10 with 9:23 left in the quarter.

Soon after, the Tigers had a chance to add to their four-point lead. Tailback Harvey Williams had consecutive gains of 6, 7 and 6 yards to lead LSU into Alabama's side of the field at the 37.

But the Tigers weren't able to go much farther and tailback Sammy Martin was stopped on an option play on third down, forcing DeFrank to punt from the Alabama 36. His soft, low kick was downed by Chris Carrier at the 6.

The Crimson Tide got a break when LSU was called for a personal foul penalty that gave Alabama a first down out to its 27. Alabama overcame a third-and-11 situation with Shula connecting with flanker Al Bell for a 24-yard gain to the LSU 39.

On the first play of the fourth quarter, Alabama jumped offsides to set up a first-and-15 from the 44. Humphrey, who rushed for 134 yards on 24 carries to set a school record with 1,138 yards this season, got loose on a draw play and was fighting for extra yardage when the ball came free and LSU's Jackson recovered at the 18.

The Tigers moved quickly in the wrong direction and had to punt. Then Shula went to work completing a 12-yard pass to Richardson, and on third-and-12, he threw deep to tight end Howard Cross for a 29-yard play to the LSU 31.

Humphrey had run the ball three times for a first-and-goal at the 5. But on his next run, he made it to just outside the end zone when Hill jolted the ball loose and Guidry recovered in the end zone for a touchback with 8:26 left.

"I almost broke my back trying to get the ball," Guidry said. "It was in the end zone. If anyone else would have fallen on the ball, it would have been a touchdown."

Trying to control the ball and run off some time, Hodson threw a third-down pass from deep in his own territory and it was intercepted by safety Kermit Kendrick, who returned it to the LSU 15, but was later ruled out of bounds at the LSU 41.

The Tiger defense made another stand in its territory and nearly came up with an interception on a tipped pass on third down. On fourth-and-5 from the 36, Alabama tried a reverse with Bell going around right end, but linebacker Ron Sancho wasn't fooled and stopped the play.

Starting at its own 38 with 4:51 left, LSU immediately crossed into Alabama territory on a 13-yard run by Williams. But a procedure call against the Tigers eventually cost them dearly and they had to punt again from the Alabama 43. DeFrank punted into the end zone, giving the Crimson Tide possession at their 20 with 2:12 left.

But Alabama's last chance went astray when Shula's pass was tipped at the line and intercepted by Hill, who returned the ball 4 yards to the Alabama 28. The Tigers were able to get down to the 15 as they ran out the clock successfully.

"We had to make them put the ball in the air," Hill said. "We knew we couldn't win if they kept the ball on the ground all night."

In the first half, Alabama controlled the action offensively and defensively at the outset, building a 7-0 lead. But the LSU defense began to stiffen and the Tiger offense came to life with two touchdown drives.

Even with Hodson knocked out of the game for two plays, the Tigers moved the ball on the opening series of the night. They completed three passes, including one by Guidry, to march from their own 20 to the Alabama 46.

A personal foul penalty against the Tide sent LSU deeper into Alabama territory at the 35. But cornerback Freddie Robinson stepped in front of Rogie Magee to intercept a Hodson pass and end the scoring threat at the 27.

On its first possession, Alabama engineered a ball-control drive that went 46 yards in 12 plays with Shula completing three passes and Humphrey gaining 25 yards on the ground. But LSU stopped Humphrey for no gain on third-and-1 from the LSU 27 and Tiffen missed a 44-yard field goal.

LSU had penalty problems on its next series. DeFrank had to kick three times before he finally got off one that counted. Penalties for illegal procedure and holding moved the Tigers back to their 11 before DeFrank was finally able to make a legal punt. It went only 37 yards and gave Alabama great field position at the LSU 44 after a short return.

Using just six plays, Alabama capitalized on the LSU mistakes by punching it in for the first points of the game. Allen took a screen pass and bolted 21 yards and Shula came right back to pass to Bell for 9 yards.

An Allen run gave the Crimson Tide a first-and-goal at the 8, but it took three more plays before Shula found Stafford over the middle for a 3-yard touchdown pass. Tiffen's point-after made it 7-0 with 1:20 left in the quarter.

Early in the second quarter, Guidry came in for his usual relief stint and passed to Davis for 10 yards to get the initial first down of the drive.

Then Garland Jean Batiste broke a draw play for 21 yards all the way to the Alabama 24. Williams got them even closer with a 14-yard pickup on an option play. On first-and-goal,

■ **Garland Jean Batiste drags two Alabama defenders with him at the end of a 25-yard run.**

Williams gained 5 more yards to the 5, but was held to just a yard on his next carry.

Guidry wanted to throw to Williams on third down, but he was covered. So Guidry tucked the ball away and found the left side wide open, dashing into the end zone with the ball raised high in the air. David Browndyke kicked the extra point for a 7-7 tie with 9:12 left in the half.

The Crimson Tide went back to work and swept down the field on a 67-yard drive. Shula threw a couple of short passes to get Alabama out to midfield and then unleashed a bomb to Richardson, who beat the LSU secondary for a 33-yard gain to the LSU 13.

But Shula was off target in trying to throw into the end zone to Stafford and Jackson picked it off just in front of the back line of the end zone.

Working with just 5:30 remaining, Hodson was perfect in the ensuing series, completing all four of his passes for 39 yards. He threw to Martin for 12 yards and to Brian Kinchen for another 8 yards to midfield.

Jean Batiste gained 7 yards to get into Alabama territory. On the next play, Hodson had to scramble when he couldn't find anyone open, picking up just a yard. But a late hit by the Crimson Tide moved the ball 15 yards farther.

Two plays later, Hodson found Davis on a short crossing route and the split end struggled for 13 yards for a first-and-goal at the 5. Tailback Eddie Fuller lost a yard on first down, but Hodson hit Davis in the back of the end zone for a 6-yard touchdown pass with just 25 seconds left.

1986: LSU vs. Alabama

Win Gives Tigers Share of SEC Lead

By Dave Moormann
The Advocate

Birmingham, Ala. — *Nov. 8, 1986*

Cornerback Willie Bryant and wide receiver Rogie Magee did an impromptu end-zone dance.

Six LSU players knelt on the Legion Field artificial turf in prayer.

Usually taciturn LSU coach Bill Arnsparger concluded an interview by hugging a group of cheerleaders. His players already had carried him off the field.

Nearly everyone associated with LSU whooped and hollered in celebration of the Tigers' stunning 14-10 victory over sixth-ranked Alabama here tonight.

"We put that on at the end as a means of expression," Bryant said of the dance orchestrated in front of the LSU end-zone crowd. "Celebration — that's what it's all about."

Better yet, it's about a victory that put 18th-ranked LSU at 6-2 overall and into a first-place tie with Alabama at 4-1 in the Southeastern Conference. Alabama is 8-2 overall. Auburn and Ole Miss are each a half-game back with 3-1 league records.

It's about a victory that saw an opportunistic defense recover two fumbles, including one in the end zone, and intercept two passes, including one in the end zone.

It's about sophomore strong safety Greg Jackson, who had one interception and one fumble recovery. It's about sophomore linebacker Eric Hill, who helped force one fumble and intercepted a pass.

It's about an entire team banding together after it lost to Ole Miss last week, 21-19, and fell behind early to Alabama, 7-0.

"All week long we practiced harder than we've ever practiced," Jackson said. "We knew we could win if we didn't make any mistakes. Coach told us all week that we had to gang tackle and try to strip the ball."

Jackson had that on his mind as Alabama sophomore halfback Bobby Humphrey neared the goal line midway through the fourth quarter. Jackson stuck his head into Humphrey, and that hit, combined with one from Hill, jarred the ball loose and into the end zone. Senior cornerback Kevin Guidry made the recovery.

"I didn't know the ball was loose," Guidry said. "Then I looked around and the ball was rolling by my leg. I thought, 'What's that doing there?'"

It was there for the taking, and so Guidry took it with 8:26 remaining and LSU ahead, 14-10. But there were still some tense times before LSU won its third straight game at Legion Field.

LSU had to stop speedy wide receiver Al Bell on a fourth-and-five reverse play, and the Tigers had to face the threat of

■ **Alabama's defense kept the game close, but Shula & Co. couldn't clinch the win.**

Alabama senior quarterback Mike Shula directing Alabama with 2:19 remaining and the ball on the Crimson Tide 20-yard line. LSU senior nose guard Henry Thomas tipped Shula's first pass attempt, and Hill intercepted to all but clinch the victory.

"We had to play good defense and shut them out in the second half," Arnsparger said, "and we did."

LSU limited Alabama to Van Tiffin's 22-yard field goal in the third quarter. The Tigers blanked Alabama in the fourth period, in part because weak safety Mike Dewitt forced Humphrey to fumble after a 25-yard gain, and Jackson recovered at the LSU 17-yard line.

144

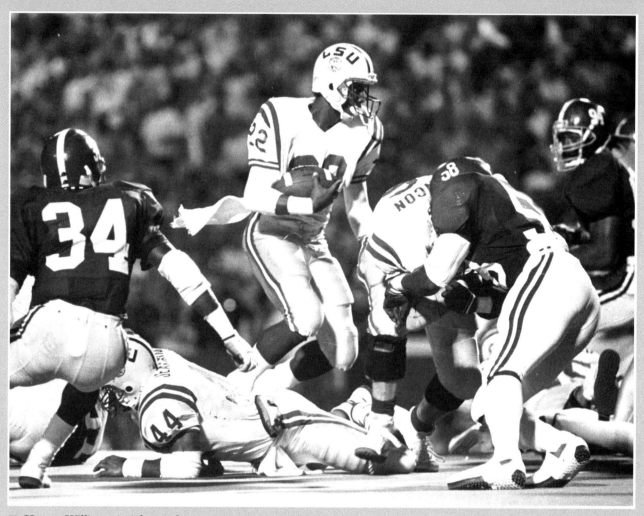

■ **Harvey Williams (22) hunts for an opening in the Tide defense.**

LSU has allowed only six fourth-quarter points this season.

"We came in at halftime and said, 'We're a better second-half team and we've already played a pretty good first half,' " Hill said, "... We made (Shula) make some bad decisions."

One of the worst came in the second quarter after Alabama had marched from its 20 to the LSU 13-yard line. A 33-yard pass to tight end Angelo Stafford put Alabama into position to break a 7-7 tie. Stafford had scored Alabama's only touchdown on a 3-yard reception at 1:20 of the first quarter.

But this time Shula overthrew Stafford and Jackson intercepted in the end zone.

"I read Shula's eyes all the way," Jackson said. "I knew where he was going to throw it, and I turned around and it was there."

The interception set up the game-winning 80-yard touchdown drive that took 12 plays and 5:05 to complete. It ended with quarterback Tommy Hodson's 6-yard pass to wide receiver Wendell Davis 25 seconds before halftime.

With primary receiver Sammy Martin covered in the right side of the end zone, Hodson said he saw Davis "running free" across the middle of the end zone. "I put it on him," said

Hodson, who had to throw the pass over Alabama cornerback Freddie Robinson. "I kind of dropped it in."

But Hodson didn't find things all that easy against a tenacious Alabama defense that sent him to the sidelines on the first series with a slightly twisted knee and limited him to 9 of 21 with two interceptions for 68 yards. Alabama also intercepted one Mickey Guidry pass.

"They did a heck of a job," Hodson said of the Alabama defense. "They took away a lot and limited us as to what we could do."

But they couldn't stop the LSU triumph and the victory celebration. "This is awesome," tight end Brian Kinchen said. "It's a great feeling."

Kinchen participated in the post-game prayer service with linebackers Darren Malbrough and Ron Sancho, safety Chris Carrier and defensive linemen Karl Wilson and Darrell Phillips. Shula also took part. Kinchen said the practice began three years ago after they met through the Fellowship of Christian Athletes.

"There's usually more out there," Kinchen said of the Alabama players. "I guess a lot of them were down."

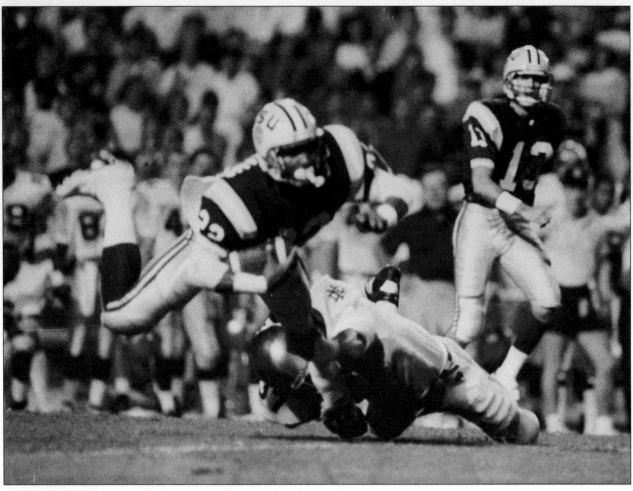

■ Harvey Williams (22) stretches for extra yardage on a pass reception across the middle.

Tiger Defense Turns Away Irish, 21-19

BY BRUCE HUNTER
The Advocate

Baton Rouge, La. — *Nov. 22, 1986*

The LSU Tigers stood up Notre Dame inches from the goal line and staked their claim to a Sugar Bowl berth with a drama-filled, 21-19 victory tonight.

Quarterback Tommy Hodson threw three touchdown passes and the LSU defense gallantly fended off Notre Dame's second-half charge to earn a close, but never-the-less, gigantic triumph in front of a sellout crowd of 78,197 in Tiger Stadium and a national television audience on ESPN. LSU is 3-0 on ESPN this season.

■ **Notre Dame's Hiawatha Francisco (33) is tripped up by Tiger linebacker Ron Sancho.**

But the crowd the Tigers were really trying to impress was the Sugar Bowl executive committee members at the game and watching on television.

"The only team that can catch us (Alabama) is the team we beat," LSU coach Bill Arnsparger said.

Taking a more direct approach to the matter, many of Arnsparger's players said they've already earned the right to represent the Southeastern Conference in the Sugar Bowl against Big Eight runner-up Nebraska. Sugar Bowl officials said they will wait until Nov. 30 to make the final choice in the event of a tie between LSU and Alabama.

"We put a bug in the Sugar Bowl committee's mind," said

Score by Periods

Notre Dame	7	0	3	9 —	19
LSU	14	0	0	7 —	21

LSU nose guard Henry Thomas. "We gave them something to think about. We wanted to show them 'Invite us to your bowl and we won't let you down.' "

Thomas helped lead the Tigers to two defensive stands in the second half, including a first-and-goal situation from the 2.

Then LSU turned back a two-point conversion attempt by the Fighting Irish that would have tied the game with 3:32 left.

By beating Notre Dame, the eighth-ranked Tigers, who earned a share of the SEC title last week, moved closer to assuring themselves of the Sugar Bowl invitation. The school announced after the game it's accepting ticket applications for the Sugar Bowl on a conditional basis. Bowl officials said the decision won't be made until after the Alabama-Auburn game next Saturday.

LSU is 8-2 overall and 5-1 in the SEC. Its only remaining game is against non-conference rival Tulane next Saturday. Alabama, idle on Saturday, is ranked ninth with a record of 9-2 overall and 4-1 in the SEC going into its finale.

Meanwhile, Notre Dame fell to 4-6 and is assured of its second straight losing season. The Irish, who never led in the game, went out with a valiant, comeback effort like they've done so many times this season. They've lost five games by a total of 14 points.

"This is absolutely unbelievable," Notre Dame coach Lou Holtz said. "What more can you tell kids after a game like this? You have to give LSU all the credit in the world. I congratulate them and Bill on a fine job. But these are getting painful and maybe our day will come."

Trailing, 14-7, at halftime, Notre Dame got a pair of field goals by John Carney and a 14-yard touchdown pass from backup quarterback Terry Andrysiak to D'Juan Francisco to rally in the second half. The Tigers managed only a 4-yard touchdown pass from Hodson to tight end Brian Kinchen, which proved to be the winning play.

In the first half, Hodson was accurate on 10 of his first 12 passes and led the Tigers on long touchdown drives the first two times they touched the ball. He threw touchdown passes of 13 yards to Wendell Davis and 4 yards to Rogie Magee in the first quarter. Both LSU's David Browndyke and Carney missed a field goal in the first half.

In between LSU's scores, Notre Dame's Tim Brown broke a kickoff return 96 yards for a touchdown to provide the Irish with their only points of the half.

With Andrysiak at the helm late in the game, the Irish needed only 1:34 to go 80 yards. A 25-yard pass from Andrysiak to split end Tony Eason moved them to the LSU 33.

Andrysiak completed two more passes before he found Francisco open in the back of the end zone. He pulled in the 14-yard pass just in front of the back line and just behind linebacker Toby Caston, bringing the Irish to 21-19 with 3:32 left.

They went for two points, but Andrysiak was pressured by linebacker Ron Sancho and threw out of the end zone.

LSU was able to clinch the victory when Hodson hit Davis and Magee on third-and-long situations in the closing minutes.

Hodson completed 20 of 28 passes for 248 yards and two interceptions. His primary receiver, Davis, collected seven catches for 121 yards and set the LSU record for most receiving yards in a season with 1,161 yards.

Running back Garland Jean Batiste gained 62 yards on 13 carries and tailback Harvey Williams added 52 yards on 20 carries. The Tigers outgained the Irish in total yards, 387 to 270.

Notre Dame quarterback Steve Beuerlein, who had thrown for nearly 1,000 yards in his last four games, completed just 7 of 18 passes for 50 yards and an interception. Andrysiak came on in relief to complete 6 of 8 for 83.

Early in the second half, LSU's defense had a couple of golden opportunities slip away with weak safety Chris Carrier and linebacker Nicky Hazard coming close to interceptions.

The Irish were able to keep the drive alive when Beuerlein scrambled 15 yards, converting the first of three straight third-down plays. But cornerback Kevin Guidry came up to throw Aaron Robb for a 3-yard loss on a pass in the flats and the Irish couldn't convert again, having to settle for a 31-yard field goal by Carney that made it 14-10 with 5:50 left in the quarter.

Notre Dame free safety Steve Lawrence picked off a

■ Notre Dame's George Streeter and Steve Lawrence force down Sammy Martin (23) after a short gain.

Hodson pass at the LSU 30 and was on his way to a touchdown before Williams bumped him out of bounds on the 2.

Spurred on by the crowd, the Tiger defense made its 10th goal-line stand of the season and one of its most crucial. Fullback Pernell Taylor plunged into the middle of the LSU line two straight times and came within inches of the goal line on his second run.

Then the Irish let tailback Anthony Johnson have a crack at the Tigers, but he was thrown back by Caston to just outside the 1. Going on fourth-and-goal, Beuerlein ran the option to the left side and was forced to pitch to Brown. Weak safety Steve Rehage was there to turn the play in and Brown went down at the 5, ending the threat.

"We have a play that we just try to beat the other team off the ball," said LSU defensive end Roland Barbay. "We try to penetrate and establish a new line of scrimmage. We take a lot of pride in our goal-line defense."

Unable to move the ball, LSU sent in punter Matt DeFrank, who fumbled the snap from center but was able to get off the kick that went for 45 yards to the Notre Dame 46.

But the Irish didn't take long to get into position to challenge for the lead again. Notre Dame, switching running backs in and out, got a couple of 10-yard runs and powered down for a first down at the LSU 13. Then Brown was thrown for an 8-yard loss by safety Greg Jackson on second down and defensive end Karl Wilson sacked Beuerlein for a 6-yard loss to the 27.

Carney still was good on a 44-yard field-goal effort, though, cutting the margin to 14-13 with 11:34 left.

The Tigers' offense awoke on their next possession. Hodson threw for 27 yards on three completions, Williams gained 20 yards on five carries and Jean Batiste added a 14-yard run.

Hodson capped the 11-play march with a 4-yard touchdown pass to Kinchen and Browndyke booted the point after for a 21-13 advantage with 7:45 left.

Then Carrier picked off a Beuerlein pass at the LSU 26 as he tried to find Brown in a crowd and the Tigers went on the move again, making the longest offensive play of the game. Hodson threw long to Davis, who beat the coverage on a streak route down the sidelines for 45 yards.

On the next play, Hodson tried to finish off the drive and threw to Magee in the end zone. Instead, cornerback Troy Wilson intercepted the pass and gave the Irish new life with 5:06 remaining.

In the first half, LSU controlled the action in every phase of the game, except special teams. Notre Dame had just four plays in the first quarter and didn't get its initial first down until midway through the second quarter.

Hodson engineered a pair of ball-control drives of 82 and 71 yards in the first quarter. On their first series, the Tigers moved steadily down the field with Jean Batiste picking up 19 yards on three carries and Hodson doing the rest through the air. He completed 4 of 5 for 57 yards on the march.

A 23-yard completion to Kinchen may have gone for a touchdown if Hodson's pass hadn't been so high, forcing him to leap into the air to pull it down at the Notre Dame 17. Hodson capped it off by hitting Davis on a curl pattern at the 1 and he fell back into the end zone for the score and a 7-0 lead after Browndyke's kick.

LSU's Ron Lewis booted a high kick to Brown at the 4 and the Irish speedster picked out a hole on the right side, sprinting through the Tigers and breaking into the clear. His 96-yard touchdown return took just 12 seconds and, with Carney's kick, tied the game at 7-7 with 9:36 left.

Undaunted by the touchdown, LSU regained control of the game with yet another sustained drive, which turned out to be its longest of the season.

Williams checked in at tailback and gained 15 yards on his first two carries. Hodson connected with Jean Batiste and Davis for 19 yards and a first down at the LSU 46. Then freshman flanker Tony Moss took a short pass from Hodson, broke a tackle and scooted 17 yards.

As they closed for the score, the Tigers had a bad break when Williams slipped and was ruled down on a run that would have gone to the 5, but actually went for a 3-yard loss. Jean Batiste finally dove for 2 yards over right guard on fourth-and-inches to get to the 4.

After Jean Batiste was held for no gain and Hodson threw incomplete, Magee broke open in the end zone on third down and pulled in a 4-yard touchdown pass with 49 seconds left in the quarter. Browndyke's kick put the Tigers back on top, 14-7.

When they kicked off for the second time, Matt DeFrank came in and squibbed it down field. But Brown still came up

with it at the 9 and returned it 22 yards. The Irish got their initial offensive play of the game with 42 seconds left in the quarter and couldn't keep the ball long enough to run out the quarter.

A 23-yard punt by Dan Sorenson gave LSU excellent field position at its own 41 and Hodson's 16-yard pass to Davis helped the Tigers moved down the Notre Dame 29. They picked up another first down, but had to settle for a 36-yard field-goal attempt from the right hash mark. Browndyke kicked the ball wide right, ending the threat with 3:20 remaining in the half.

On Notre Dame's third possession, it finally came up with a first down. Andrysiak scrambled 22 yards out to the Irish 48, but fumbled the ball away two plays later when Barbay delivered a hit on him. The fumble was recovered by Thomas at the LSU 49.

Although the Tigers couldn't move the ball, DeFrank was able to pin the Irish at their own 15 with a 36-yard punt.

Working with 4:17 left before halftime, Andrysiak led the Irish on their best drive of the half. The play that started the march was a 20-yard pass to split end Milt Jackson.

The Irish continued to move until LSU finally held and forced them to go for a 49-yard field goal by Carney. He made the kick, but LSU was offsides before the snap.

So Carney had to try again, this time from 43 yards out. His kick went off to the left with 17 seconds left.

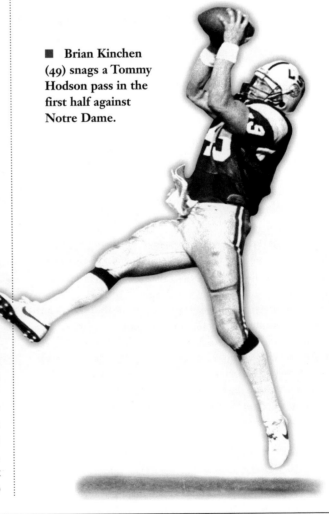

■ **Brian Kinchen (49) snags a Tommy Hodson pass in the first half against Notre Dame.**

Everything Went Right For Tigers' Dramatic Win

BY DAVE MOORMANN
The Advocate

Baton Rouge — *Nov. 22, 1986*

LSU defensive teammates Steve Rehage and Ron Sancho found themselves in the right place at the right time Saturday night, and senior linebacker Toby Caston is glad they did.

Caston also thought he was in the right place in the end zone. But his timing wasn't right, as Notre Dame quarterback Terry Andrysiak lofted a 14-yard touchdown pass to D'Juan Francisco with 3:32 remaining in the Irish's game against LSU in Tiger Stadium. Caston was covering on the play that went for the first fourth-quarter touchdown against LSU's defense this season.

"I don't know how the guy caught it," Caston said. "I bumped him and then looked, and saw he still had the ball and his toes were in bounds."

The score narrowed LSU's lead to 21-19, and Caston felt responsible for allowing a play that might have resulted in a tie for LSU. But on the ensuing two-point conversion try, Sancho hurried Andrysiak into throwing an incompletion in the end zone. Caston was relieved.

"I would have been crushed," Caston said of what a tie would have meant to him. "After we stopped the two-point conversion, I felt good."

Sancho did, too. And with good reason, for it was pressure from the sophomore linebacker that forced Andrysiak to throw incomplete for Joel Williams in the end zone.

Sancho said LSU had an "inside defensive play" called before Andrysiak dropped to pass. When Sancho saw that, he said he "aborted what I was doing and ran" after Andrysiak, who hurried his pass and threw it out of bounds.

Defensive coordinator Mike Archer said LSU had called the same blitz it had used on the preceding touchdown. "You live by the blitz and die by the blitz," he said.

Eighth-ranked LSU survived with a 21-19 victory that improved its overall record to 8-2 and its chances of appearing in the Sugar Bowl on New Year's Day. Should Alabama and LSU tie for the Southeastern Conference title at 5-1, Sugar Bowl officials said they will decide upon the SEC representative on Nov. 30.

Alabama must play Auburn on Nov. 29. LSU ends its regular season that same day at home against Tulane.

LSU coach Bill Arnsparger said again he believes his team belongs in the Sugar Bowl because "the only one who can catch us, we beat."

Notre Dame found itself trying to catch LSU the entire game. The Irish did once, when Tim Brown returned a kickoff for a 96-yard touchdown that tied the score, 7-7, at 9:48 of the first quarter. LSU had taken the opening drive 71 yards, with quarterback Tommy Hodson throwing a 13-yard touchdown pass to Wendell Davis.

Davis, who finished with seven catches for 121 yards, became LSU's single-season yardage leader with 1,161 yards. Eric Martin set the old record of 1,064 in 1983. Davis has a school-record 75 catches. He was named the ESPN-TV Player of the Game and Coach Bill Arnsparger said he has "invited ESPN back for next week's game." LSU is 3-0 on ESPN this season and 5-0 overall.

"It was one of those football games where things went well for awhile and things didn't go well for awhile," Arnsparger said.

Things looked bleak for LSU in the third quarter when Notre Dame free safety Steve Lawrence intercepted Hodson's pass and returned it 28 yards to the LSU 2-yard line. But two runs up the middle by fullback Pernell Taylor gained only 1 yard, and Anthony Johnson gained nothing on a third-down play over the top, where he was met by Caston, who participated on all three tackles.

On fourth-and-1, Notre Dame quarterback Steve Beuerlein rolled left on an option and pitched to Brown. But Rehage shed a blocker and dropped Brown for a 4-yard loss.

"I knew the whole way," said Rehage. "I figured they had run three times to the middle and then were going to try either a toss sweep or the option ... I knew they were going to go to Brown. He's their horse."

But Rehage didn't even know if he was going to get in the game. Rehage returned to action briefly last week after missing three games with a knee injury. And up until Notre Dame reached the 2-yard line with 5:33 remaining in the third quarter and LSU ahead, 14-10, Rehage wasn't sure if he would play against the Irish. Then Archer sent him in for the goal-line series.

Archer said he intended to insert Rehage because sophomore Greg Jackson had begun to tire. Rehage figured he was in on only about 10 plays and Archer said Rehage's left knee "still isn't 100 percent."

But Rehage was feeling fine after he shed a blocker and tackled Brown. Rehage said he was assigned to the pitch man and senior cornerback Norman Jefferson was to take the quarterback.

"The last three weeks we've played option teams," Rehage said, "and Coach Archer does a great job of telling us what he wants us to do."

After sitting on the bench with an stretched knee ligament, the intense Rehage was ready to vent his emotions.

"A game like tonight is three-fourths frustration coming out," he said. "The whole first half I was wondering when I would come in."

■ Texas A&M's gang-tackling finally brought down this Tiger on the loose.

Van Buren Stars in 19-14 Orange Bowl Win

BY MAURICE McGANN
The Advocate

Miami — *Jan. 1, 1944*

Striking swiftly in the first and third quarters, the Louisiana State Tigers piled up three touchdowns and scored a well-earned 19-14 victory over the Texas Aggies here today before an overflowing crowd. Steven Van Buren was the big gun for the Bengals, sprinting 13 and 62 yards for touchdowns and tossing a scoring pass to Burt Goode.

Bernie Moore had put in some special plays for this game and he lost little time in seeing that they were made the most of. After the Tigers had worked the ball down to the Aggies' 12 the second time they got their hands on it, Van Buren caught the Aggies by surprise on a delayed double reverse and he sped over the goal without a hand being laid on him.

The Tigers failed on the extra-point attempt, but they lost little time in moving further out in front when Charley Webb recovered a punt fumbled by Jess Burditt on the Aggies' 22. Two running plays gained only two yards and then Van Buren passed neatly to Goode who stepped across the goal line for the score. Van Buren's extra-point attempt failed.

The Aggies quickly got back in the game, however, when they took the following kickoff and marched 70 yards for their first touchdown. Babe Hallmark had his pitching arm in fine

■ **Steve Van Buren raced for 13-yard and 62-yard touchdowns and passed for a third touchdown.**

trim and aided by a 15-yard roughness penalty the Aggies passed their way to the Tigers' 21.

The Bengals stopped a couple of Aggie running plays, but Hallmark found his mark, passing to Burditt for 11 yards and a touchdown. Stan Turner booted the extra point and the scoreboard read, LSU 12, Aggies 7.

The Tigers had three fine scoring chances in the second period but lacked the punch to add to their total. Van Buren faked a punt and raced 40 yards only to stumble and fall from exhaustion when he had a clear field. On another occasion, the Tigers made a first down on the Aggies' 5-yard line, but four smashes failed to put it over.

The Bengals came back strong at the start of the second half and within a few minutes, Van Buren showed his all-American form by breaking loose from scrimmage for 62 yards through the entire Aggie team and the third LSU touchdown. This time he converted the extra-point kick and the Bengals held a 19-7 advantage.

But the Aggies weren't through by any means and they went all out with their aerial game. Making the most of a stiff breeze at their backs, the Aggies worked the Bengals into a hole, and made the most of a break when they got it — recovering Joe Nagata's fumble on the LSU 25.

Score by Periods

Texas A&M	7	0	7	0 —	14
LSU	12	0	7	0 —	19

E.G. Beesley passed to Burditt for seven yards and then Hallmark shot a neat one to Marion Settegest on the LSU 5-yard line and he raced over for the score. Turner booted the point-after kick which reduced the Tigers' lead to five points, 19-14.

The Bengals held on gamely to their small lead and until the closing minutes of the game it was a defensive battle. In the final minutes, fumbled pass interceptions and laterals thrilled the fans of both teams, but failed to produce a score. The Bengals were in possession of the ball on the Aggies' 22 when the game ended.

The victory was especially sweet to the Tigers because they had been defeated, 28-13, by these same Aggies earlier in the year. It was even sweeter to LSU coach Bernie Moore since it marked his first bowl victory in four trips.

■ Wendell Davis (82) had 11 receptions for 128 yards against the Bulldogs.

Tigers Outduel Stubborn Georgia, 26-23

By Bruce Hunter
The Advocate

Athens, Ga. — *Oct. 10, 1987*

LSU and Georgia lived and died by the big play, of which there were many on this wild afternoon.

The final two — a leaping touchdown catch by Brian Kinchen and a div-ing interception by Kevin Guidry — went LSU's way, allowing the Tigers to escape with a 26-23 victory before a thunderous, sold-out crowd of 82,122 in Sanford Stadium and national television audience on ESPN.

"I feel like I'm 34 years old going on 60," said LSU coach Mike Archer. "I was really feeling my age that last drive. We let them back into the game with the big plays, but our kids showed a lot of heart and desire. I can't say enough about our players and coaching staff and how we hung together."

LSU, leading 16-3 at halftime, had to come from behind in the final minutes after the Bulldogs, as they have done so often in 24 seasons under Vince Dooley, found a way to get back in the game and make it close. But Georgia's 20-point comeback with three long touchdown plays in the second half was completely out of character for the Bulldogs.

Quarterback Tommy Hodson connected with Kinchen for a 5-yard TD pass to provide LSU with the winning margin with 3:36 left to play. But the explosive Bulldogs weren't out of it until a James Jackson pass deflected off tailback Rodney Hampton and into the hands of Guidry, who caught the ball just off the grass. Guidry's interception Georgia's final drive at the LSU 28 with 1:01 left and atoned for a touchdown pass that he surrendered earlier in the second half.

"I felt like the difference in the two halves was big plays," Dooley said. "In the second half, we had the long catch by (John) Thomas, then (Cassius) Osborn got loose by breaking a tackle and scored on the long run. We also had a big play on Vince Guthrie's interception. It was a great game for everybody involved, but unfortunately someone had to lose. And this time it was us."

Engaging in close games like this one was nothing new for either team. The seventh-ranked Tigers have found ways to survive these tests, while the 16th-ranked Bulldogs continue to falter in the clutch.

LSU, 5-0-1, moved into sole possession of the Southeastern Conference lead, going to 2-0 in defense of its league championship. The Tigers went to the wire for the third straight Saturday, including a 13-10 decision over Florida last week and 13-13 tie with Ohio State two weeks ago. All three opponents were nationally ranked.

Georgia, on the other hand, hasn't won the crucial SEC

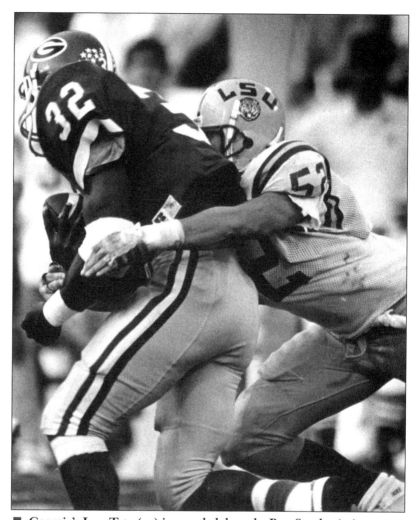

■ **Georgia's Lars Tate (32) is wrestled down by Ron Sancho (52).**

games since Herschel Walker left school after leading the Bulldogs to conference titles from 1980-82. The Bulldogs, 4-2 overall and 1-1 in the SEC, have lost twice this season by a combined total of just four points.

"It was a great win today," Kinchen said. "It seems like every week it gets closer and closer. But this was better because it was in their backyard."

Georgia, which lost for just the sixth time at home in the 1980s, appeared to be on its way to another miracle "Between the Hedges" that surround the 58-year-old stadium.

Jackson, who passed for 170 yards and rushed for 85 more in the game, threw touchdown passes of 31 yards to Thomas and 74 yards to Osborn. Then Hampton raced 14 yards for the go-ahead points, giving the Bulldogs a 23-19 lead with 6:58 left.

LSU's first-half points came on a 36-yard touchdown pass from backup quarterback Mickey Guidry to Tony Moss and three field goals by David Browndyke. Another Browndyke field goal early in the fourth quarter enabled him to tie his own school record of four in a game and set the stage for the final offensive fireworks.

Score by Periods

LSU	3	13	0	10 —	26
Georgia	3	0	6	14 —	23

■ **Tailback Sammy Martin (23) finds a seam in the Georgia defense.**

After Georgia went in front, the Tigers responded with a 39-yard kickoff return by Eddie Fuller that led to a nine-play scoring drive. Even with Hodson knocked out of the game for two plays on a late hit by Georgia's Ben Smith, LSU was relentless on its 61-yard touchdown march that used up 3½ minutes.

"I was really confident," Hodson said. "It was kind of like Kentucky last year (when he rallied LSU to a 25-16 victory after being knocked out of the game). I really felt confident then and I was confident today that we could drive down and score."

Although Hodson was dizzy on the sidelines, he spelled Mickey Guidry at quarterback and completed four passes, including two 11-yard strikes to split end Wendell Davis, who had 11 catches for 128 yards. Davis' second reception left the Tigers with a first-and-goal at the 7, a position from which they've been unsuccessful in the last three games.

This time Fuller picked up 2 yards on a first-down carry around left end. On the next play, Hodson faked a handoff and dropped back to pass, looking for tailback Sammy Martin or

tight end Willie Williams. Instead, he had enough time to find Kinchen going all the way across the field.

"He got out of the pocket and just happened to roll my way," Kinchen said. "I think Willie picked off my man and it left me open. It was kind of a fluke play."

Kinchen's touchdown sent LSU back on top, but left plenty of time for the Bulldogs. Hampton returned the kickoff out to the 24 and Jackson quickly tossed first-down passes to Troy Sadowski and Lars Tate, sending Georgia to midfield.

Staying in the air, the Bulldogs advanced into LSU territory on a 19-yard reception by Osborn over the middle with 1:50 remaining. But Georgia's comeback bid ended two plays later when Jackson's pass slipped away from Hampton and was corralled by Kevin Guidry.

"We were in zone coverage and my primary responsibility was to come up and make the tackle," Guidry said. "I just think the Lord that the guy bobbled the ball. ... I had some breakdowns early in the game, but I did something to get the respect of my teammates back."

Guidry, a fourth-year starter at cornerback, walked off the field with tears welling in his eyes. "This was the biggest game of my life," he said later.

The interception provided Guidry with a memorable ending to what had been a nightmare of a second half. It began with Thomas sprinting down the left sidelines and Guidry running with him step-by-step.

However, Thomas caught Jackson's 31-yard pass over his left shoulder in the end zone before Guidry could even get his hands up. The Georgia touchdown, coming three plays after Bill Goldberg recovered a Harvey Williams fumble, pulled the Bulldogs to within 16-9 after Steve Crumley missed the extra point with just four minutes gone in the third quarter.

Almost 10 minutes of hard-knocks defense went by before either team threatened. And it was Thomas who put Guidry in an awkward position again.

The junior split end was 15 yards behind Guidry on a flea-flicker pass from Jackson late in the third quarter. Thomas, the fourth Georgia player to touch the ball on the reverse-pitch-back pass, was pulling it down with the official signaling a touchdown, only to let it slide through his hands in the end zone, spoiling a 48-yard touchdown pass.

Another incomplete pass forced the Bulldogs to punt back to LSU, which seemingly was motivated by the near miss. The Tigers, starting at their 14, were quickly off to the races with a 41-yard run by Martin, who rushed 13 times for 84 yards and caught six passes for 55 yards in the game.

Martin and Fuller kept gaining large chunks of ground against the Georgia defense, leading the Tigers to a first-and-goal at the 2. Then a delay-of-game penalty stymied the march and Browndyke came on to kick a 21-yard field goal, increasing the margin to 19-9 with 11:17 left in the game.

Backed up against the wall, the Bulldogs broke loose with consecutive scoring drives. Osborn was running a basic down-and-out pattern on third down, but cornerback Willie Bryant

■ LSU quarterback Mickey Guidry (10) attempts to recover his fumble, which is between the legs of Nacho Albergamo (56).

missed the tackle, giving Osborn room to run away from the pack down the right sidelines.

Osborn's 74-yard touchdown play sliced the Bulldogs' deficit to 19-16 with 9:45 left and Guthrie put them back in business with an interception of Hodson, who completed 21 of 31 for 209 yards with just one turnover. The Georgia linebacker returned the interception 28 yards to the LSU 17 before being tripped up by Rogie Magee, the intended receiver.

The Bulldogs needed just two plays to take their first lead since early in the game. Tate gained 3 yards around left end and Hampton dashed the remaining 14 yards, breaking two tackles

to get across the goal line. Crumley's kick put the Bulldogs in front by more than a field goal at 23-19, putting LSU in a position to play for a touchdown.

The Tigers were up to the test, just as they were in the first half when they scored on four of their six possessions in taking a 13-point lead.

After Browndyke kicked a 27-yard field goal to match Crumley's 34-yarder earlier in the first quarter, LSU dominated the rest of the first half, scoring on its final three offensive series. Mickey Guidry, seeing his first action at quarterback in two weeks, engineered the only touchdown drive of the half by completing 4 of 5 for 72 yards and a TD strike to Moss.

Hodson Rallies Tigers in Win over Georgia

By Dave Moormann

The Advocate

Athens, Ga. — *Oct. 10, 1987*

It was shades of Kentucky.

An injury. A trip to the sidelines. A re-entry into the lineup. The need for a rally. The game-winning points.

So how did LSU quarterback Tommy Hodson feel about this sense of deja vu?

"It was Georgia," he said, the ringing of a late tackle still fresh in his ears.

Georgia it was. Hodson hadn't lost his senses. Nor had he lost his flair for the dramatic. His Bulldog-induced headache kept him on the bench for two plays. Upon returning, Hodson took six plays to push LSU into the end zone, hitting tight end Brian Kinchen with a 5-yard pass that rallied LSU to a 26-23 victory.

"It (the pain) was like Kentucky," said Hodson, shaken up today when Georgia cornerback Ben Smith hit Hodson, who was out of bounds, "only not as bad."

Against Kentucky last year, Hodson bit through his tongue, requiring five stitches. He missed most of the first half. Upon his return LSU trailed, 7-0. Hodson promptly rallied LSU to a 12-7 halftime lead and a 25-16 victory.

Against Georgia, Hodson didn't feel as bad, but the situation was worse. LSU trailed, 23-19, with 6½ minutes left and the ball 42 yards from the end zone. Hodson had just run 3 yards and out of bounds and Smith's personal-foul penalty added 15 yards to the play.

Smith said he couldn't tell if he was out of bounds, but he had committed himself and made a mistake. He also said LSU coach Mike Archer grabbed him and berated him but apologized on the next play.

"I lost my cool in that situation," Archer said. "I apologized. That was uncalled for."

Hodson was more restrained.

"That's all part of the game, it happens," said Hodson, who admitted he was still somewhat woozy when he re-entered the game.

Hodson had a handful of Tylenol packages next to him in his locker-room stall.

"I'm sure he's (Smith) a nice guy," Hodson said. "He probably didn't mean it."

Hodson vented his frustration on the field, hitting 3 of 4 passes before Eddie Fuller gained 2 yards. Then came the play that eased whatever pain Hodson felt, excited a faithful LSU throng in sold-out Sanford Stadium, and brought Kinchen his second touchdown of the season.

It was the second time this season that LSU ran its "Cougar Route."

"We name all our goal-line stuff after animals," Kinchen said.

The first time, Kinchen, who is not the primary receiver, wasn't involved in the play. This time, with wide receiver Rogie Magee running a deeper route in the end zone and tight end Willie Williams running a crossing pattern underneath Kinchen, Kinchen found himself free. After a play-action fake and a rollout to his left, Hodson located Kinchen.

"It wasn't a dead spiral," said Kinchen, who jumped to make the catch. "Anytime it's a little wobbly, there's a chance you could drop it."

Despite an injury to his right hand, which Kinchen said has ached for two weeks and was reaggravated today when someone stepped on his two outside fingers, Kinchen clutched Hodson's 31st pass attempt with 3:36 remaining. Hodson completed 21 passes for 209 yards. Junior Mickey Guidry, who replaced Hodson for a second-quarter series and again when Hodson was sidelined, hit 4 of 5 passes, including a 36-yard touchdown toss to Tony Moss.

The pass to Kinchen was designed for a touchdown. The sideline pass to Moss was meant only to gain a first down. But Moss turned the third-down pass into a touchdown with nifty footwork along the sideline, as he avoided three potential tacklers. It was Moss' first collegiate touchdown.

"I was just trying to get to the outside for more yardage," Moss said. "I was trying to get away from 15 (Mark Vincent). All of the sudden I had one man to beat. I really like a one-on-one situation."

In a game featuring two defenses with reputations for preventing big plays, numerous one-on-one confrontations developed. Georgia's Cassius Osborn raced for a 74-yard touchdown catch-and-run after cornerback Willie Bryant missed a tackle. The Bulldogs' John Thomas slipped behind cornerback Kevin Guidry to make an over-the-shoulder 31-yard touchdown catch, later dropping an apparent 48-yard touchdown pass after the ball changed hands three times in the Georgia backfield.

Finally, Guidry found himself one-on-one against freshman Rodney Hampton, who earlier had scored Georgia's go-ahead touchdown on an 14-yard run. Following Kinchen's touchdown, Georgia had driven 45 yard to the LSU 31-yard line when quarterback James Jackson passed to Hampton.

"My primary goal is to make the tackle and keep him to a 4- or 5-yard gain," Guidry said. "The guy bobbled the ball."

And Guidry made the interception, securing the victory for LSU, which improved to 5-0-1 and 2-0 in the Southeastern Conference. Georgia, losing for only the sixth time in 47 home

■ **LSU receiver Wendell Davis looks for extra yardage with Georgia's Will Jones in tow.**

games this decade, fell to 4-2 overall and 1-1 in the SEC. Guidry, a senior, left the field in tears.

"That's something I can't explain," he said. "That's the first time I've ever cried at LSU. To know you made the deciding factor in winning the game is a great feeling."

"It was a total team effort," Archer said. "We need all the people."

No one was more valuable then sophomore place-kicker David Browndyke, who kicked four field goals, matching a school record he tied twice last season. Browndyke has made eight straight field goals. He began his career with seven consecutive kicks.

Browndyke's success also pointed to LSU's growing frustration around the goal line. One LSU drived stalled when the Tigers lost yardage on third-and-1 at the Georgia 2. Another drive fizzled after a delay penalty on first-and-goal from the 2.

"We made two or three glaring errors," LSU offensive coordinator Ed Zaunbrecher said. "We thought we had corrected those things. It's a matter of concentration."

Hodson concentrated. But no matter how hard he thought, the latest drama didn't remind him of Kentucky.

It was Georgia.

Hodson's 4th Down Strike Clinches Win Over Auburn

By Bruce Hunter

The Advocate

Baton Rouge, La. — *Oct. 8, 1988*

It will go down in the LSU record book as Tommy Hodson's 40th touchdown pass. He's never thrown a more important one at a more crucial moment in a more exciting football game.

His 11-yard pass, coming on fourth down with 1:41 left, was pulled down by tailback Eddie Fuller in the back of the end zone, almost in the same spot where he had been ruled out of bounds only three plays earlier.

The dramatic touchdown pass, along with David Browndyke's extra point, lifted LSU to a 7-6 victory over fourth-ranked, previously unbeaten Auburn tonight in Tiger Stadium.

"That was the only throw I had left in me," Hodson said. "If football had five downs, I don't know if I would have had it left in me."

Hodson, who was 17 of 38 for 167 yards, led LSU on a last-ditch drive that went 75 yards on 15 plays. All but one of those plays were passes, including a fourth-down throw to tight end Willie Williams that set up the game-winning pass.

It was only the second time all night that LSU had crossed midfield. It also broke a string of seven quarters without a touchdown.

When Fuller came down with the touchdown catch, the LSU players on the field, those on the sidelines and the majority of the 79,431 fans in the stands exploded in celebration.

"I've been around a lot of college football games," LSU coach Mike Archer said. "But I've never been around a bunch of kids that have made a gutsier effort than our players just have. They never got down on themselves."

■ It was a night of hard knocks for LSU quarterback Tommy Hodson, whose late pass won the game.

In the nationally televised game on ESPN, Auburn built a 6-0 lead on field goals of 41 and 33 yards by Win Lyle. And its defense had held LSU to just nine first downs until the fateful final march.

To start that drive, Hodson threw over the middle to flanker Tony Moss for a 17-yard gain out to the 42. Then he hit Williams for 12 yards to move into Auburn territory.

A third-down reception by Moss went for 20 yards to the Auburn 21. And then the excitement really started.

Fuller dropped a possible touchdown pass. It was a high throw from Hodson, but definitely catchable.

Faced with fourth-and-9, Hodson rolled out under pressure

Score by Periods

Auburn	0	3	0	3 —	6
LSU	0	0	0	7 —	7

■ Eddie Fuller's touchdown leap gave the Tigers a come-from-behind victory.

and connected with Williams on an out route. The 6-6 tight end fell forward to reach the first-down marker. LSU was still alive.

On first down, Fuller, missing a second chance to score, was ruled to have come down out of the end zone on an apparent touchdown reception. It was the same route he would soon run again.

Then Hodson misfired on his next two attempts. That set up fourth-and-10 and in all likelihood LSU's last shot.

"I didn't know if I was going to get the ball again," Fuller said. "I'm just glad Tommy had enough confidence in me to come back to me."

Although Fuller wasn't the primary choice, Hodson had enough time to find him over the middle and behind the Auburn secondary.

"The (line)backer kind of lost him," Hodson said. "And the free safety moved over to cover the wide receivers. And it left a little seam in there for Eddie."

Fuller caught the pass and immediately looked down to see where his feet had landed this time. He didn't need to look. The crowd gave him the answer.

"This is beyond me," he said afterwards. "I can't even describe this feeling."

LSU, 3-2 overall, broke a two-game losing streak, its longest since 1983, and climbed back into the Southeastern Conference race at 2-1. Auburn fell to 4-1 and 2-1 in the SEC.

"You've got to give LSU an awful lot of credit because they didn't have a lot of success driving the ball until that last drive of the game," Auburn coach Pat Dye said. "When it came down to winning and losing, they did what they had to do to win the football game."

Up until those closing minutes, defense had ruled the battle of the SEC's Tigers, their 25th meeting overall and first since 1981.

The defensive war consumed most of the game. The second half started with LSU failing to move beyond its 23 and Rene' Bourgeois punting for the eighth time.

Auburn quarterback Reggie Slack, throwing to Alexander Wright and Walter Reeves, directed Auburn down to the LSU 24. After an illegal motion penalty, Slack tried to hit Wright again, but cornerback Mike Mayes tipped the pass and weak safety Greg Jackson intercepted it at the 18.

What ensued was LSU's longest drive to that point. Hodson connected with Ronnie Haliburton for 17 yards and then went to Moss for back-to-back receptions for 32 yards. Moss got most of it on his own, taking a quick out 23 yards to the Auburn 33.

A defensive holding call against cornerback Carlos Cheattom gave LSU another first down at the 23. But Auburn held and was helped by a third-down clipping penalty that pushed LSU back to the 40 and out of field-goal range.

Brian Griffith, LSU's pooch punter, narrowly missed the coffin corner. His punt went into the end zone, and Auburn took over at the 20.

Neither offense could mount an attack the rest of the quarter. LSU got the best of the punt exchanges, however.

"I love that kind of game," LSU outside linebacker Eric Hill said. "It was a tough, physical game. I wish they were all like that."

Auburn finally put together a 71-yard drive that took 15 plays and almost six minutes.

Tailback James Joseph rushed 3 yards for a first down to the 25. Then Slack threw to Freddy Weygand for a 21-yard completion to midfield.

After that, Slack converted on two third-down plays. On third-and-18, he found Lawyer Tilman on a deep out that went for 19 yards. Then on third-and-10, he connected with Greg Taylor on a crossing pattern that gained 19 yards to the LSU 20.

LSU's defense held Stacy Danley to 3 yards on back-to-back carries, and fullback Vincent Harris picked up a yard on a third-down reception. Lyle finished off the drive with a 33-yard field goal for a 6-0 lead with 10:12 left.

Mickey Guidry took his second turn at quarterback for LSU. Despite a personal foul against Auburn, Guidry couldn't mount a drive and LSU punted back to Auburn.

After LSU's defense held, the homestanding Tigers got another opportunity with 6:07 left and Hodson back at quarterback. He completed six passes on the march and saved his biggest throw for last.

In the first half, Slack's third pass was well behind Wright and was picked off by cornerback Jimmy Young at the LSU 20.

LSU wasted the opportunity when Haliburton dropped a pass over the middle at the LSU 48.

Auburn had the first scoring threat, driving from its own 34 to the LSU 33. Harris had two carries for 15 yards to lead the way.

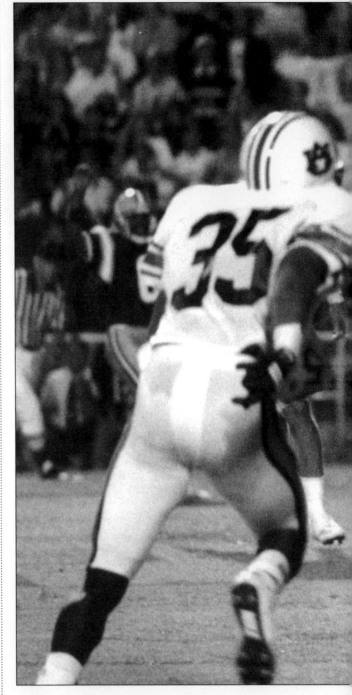

But on third down, defensive end Clint James batted Slack's pass into the air. Slack caught the ball, but was thrown for a 2-yard loss by Ron Sancho. Auburn chose to punt, rather than attempt a 52- yard field goal.

Ironically, LSU had an identical play on its next series. Hodson's pass was deflected by inside linebacker Brian Smith, and he caught his own pass, but was thrown for a 4-yard loss by Tracy Rocker.

Hodson hit Alvin Lee on a third-down pass over the middle that went for 21 yards. But on LSU's next third-down play, Fuller was stopped a yard short on a pass reception to the LSU 41, forcing a Bourgeois punt.

■ **Eddie Fuller missed his first two possible touchdown receptions, but the third one made the difference.**

Once again, Auburn drove into LSU territory. Slack threw to Joseph on third down, connecting on a deep out that went for 20 yards. He went right back to the air and hit Wright over the middle for 19 yards to the LSU 37.

But major infractions for clipping and a personal foul pushed Auburn all the way back to its 46, spoiling another scoring chance.

Auburn's defense came up with a big play to get the ball right back. Outside linebacker Craig Olgetree blitzed on third down and threw Hodson for a 7-yard loss, breaking LSU's

seven-game streak without allowing a sack.

Then Bourgeois shanked the punt. It rolled only 24 yards to the LSU 38, giving Auburn its third opportunity to get on the scoreboard.

Slack threw three straight incomplete passes, two that were broken up by LSU. Hill delivered a a hard hit to dislodge the ball from Danley on a third-down pass. And Auburn's Brian Shulman punted for the third time.

On LSU's first possession of the second quarter, Guidry

took a turn at quarterback and completed his first pass to Fuller. But he couldn't move LSU, either. Bourgeois came on and punted 42 yards.

LSU's defense finally prevented Auburn from crossing midfield, and Shulman punted only 29 yards to LSU 34.

With Hodson back, LSU picked up one first down, but was hurt by an illegal prodecure call and stalled out at its own 36.

That led to three more punt exchanges before Auburn finally broke the scoreless tie with a 45-yard march. Starting at its own 33, Auburn got two first-down runs by Harris and a personal foul call against LSU to move down to the LSU 28.

Wright gained nothing on a reverse, and Harris netted only 6 yards on back-to-back carries. That brought on Lyle to score the first points with 1:41 left in the half.

A 26-yard kickoff return by Slip Watkins set up LSU at its 33. But the third illegal procedure penalty against LSU backed the offense into a second-and-12. Hodson connected with tight end Willie Williams for 10 yards, but overthrew Lee on third down. Bourgeois made his seventh appearance and booted a 54-yarder to the Auburn 5 with 11 seconds to play.

■ The Tigers' last-ditch drive went 75 yards on 14 plays.

■ Mickey Guidry wasn't able to kick-start the LSU offense in relief of Tommy Hodson.

LSU & Razorbacks Can't Break 0-0 Tie

By Dan Hardesty
The Advocate

Dallas, Tex. — *Jan. 1, 1947*

The Tigers of LSU shoved the Arkansas Razorbacks all over the rain and sleet-swept Cotton Bowl gridiron here this afternoon but couldn't breach the Porkers' Red line when the chips were down and had to settle for a scoreless tie in what was probably the coldest game in college football history.

The bayou Bengals piled up 15 first downs and three times had first downs inside the Arkansas 10, but great defensive play aided by the impossible weather halted the attack each time as an estimated 38,000 half-frozen fans sat in snow, ice, rain and freezing temperature.

Arkansas made a first down on an 18-yard smash by its terrific fullback, Leon Campbell, four minutes after the opening kickoff, and that was the only time during the afternoon that the defense-minded Razorbacks succeeded in gaining 10 yards on one series of downs.

Throughout the contest it was all LSU, but down near the goal line, it just wasn't LSU's day. They stormed down the field several times on powerful marches but always the rugged Arkansas defense halted them in time. Three times penalties nullified plays on which the Tigers had made first downs in scoring territory, and at least two more times frozen fingers couldn't hang on to passes which might have meant touchdowns.

There will probably be a lot of second-guessing on LSU's quarterbacking near the goal line, but under those playing conditions it's a wonder the teams could even line up to put the ball in play. The Arkansas line — one of the most vicious faced by the Tigers all season — had a lot to do with the Tigers' lack of success on some of those crucial plays. The Razorbacks charged hard and tackled for keeps.

An account of today's game wouldn't be complete without first describing the contest's weather conditions.

The snow stopped falling yesterday and this morning everything was frozen solid. But a sudden thaw at midmorning sent the temperature slightly above the freezing mark. When the Tigers reached the stadium, the ice and snow were slightly melting. The big tarpaulins were rolled back and the field was in almost perfect condition.

The LSU board of strategy had 40 bales of hay delivered to the Tigers' bench. This was piled along the sideline and stacked deep in front of the bench. Most of the players stuck their feet in the hay to keep them warm, but there were at least a dozen people simply buried in it with their heads sticking out.

The Tigers were enthusiastic about the condition of the playing field itself before the game, got into grid togs and went on into the dressing room.

And then it happened.

First, it was just a light sprinkle. Gradually, it increased to a steady drizzle, and then it turned to sleet. Throughout the entire game, either sleet or freezing rain was falling. The spectators, who turned out in surprising numbers, huddled in snow-covered seats.

UNIVERSITY OF ARKANSAS vs. LOUISIANA STATE UNIVERSITY
Annual COTTON BOWL CLASSIC
NEW YEAR'S DAY
1947
DALLAS, TEXAS
25c

LSU kicked off and after an exchange of punts, Arkansas took over on its own 20. Campbell, who played a tremendous defensive game for the Porkers, pounded through center, bounced off Buck Ballard and churned 18 yards for the one and only first down made by Arkansas all afternoon. Then Aubrey Fowler got off a great quick kick to the Tiger 3-yard line.

Red Knight punted back to the LSU 45 and Fowler returned to the 37. The Tigers dug in and forced Arkansas to punt.

Starting at their 20, Dan Sandifer circled left end for 11 yards and Ray Coates and Rip Collins pounded out

■ **LSU and Arkansas battled to a 0-0 tie on the icy field of the Cotton Bowl.**

yardage for another first down on the Arkansas 49. Two plays lost three yards. Y.A. Tittle flipped a screen pass to Collins who gained almost 13 yards but it was inches short of a first down.

Knight fumbled trying to plunge on fourth down and John Hogman recovered for Arkansas on the Porkers' 42.

Hogman promptly fumbled back and Tittle grabbed the ball on the LSU 43. Knight got off a great punt which rolled to the Arkansas 3, but Jeff Adams raced in and fell on the ball, thus making it an automatic touchback and pulling the Porkers out of a big hole in the opening minutes of the second quarter.

Knight broke through the middle for 16 yards a few minutes later, and then ran for another first down but LSU was penalized for backfield in motion. Knight's fourth-down punt was blocked by tackle Charles Lively and end Alton Baldwin scooped up the ball and took off for the Tiger goal line, but little Jim Cason dove right over a blocker and pulled him down from behind on the LSU 43 to save a probable touchdown.

Later, Tittle intercepted a Porker pass at the Arkansas 23 and returned it to 16. Two passes failed and two running plays lacked a foot of 10 yards. Unable to move the ball, Fowler punted to the Arkansas 42 and Cason returned it to the 19 with three minutes left in the half. In four plays, the Tigers moved to a first down at the Porkers' 8, with only 40 seconds remaining. In one running play, which lost two yards, and an incomplete pass the Tigers failed to score before the clock ran out.

The second half was completely LSU — except that the Tigers didn't score.

Taking a punt on their eight, LSU staged a powerful drive

with Ray Coates smashing through the middle of the line for 18 yards and then for 17 more. Sandifer picked up 19 yards over the middle as the Porkers continued to play their linebackers wide. Coates and Knight pounded for a first down at the Arkansas 21. Then the attack bogged down and the Porkers took over on the 18.

Early in the fourth quarter, the Bengals began a drive from the Arkansas 42 — and this time they almost made it. Almost — but not quite.

Sandifer picked up six yards and Collins swept through left tackle and churned for 16 yards to the Arkansas 19. Coates roared through right guard for 10 yards and another first down at the Porkers' 9. Collins made another yard, then Tittle whipped a pass to Adams who was knocked out of bounds just as he caught the ball on the 1-yard line by Clyde Scott. The entire Arkansas lineup ganged up to stop Zollie Toth, the expected ball carrier, on the plunge — and stop him they did. A couple of feet from the goal line.

The Bengals got another chance again on the next series with six minutes left in the game. Dale Gray returned a Fowler punt from the Arkansas 29 to the 20. Gray made 3 yards, then Willard Landry blasted through the line for a first down at the Arkansas 20. Landry carried two more times to pick up a first down at the Porkers' 9.

Gray added 3 yards and Toth picked up two more to the Porkers' 4. Landry then lost a yard. The Tigers' field goal attempt never worked due to a botched center snap.

In the final three minutes, both Arkansas and LSU failed to get a drive started.

■ Tiger Stadium, originally built in 1924, now seats 79,940.

The Mystique of Tiger Stadium

BY SAM KING
The Advocate

How dare you call it a mere football stadium. It is the heart of a university — the cornerstone of a community — the focal point for a state. It has stood as a shrine for 105 years of football ... a temple for Tiger faithful to pay homage to the team and to the program in which they so strongly believe. It is the body, soul and spirit of a football program laden with rich tradition and glory.

■ **Tiger Stadium before the north end zone was completed in the 1950s.**

The mystique that has enveloped Tiger Stadium going into this its 75th year has become unforgettable for those — coaches, players and fans — who have experienced it.

There's something about this home of LSU's football warriors that makes men rise past their capabilities, play to heights they never dreamed possible.

"Running into Tiger Stadium was an enormous uplift — the people hollering and the crowd roaring," recalled former Tiger Hart Bourque. "We would go running out on the field five feet off the ground.

"Nothing could get your adrenaline going quicker than having 60,000 fans screaming to try and get you to do something. It rejuvenates you and makes you want to do something. In a few games it made me play way, way above my skills," said Bourque.

"It did things to a guy like Bert Jones who came into the game from out of nowhere and threw three touchdowns passes," said former LSU player and coach Jerry Stovall of the future pro who starred from 1970-72.

"It did something to a little kid like (running back) Dalton Hilliard, who comes from out of nowhere to play great.

"They were both good players, but 70,000 to 80,000 people

had something to do with that. It excites you to another degree of excellence."

It is no wonder that in a recent poll conducted by ESPN, Death Valley is deemed the greatest site anywhere for a college football game. The TV network noted, "for the college football fan, there is no better place to be on planet Earth on Saturday than LSU's Tiger Stadium."

It's a mystique you can't explain. You have to be there. Tiger Stadium, you see, is much more than a football stadium. It has been home for 118 All-Southeastern Conference performers, 38 All-American selections, one Heisman Trophy winner and one national championship team.

It is the birthplace of the legendary Chinese Bandits, a heroic bunch of defensive demons who played far, far above their heads. The specially-written Chinese Bandits song was played and hundreds of fans would don coolie hats as their Bandits took the field. That explosion of roars, music and excitement lifted third-team players to heights unknown.

"I don't know what it did to them, but they went wild," recalled former LSU coach Charles McClendon.

"It made them play exceptionally well," said Dietzel. Both coaches concurred: "they really weren't that good, but no one told them."

■ LSU quarterback Herb Tyler (14) outruns a pair of Razorback linemen in the 1995 LSU-Arkansas game.

■ **Harvey Williams (22) rushed for 52 yards and caught two passs for 18 yards against Notre Dame in 1986.**

In fact, thousands told them just the opposite every week. Death Valley has seen its great plays, few — if any — causing a bigger roar from the Tiger loyal than when Tommy Hodson's touchdown pass to Eddie Fuller defeated Auburn, 7-6, in 1988, in the game dubbed "the night the Tigers moved the earth." It registered a reading of earthquake proportions on a seismograph machine in the geology department.

The most famous of all plays here, though, was "The Run" — that 89-yard, Halloween night return of a punt by Billy Cannon in 1959 that lifted LSU to a 7-3 victory over Ole Miss and won Cannon the Heisman Trophy.

Almost every year on the eve of the Ole Miss-LSU game you will hear a replay of the run. For 30 years after the run you heard it two, three or four or more times.

This great series, especially in the 1950's and early 60's, produced some great moments.

How many games the mystique of Tiger Stadium helped the Tigers win, with goal line stands, final second plays, in the LSU-Ole Miss series is unbelievable — Cannon's run, the ensuing goal line stand, so many other goal line stands in so many other games and Billy Ezell's Halloween night, two-point pass to Doug Moreau in 1964.

And, what a deafening place it was when LSU managed to run two plays in eight seconds in their 1972 game. LSU defeated the Rebs, 17-16, on the PAT after Bert Jones' TD pass to

Brad Davis as regulation time expired. What a setting for such a fierce rivalry. Getting inside Death Valley wasn't always cheap and sometimes it was almost impossible.

But, Jackson, Miss., native Bill Rogers did to watch Cannon make his great run. Rogers was a high school official in Jackson, caught a ride down to go to the game but could not find a ticket — not one that he could afford. He came prepared, though. He also brought his official's uniform. So, he went to work, so to say. Rogers said he dressed and managed to file through the gate where the game officials entered without attracting any special attention. Once in the stadium he said he went to the sideline and was finally seated on the Ole Miss players' bench.

Just prior to the kickoff, however, Rogers said one of the game officials wanted to know what he was doing out there. He confessed, but pleaded with the official not to kick him out. They didn't. Few people ever noticed him — until near the end of the game and then thousands saw him and cheered.

If you notice the end of Cannon's run, Rogers — a car salesman — is standing on the 30-yard line. He is the first to signal a touchdown for Cannon.

And this writer, a part-time LSU student who played basketball against Cannon in high school, was the only one to outrun him down the east sideline.

The traditions are many in Tiger Stadium, none more unbelievable than the number of goal line stands at the south

■ **Tiger Stadium on Opening Day against Tulane in 1924.**

end zone. So many opponent drives, so few points.

Mike the Tiger is paraded around the stadium in a cage topped by cheerleaders prior to the game, bringing Tiger fans to a standing roar, but sometimes making opponents feel uncomfortable.

Tradition has it, LSU will score one touchdown for each time Mike roars.

But the tradition starts much earlier in the week than at kickoff. The fans start gathering in motor homes, campers and the like as early as Thursday or Friday. They party and let the good times roll. They're up well before game time, cooking, partying and getting the proper attitude adjustments to cheer their Tigers to victory.

The mystique of Tiger Stadium has been most valuable to football teams playing so great, to players rising to the occasion. However, Cannon when asked about the mystique of Tiger Stadium, questions back, "Mystique? What mystique? It was the people.

"We played as freshmen in 1956 and would draw like 15,000 people. In '57 we lose four games in a row and we're playing to 30,000 empty seats. We had to beat Tulane to finish 5-5.

"Jimmy Taylor was an All-American, a great player, but you didn't feel any mystique," said Cannon. "But, in '58, we're going 11-0 — and now it's full of mystique," said Cannon. "But, let me tell you, there's always something special about a night game in Tiger Stadium.

"Playing in there in the evening helped the mystique even back then," said Cannon.

Stovall remembers his days as a player and said the tradition of goal line stands didn't come about accidentally.

"It started in practice. Coach (Paul) Dietzel and (Charles) McClendon, in spring practice, would go into the stadium to scrimmage. They would put the Chinese Bandits on defense and give us first and goal at the nine. It seemed like we never got it in.

"They would make it first-and-goal at the three — and we never got it in," said Stovall. "The tougher it got, the more adamant the coaches and players got.

"I think the fans picked up on that in the south end zone," said Stovall, noting the fans were not only louder and more aggressive, but closer to the field.

"It seemed like they could reach out and touch you. I remember when LSU stopped Ole Miss four downs near the end zone. They were trying to stick it down our throats. Here we were sitting there fixing to lose a national championship — but (Warren) Rabb, Cannon and 30,000 people in the end zone stopped them."

The mystique of this stadium that has earned the nickname of Death Valley is indisputable. It cannot be denied. As easily as it can strike fear into the heart of an opponent, it can send goose bumps up the backs and necks of Tigers, spur them on to do things on a football field that they are not capable of doing.

It's an emotional place where women have wept and grown men cried. Countless are the number of times when those Saturday evening heroes felt a lump in their throat and tears in their eyes when they made that final trip through the north end zone chutes.

Or, the mystique of this great arena could leave you in awe as you entered your first time.

Stovall gave his recollections.

"I was being recruited from West Monroe in 1958. I was standing in the tunnel, came out and there were more people in there (Tiger Stadium) than in it was in my whole home town — and so much noise," said Stovall. "It made the hair stand up on the back of my neck. The initial impression was awesome."

His first time out the chute as a player was as a sophomore against Texas A&M.

■ Auburn's Reggie Slack (17) rifles a pass downfield against LSU in 1988.

■ Alabama quarterback David Smith, while looking downfield, doesn't see Ron Sancho (52) closing in for the sack.

Archer's Tongue-Lashing Inspires Tigers To Win

By Bruce Hunter
The Advocate

....

Tuscaloosa, Ala. — *Nov. 5, 1988*

With less than six minutes left in the first half today, LSU was in near-desperate straits. The Tigers had no points and no first downs and were headed nowhere.

Alabama, on the other hand, had scored on four consecutive possessions and secured a 15-0 lead at home in Bryant-Denny Stadium.

It could have been much, much worse.

By halftime, LSU had pulled to within 15-7. But LSU coach Mike Archer was furious with his team's "lackadaisical" play, especially on defense. He gave the players a tongue lashing during the break.

"I told them, 'We're very lucky to be down 15-7. We've got to go out in the second half and be patient offensively and create some turnovers,'" Archer said. "And that got us some points."

■ **Tommy Hodson (13) tries to escape from Alabama linebacker Derrick Thomas.**

The game was played in two segments with a frantic finish to cap it off.

Alabama totally dominated the first 25 minutes in mounting the 15-0 lead. LSU took over and rallied for 16 unanswered points over the next 27 minutes. Then it was up for grabs in the thrill-a-second final minutes.

LSU finally prevailed, 19-18.

"I think the key thing was the drive Mickey (Guidry) put together to bring us back in the ballgame," Archer said. "And we came out in the second half and made some things happen."

Guidry, spelling Tommy Hodson on LSU's last series of the first half, completed three straight passes for 37 yards, including a 21-yard strike to Alvin Lee. That led to a 3-yard touchdown run by Jay Egloff.

"That's the number one job of the second-string quarter-

Score by Periods					
LSU	0	7	9	3 —	19
Alabama	6	9	0	3 —	18

back, to change the tempo of the game," Guidry said. "The problem was field position."

Alabama had excellent field position in the first half, starting twice inside the LSU 45. Meanwhile, the Tigers didn't get outside their own 33 until the closing minutes of the half.

Hodson was just two of five for 9 yards in the first half and failed to lead the Tigers to a single first down. He was sacked twice for losses of 28 yards.

"I think we started mixing it up (in the second half)," Hodson said, explaining the turnaround. "You can mix it up with better field position. I think Mickey came in and got them off balance. Then we got some field position and things started to work."

Despite three interceptions, Hodson completed 10 of 18 for 213 yards and a touchdown in the second half.

The Hodson-Tony Moss combination ignited the Tiger offense. Moss turned a 4-yard pass into a 48-yard touchdown and totaled four catches for 124 yards in the second half. He finished with six catches for 133 yards.

"That's my main goal, just to improve each week," said Moss, who had six catches for 128 yards and two touchdowns against Ole Miss last week. "I just want to help my team as much as I can and I'll be happy."

Moss was indeed a happy young man as dusk approached today. He caught two passes for 41 yards on the Tigers' final drive.

Hodson, rebounding from an interception and fumbled snap, was three of four for 63 yards on the march.

"Tommy did a good job of fighting back," LSU offensive coordinator Ed Zaunbrecher said. "He made some mistakes, but he came right back. He made some great throws."

It marked the third time in the Tigers' last four games that Hodson rallied them to victory. He threw fourth-quarter touchdown passes to beat Auburn and Kentucky.

"I think it has a lot to do with experience," Hodson said. "Hopefully, it has a lot to do with my personality. I want the ball in clutch situations."

David Browndyke's 34-yard game-winning field goal came with the help of Mike Hebert, who was making his first college snap.

Jim Hubicz snapped on Browndyke's first two kicks, a field goal and extra point. But the snaps rolled to holder Chris Moock, who had to make nifty plays to get the ball on the tee.

"I did not worry about having to change snappers during the week," Browndyke said. "As a kicker, if I would have let that bother me, it would have affected my kicking. I thought Hebert did a good job of snapping."

LSU's snapping problems resulted from Pat O'Neill quitting the team on Thursday. His departure was not announced by LSU. Archer said he didn't want to give anything away to Alabama.

"It was just a tremendous effort by our players and coaches," Archer said. "I've been around some good things, but nothing like this on the road, for what the game meant, playing for the opportunity to win the Southeastern Conference against a very good football team."

The Tigers, tied with Georgia for the SEC lead, can clinch a share of the title by winning at Mississippi State on Saturday. They were in a similar situation in 1984 and lost to the Bulldogs, 16-14.

"What you've got to do is know what you're playing for," Guidry said. "In '84, we hadn't played for a championship in about 14 years. It's different now. We have our goals now. We know what we're striving for."

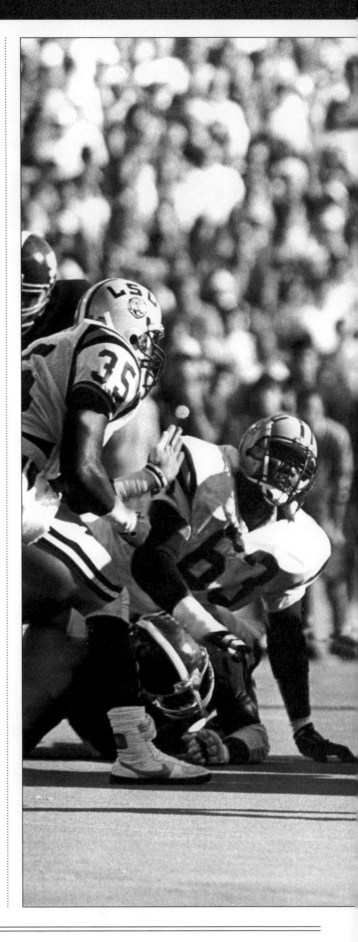

■ **Alabama halfback David Casteal (28) attempts to hurdle the LSU defense.**

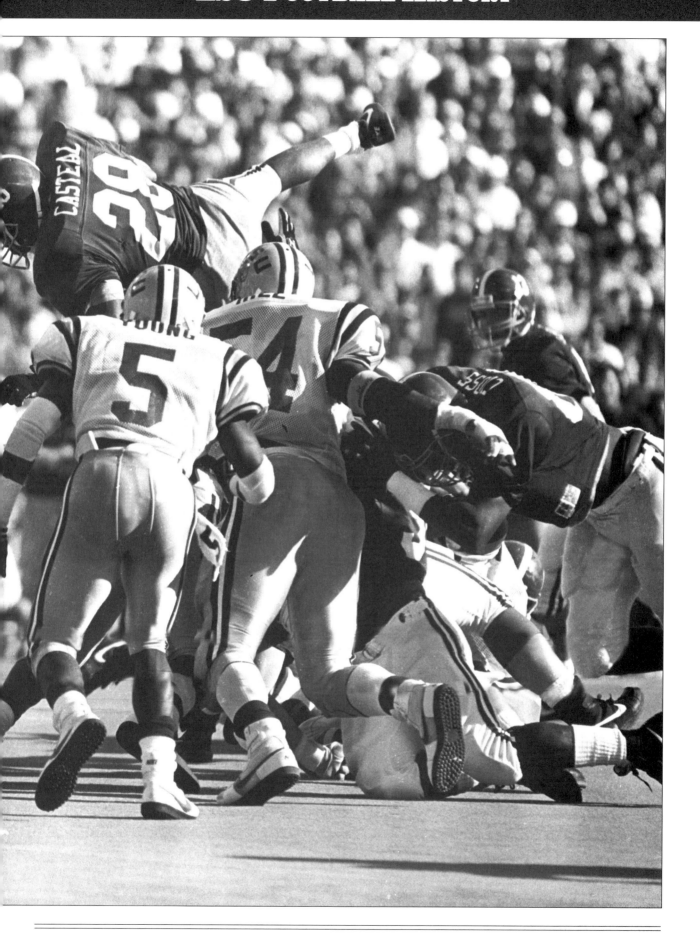

Bronwndyke's 34-yard FG Stuns Alabama

BY BRUCE HUNTER
The Advocate

Tuscaloosa, Ala. — *Nov. 5, 1988*

They just don't get any closer. They don't often matter any more.

As the final four seconds ticked off, Alabama place-kicker Philip Doyle's 54-yard field-goal attempt faded just right, a mere foot outside the uprights.

LSU, by virtue of David Browndyke's 34-yard field goal with 28 seconds left, survived a rare trip to Bryant-Denny Stadium, 19-18, this afternoon.

It was a fitting finish to a Southeastern Conference showdown that was as glorious as the scenic fall setting in the Capstone. A sellout crowd of 70,123 and a split-national audience on CBS-TV were treated to a classic, matching two teams with three-game winning streaks and championship hopes.

The 13th-ranked Tigers, overcoming a 15-0 first-half deficit and four second-half turnovers, made enough crucial plays to move within a game of clinching a share of the SEC championship. LSU, 6-2 overall, is tied with Georgia for the league lead at 5-1.

"The bottom line is we just wouldn't give up," LSU offensive guard Ruffin Rodrigue said. "We knew we would come back. We did it against Georgia and Florida last year. We did it against Auburn earlier this year. And now we've done it against Alabama. We're a team of pride. We never give up."

LSU split end Tony Moss caught six passes for a career-high 133 yards, including a 48-yard touchdown catch and two fourth-quarter receptions that put Browndyke in position for the game winner.

Outside linebacker Ron Sancho led the Tigers' defense with nine unassisted tackles, two sacks and a pass deflection, helping LSU hold Alabama to only a field goal in the second half. And Mike Hebert, in his first attempt as a kick snapper, made a perfect delivery to Chris Moock on Browndyke's final field goal.

But 18th-ranked Alabama, 6-2 and 4-2, had its own heroes in this hotly contested rivalry that has had a direct bearing on the SEC title for the last five years.

■ Kicker David Browndyke (4) goes airborne as he and holder Chris Moock (7) celebrate LSU's winning field goal.

Quarterback David Smith was almost flawless in completing 22 of 34 passes for 241 yards. Middle linebacker Willie Shephard charged up the Tide defense with 12 tackles, an interception and a 23-yard loss on a sack.

"It was a great effort by both teams," Alabama coach Bill Curry said, "but the little fine details, the kind that win championships, were not there. The great catch, the great kick, the great run — we didn't have them."

To many, it appeared the Tide had its great kick. Doyle's attempt soared into the cool, early-evening air with plenty of distance. It just didn't have quite enough accuracy.

Alabama's dreams for its first title since 1981 faded with Doyle's miss.

"It just wasn't it for us today," said Doyle, who tied a school record with four field goals, but missed three times from outside 50 yards in the final 19 minutes.

Doyle kicked field goals of 35, 24 and 33 yards and David Casteal scored on a 2-yard run to stake Alabama to its 15-0 lead. LSU backup quarterback Mickey Guidry led the Tigers to their only first-half score, a 3-yard touchdown run by fullback Jay Egloff. It was 15-7 at halftime.

Moss' touchdown and two Browndyke field goals enabled LSU to outscore the Tide 12-3 in the second half.

LSU quarterback Tommy Hodson completed 12 of 23 for 222 yards and a touchdown, but lost a fumble and was intercepted three times in the second half, twice by Lee Ozmint.

But Hodson took charge on LSU's final drive. After Doyle hit a 20-yard field goal to put the Crimson Tide ahead, 18-16, with 7:13 left, there ensued a wild finish with three turnovers in a span of less than two minutes.

Starting at its own 15 with 2:57 left, LSU drove to the Tide 17 with Hodson connecting on three passes for 63 yards. Tailback Eddie Fuller dropped a potential touchdown catch. But Browndyke finished off the drive.

"During the drive, I tried to keep to myself on the sidelines," Browndyke said. "I tried to relax before going in. When I was called on, I wanted to prove that I could kick it through in the last seconds."

Browndyke's squib kickoff was returned by John Cassimus to the Alabama 31 with 22 seconds remaining and the Tide out of timeouts.

Making a daring effort to rally, the Tide picked up 18 yards on a Smith pass to flanker Marco Battle. Then tight end Lamonde Russell found an opening near the left sidelines and caught a 14-yard pass to the LSU 37 with four seconds to play.

That brought on Doyle for his seventh field-goal try.

"I thought it was going through," Browndyke said of his counterpart's attempt.

After the kick missed, LSU broke out in celebration. It must still win at Mississippi State on Saturday to get at least a share of the title.

For most of the first half, it didn't look like LSU would ever get started offensively, while Alabama lived in LSU territory.

Casteal and Smith keyed the Tide's first drive. Casteal had a 12-yard run and Smith completed two passes for 24 yards. On third-and-2 from the LSU 18, Smith was pressured by Clint James and Karl Dunbar and threw incomplete. Doyle put the

Tide on the board with a 35-yard field goal.

Alabama's defense made its first big play of the day when Shephard came on a blitz and threw Hodson for a 23-yard loss back to the LSU 2. Rene Bourgeois punted out to the LSU 49, but Murry Hill returned it to the 35.

On first down, Hill rushed for 9 yards, but sustained a lower back injury on a tackle by Greg Jackson. He was taken off on a stretcher. The injury was later determined to be only a bad bruise.

With Hill out, Casteal ran 10 yards on a sweep around right end to the 7. A procedure penalty cost the Tide, and Doyle kicked a 24-yard field goal for a 6-0 lead still in the first quarter.

After Hodson was sacked by Derrick Thomas, Bourgeois punted from just outside his end zone. Cassimus returned the 39-yard kick to the LSU 41.

Smith threw a swing pass to Casteal who bolted 16 yards to the 25. Smith connected with Russell for a 6-yard gain, setting up first-and-goal at the 4.

Casteal went the final 2 yards around left end, running over cornerback Mike Mayes to get into the end zone. On a two-point conversion attempt, Casteal was stopped short by Sancho, but the Tide led, 12-0.

After LSU punted a fourth time, Smith engineered another scoring drive. Defensive facemask and pass interference calls helped Alabama.

But when it appeared the Tide was about to pull away, Sancho came up with back-to-back key plays. He sacked Smith and stopped Robert Stewart on a run up the middle. That led to Doyle's 33-yard field goal and a 15-0 lead.

Guidry finally gave the Tigers an offensive spark. The drive's key play was Guidry's 21-yard pass to Alvin Lee.

On second-and-goal from the 3, Fuller went in motion to left, and Guidry handed off to Egloff up the middle. The fullback scampered through a massive hole to score standing up. Browndyke, despite a poor snap by Jim Hubicz, kicked the extra point to make it 15-7 with 2:52 left.

In the second half, Hodson returned to the game and led the Tigers to two first downs out to the 44. Then he was pressured and forced into an intentional grounding that sent the ball back to the 21.

He came back to throw to Fuller for 16 yards over the middle, but his third-down pass was intercepted by Ozmint at the Alabama 25.

LSU's defense held the Tide to three plays and a punt, and Hodson had another chance from the LSU 26. His first-down pass went to Moss for 35 yards.

From Alabama 39, Hodson tossed a short pass to Darrell Williams, who rambled for 17 yards. A holding penalty stalled the Tigers, and they settled for Browndyke's 36-yard field goal, again coming on a poor snap by Hubicz, that made it 15-10.

Alabama kept the ball just one play. Smith threw over the middle to Russell who made the catch but was hit and fumbled away to Jimmy Young at the LSU 46.

After two running plays, Moss made the play of the day. He lined up in the slot left and came across the field in motion. Then he ran a short crossing route, making the catch at the 44

■ **Tommy Hodson (13) airs out a deep pass against the fierce Crimson Tide rush, led by Derrick Thomas.**

in front of linebacker Vantreise Davis.

Running hard to the left, Moss changed directions to fake out Ozmint and Charles Gardner on his way to a 48-yard touchdown. On a two-point try, Hodson was sacked by Thomas, but the Tigers still led, 16-15, with 5:19 left in the third quarter.

Alabama came up empty on field-goal attempts from 59 and 55 yards. But in the fourth quarter, Smith completed 6 of 7 passes to set up Doyle's 20-yard field goal, putting the Tide back on top, 18-16.

The rash of turnovers followed before Browndyke and Doyle each had a final kick.

LSU Holds Off No. 5 Crimson Tide, 17-13

■ Alabama coach Gene Stallings congratulates LSU coach and former pupil Curley Hallman at midfield.

By Dave Moormann
The Advocate

Tuscaloosa, Ala. — *Nov. 6, 1993*

From bowled over to bowl gazing. Imagine that.

How the tide has turned.

In one afternoon, LSU went from an uncertain football team to one toying with the possibility of postseason plans.

A centennial season that produced the worst loss in school history featured perhaps its most improbable victory when LSU stunned fifth-ranked Alabama, 17-13, today.

Looking more like the defending national champion than Alabama, LSU intercepted four passes, recovered a fumble and turned to backup quarterback Chad Loup en route to the dramatic upset.

The verdict touched off a celebration among LSU fans in

■ Tiger kicker Andre Lafleur boots a 36-yard field goal in the fourth quarter to ensure LSU's 17-13 win.

Bryant-Denny Stadium, and numerous players rushed over to join in an impromptu singing and dancing.

It was sweet vindication for third-year coach Curley Hallman, who returned home as an embattled figure and will leave buoyed by the memorable triumph.

"I love my hometown ... I have a lot of ties here ...," said Hallman, who grew up about five miles away in Northport. Looking back, its hard to imagine LSU rose above the ashes of a 58-3 loss to Florida and the other mistakes that have characterized much of the season.

But LSU surprised Ole Miss last week, 19-17, and in beating Alabama put together two Southeastern Conference victories for the first time since beating Kentucky and Ole Miss in 1991.

More than that, LSU snapped the nation's longest unbeaten streak at 31 games in a feat reminiscent of the 22-game victory string LSU ended when it beat Arkansas, 14-7, in the 1966 Cotton Bowl.

Alabama had defeated LSU twice in fashioning its 30-0-1 mark. But by winning in Tuscaloosa for only the third time

Score by Periods					
LSU	0	0	14	3 —	17
Alabama	0	0	0	13 —	13

ever, LSU halted a four-game losing streak.

LSU also improved to 4-5 overall and 3-4 in the Southeastern Conference and put itself in contention for its first bowl berth since 1988.

Victories over Tulane and Arkansas in its last two games will likely send LSU to the Peach Bowl as the fourth-seeded SEC team in the bowl coalition, or to the Carquest Bowl as the fifth-seeded team.

LSU is idle next week.

Alabama, which clinched the SEC Western Division title by virtue of LSU's victory over Ole Miss, fell to 7-1-1 and 4-1-1 in the SEC. Alabama entertains Mississippi State next week.

"Yesterday (Friday), we came to the stadium and walked through just to clear our minds and visualize what would happen," LSU senior center Kevin Mawae said.

"I pulled the team together on the 50-yard line and told them we were playing for a bowl game tomorrow.

"It's the best win I've ever had. I've always dreamed about beating Alabama, and I did it today. There's no better time to do it than your senior year."

LSU battled Alabama to a scoreless halftime tie, just as it had against Texas A&M, then ranked fourth, in the season opener.

But unlike before, when LSU wilted under an Aggie onslaught, 24-0, the Tigers erupted in the second half.

Alabama tried three quarterbacks, including David Palmer to no avail, as LSU intercepted all three and scored after three of the interceptions.

Alabama sophomore Brian Burgdorf started his second straight game for Jay Barker, who remains sidelined with a shoulder injury.

Burgdorf was ineffective, though, and threw Alabama's first interception to end the opening series of the third quarter.

Anthony Marshall's theft and 4-yard return left LSU on Alabama's 38-yard line at 12:48. Five plays later, sophomore tailback Jay Johnson took a pitch 2 yards into the end zone for a 7-0 lead at 10:41.

Sophomore fullback Robert Toomer carried four times for 27 yards during the drive and finished with a 18 carries for a career-high 72 yards. Johnson gained a game-high 83 yards on 14 carries.

LSU finished with 227 yards against the SEC's best defense. Alabama gained 341, but its three quarterbacks completed only 14 of 27 passes for 189 yards and were sacked four times. LSU had only seven sacks in its first eight games.

"This is the biggest victory for me," said Marshall, a product of Mobile, Ala., who returned to his home state for the first time in eight months.

Loup, a senior who has played sparingly the last two years, kept the victory in perspective despite the thrill of helping to contribute to a victory again.

"We've got two games left to worry about," he said. But the prospect of a bowl is compelling.

"It'd be fun," he said. "I've never been associated with one."

It's been a long time between wins for Loup, who found himself taking over for starter Jamie Howard, who completed only 3 of 10 passes for 16 yards, at 8:21 of the second quarter and LSU on its 9-yard line.

LSU punted after the two series Loup played in the quarter, but he returned in the second half and was the beneficiary of LSU's stingy defense. Loup finished 4 of 9 for 45 yards.

After Marshall's theft, Alabama coach Gene Stallings inserted freshman quarterback Freddie Kitchens. LSU junior strong safety Ivory Hilliard intercepted Kitchens on two straight series with the first swipe resulting in Toomer's 2-yard touchdown run and a 14-0 lead at 4:38.

"We couldn't get any continuity going, we had penalties at critical times and turnovers at critical times," Stallings said.

"We couldn't stop them. When it came down to it, we didn't perform like a championship-caliber team."

Stallings finally went with Palmer at 3:16 of the third quarter, and although Palmer staged a furious rally, it wasn't enough to offset the Tigers' defense.

Palmer narrowed the deficit to 14-7 on a 3-yard touchdown pass to fullback Tarrant Lynch with 14:14 remaining, and he tacked on the final six points with a 22-yard touchdown pass to Kevin Lee with 2:41 left.

But in between, LSU junior cornerback stole a Palmer pass

■ **LSU's Ivory Hilliard (3) celebrates after tackling Alabama's David Palmer (2).**

intended for Lee and returned it 23 yards to LSU's 47-yard line with 9:04 left.

Loup then directed a 10-play, 47-yard march that resulted in Andre Lafleur's 36-yard field goal and a 17-7 advantage with 4:22 remaining.

After Alabama's last score, Palmer was stopped on a two-point conversion run and LSU recovered the ensuing onside kick with 2:41 left.

LSU ran out the clock, as Johnson scampered 11 yards for a critical first down in the middle of the possession.

Harking back to Mawae's earlier comments, sophomore defensive end Gabe Northern said LSU has renewed vigor.

"He said we had a chance to win our last three, and if we did we'd go to a bowl," Northern said. "He said he didn't know if everybody felt the same. It's good to know everybody is on the same page."

It is a page of history.

■ A group of LSU defenders team up to bury Arkansas quarterback Barry Lunney Jr. in the second quarter.

Tigers Stun Arkansas, 28-0

BY DAVE MOORMANN
The Advocate

Baton Rouge — *Nov. 18, 1995*

No need to call a psychic hot line. Junior linebacker Pat Rogers has seen the future of LSU football. Rogers relied on LSU's 28-0 victory over 14th-ranked Arkansas to clue him in about impending events. "In coming years that's going to be LSU, as long as Gerry DiNardo is the head coach at the school," Rogers said.

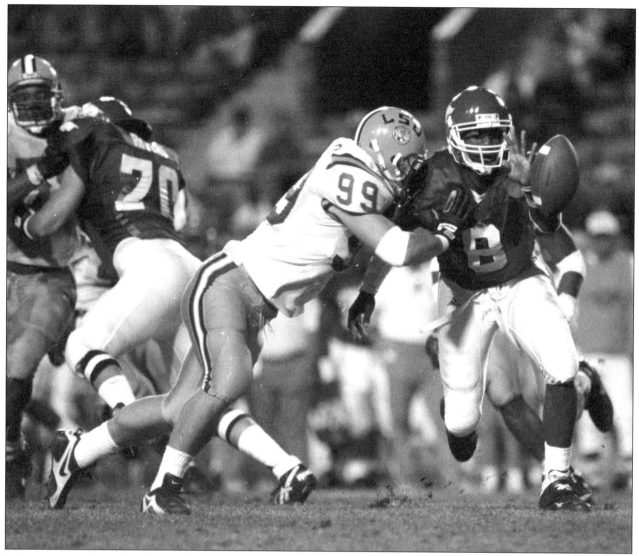

■ Hog quarterback Barry Lunney (8) attempts to make a pitchout before being tackled by a Tiger defender.

If so, that will mean more bowl games and more winning seasons. But, perhaps, nothing short of a championship will match the magnitude of today's victory before an announced crowd of 66,548 in Tiger Stadium.

LSU took out its frustrations of six losing seasons on an Arkansas team that offered little resistance against a Tiger onslaught that featured Kendall Cleveland's three touchdown runs and first 100-yard game.

"We gave Kendall an inch," senior offensive guard Mark King said, "and he made it a mile."

Actually, it was more like a game-high 102 yards on 24 carries, but it went a long way toward securing the victory in LSU's regular-season finale. After Sheddrick Wilson's 9-yard touchdown catch at 5:05 of the first quarter, Cleveland rushed for first-half touchdowns of 4, 20 and 1 yards. It didn't matter that LSU failed to score in the second half. The damage was complete.

The redshirt freshman tailback did it, too, against an SEC defense that ranked second overall and first against the run.

Score by Periods

Arkansas	0	0	0	0 —	0
LSU	7	21	0	0 —	28

"I don't see how they're only 6-4-1," said Arkansas senior quarterback Barry Lunney, who was sacked five times. "That blows my mind that they're only that."

LSU blew Arkansas away to reach that point and a likely Independence Bowl invitation. The fact that LSU finally realized those once unobtainable goals is mind-numbing, in itself. Two years ago, Arkansas denied LSU, 42-24.

"I can't tell you how happy I am for the players," said DiNardo, who when hired last December promised to "bring back the magic" to Tiger Stadium. "It's been a hard year for them ... For the guys who stayed, it's a chance to play in anoth-

■ **NOWHERE TO RUN: This was the story for the Arkansas offense all afternoon.**

er game. That makes it all worth it."

Arkansas, the Southeastern Conference Western Division champion, has two games ahead of it. The Razorbacks will meet Florida in the SEC Championship Game before finishing in a bowl game. Wilson would have none of the notion that LSU caught Arkansas at a time when the Tigers' had more at stake.

Arkansas fell to 8-3 overall and 6-2 in the SEC. LSU hiked its SEC record to 4-3-1.

"All I can tell you is that we went out and did our job to the best of our ability, and things worked out," said Wilson, a senior flanker who caught a game-high eight passes for 81 yards. "To say they were flat takes away from what we did tonight."

Wilson ignited the explosion with his 9-yard touchdown catch on third down. That helped LSU atone for an illegal-motion penalty on first down at the one. It also completed a 19-play, 80-yard march to begin the game.

"I knew from there, there was no stopping us," freshman quarterback Herbert Tyler said. "We could only stop ourselves."

With Tyler in control, there was none of that. Tyler won his third game in as many starts in replacing senior Jamie Howard,

who remains sidelined with a bruised right shoulder. Howard stood on the sidelines with his right arm in a sling.

Tyler completed 12 of 17 passes for 188 yards with a touch-down and an interception. He also accomplished what Wilson deemed important to the Tigers' welfare.

"All we wanted to do was come out and get points early because we knew the defense would hold them," Wilson said.

Even at that, Wilson said he didn't expect a shutout. But LSU cast Arkansas away at every turn in recording its first shutout since a 27-0 victory over Texas A&M in 1988. LSU held Arkansas to 21 yards on 20 first-half plays and a season-low 144 for the game. LSU registered 348 yards.

"The defense got together and said we were going to stop the run," LSU sophomore defensive tackle Chuck Wiley said. "That was the main focus."

In so doing, LSU held tailback Madre Hill, the SEC's second-leading rusher, to 64 yards on 22 carries. Lunney completed 10 of 28 passes for 78 yards with an interception.

"We kind of caught on to his checks," Rogers said of how the Tigers managed to contain Lunney and his teammates.

■ **Tiger head coach Gerry DiNardo signals in an offensive play.**

Stansberry said Lunney's audibles usually had Arkansas running away from LSU's strong safety.

Stansberry took advantage of it to share the team lead in tackles with eight, including 1½ quarterback sacks. Rogers intercepted a second-quarter pass and returned it 37 yards to the 1-yard line. Cleveland scored on the next play just 2:37 before halftime.

Cleveland first scored on a 4-yard run at 13:17 of the second quarter. That completed LSU's second possession after 10 plays, 58 yards and 4:16. Cleveland's 20-yard touchdown run at 3:50 was highlighted by his twists and turns and what Cleveland said was Wilson's critical block.

"It was great blocking by the offensive line, mostly," Cleveland said in assigning credit for his overall success. "It felt real good to get the win. It means a lot to me because last year I didn't play. I look at it as the start of a good trend."

Not only did Cleveland upstage Hill, but he also compensated for the thigh bruise that slowed teammate Kevin Faulk to 18 yards on eight carries. And Tyler overshadowed Lunney, despite losing two fumbles, throwing two interceptions and getting sacked three times. Only one of Tyler's turnovers came in the first half when he completed 8 of 10 passes for 121 yards.

"His composure and competitiveness are two of Tyler's finer attributes," DiNardo said. "I like a lot of things about him."

Despite the game's significance, Tyler said he felt no different than he did before any of his other starts. Tyler has opened three of the last four games and played briefly in a 10-3 loss to Alabama.

"There's pressure every week," Tyler said. "You just have to take each week one at a time."

LSU now will have several weeks to prepare for a bowl game, which DiNardo said will help to fortify the Tigers.

"I think that helps you as a program," said DiNardo, who will be coaching in his first bowl since Colorado with DiNardo as offensive coordinator won the Orange Bowl to clinch the 1990 national championship. "The strong get stronger ... It helps the development of the younger players."

It also represents a reward for the older players, whose dream finally came true. King celebrated by helping to dump a bucket of ice water on DiNardo's head with less than 90 seconds left. King said he was on the sidelines as freshman Ryan Thomassie played in an effort to earn a letter.

"That had to be the worst part of the evening," a smiling DiNardo said of the dousing.

But for the most part, the Tigers found it to be an exquisite affair.

"I think it's the best game I've ever played in," Wilson said. "It was the best thing I've ever been a part of. I love the guys for what they did for the senior class tonight."

Determined Tigers Were on a Mission

By Sam King

The Advocate

Baton Rouge, La. — *Nov. 18, 1995*

LSU was not to be denied.

Focused, intent and determined, it was obvious from the outset, LSU came to win.

It would settle for nothing less.

It dominated offensively.

It destroyed defensively.

It manhandled Southeastern Conference Western Division champion Arkansas like no one else has been able to do this year.

Piling up 115 yards rushing on the league' best defense against rushing and 236 yards of offense against the SEC's second-best total defensive team, LSU scored four first-half touchdowns en route to its 28-0 victory.

The Tigers' sixth win of the season against four losses and a tie not only provides them with the school's first winning season since 1988, but puts LSU in a bowl game, most likely the Poulon Weed Eater Independence Bowl at Shreveport.

The chips were down and LSU responded in a fashion seldom seen in six previous seasons in which the Tigers lost 41 (of 66) games, two head coaches and a score of assistants.

It was LSU's first shutout since a 27-0 win over Texas A&M in 1988 and the first SEC shutout since a 47-0 rout of Mississippi State in 1986.

It showed just what this team is capable of doing. That was not a bad football team on the other side of the ball, although LSU left it standing in an upright position only on a few occasions.

It wasn't just the offense that dominated in the first half, although scoring 28 points speaks awfully good for it. The defense was a bit unreal, maybe a little unbelievable, allowing the Razorbacks only 21 yards on 20 plays.

Sooey Pigs!

When the Tigers' offense faltered in the third quarter, the defense again rose to the occasion. Freshman quarterback Herbert Tyler fumbled the ball away twice and threw two interceptions, but the Razorbacks were stymied despite getting great possessions on the LSU 21 and 31 and Arkansas' 46.

It was obvious the Tigers were determined to deny a repeat of 1993 when they were routed by Arkansas (42-24) in this same stadium in an identical situation — a winning season and

■ **LSU's 28-0 shutout of Arkansas gave Tiger players and fans a lot to shout about.**

bowl bid awaiting.

LSU quite likely played its best ball of the year.

"I think so, considering the pressure," said a happy Gerry DiNardo, who is headed to his first bowl ever as a head coach. "We probably played a more complete game last week (in beating Ole Miss), but I think the fact that we needed a win for a winning season and to go to a bowl game makes it much better.

"Although it may not look as good statistically as last week because we didn't score points in the second half, I still think it was best of the year because of what was at stake," said DiNardo.

Admittedly, it was DiNardo's finest hour as a head coach.

"This is my fifth year I've been a head coach and the first bowl we've gotten and the best team we've had," he said. "I've had fun since I've had this job ... all the obvious things and the locker room scene after the game."

Appropriately, DiNardo was doused with a barrel of "Power Aid" drink by celebrating players at the end of the game. It was a fitting, even if chilling, climax to an up-and-down season in which players were left by the wayside as the Tigers continued to improve and get on with the DiNardo program.

"That'll give you a heart attack," he said of the sudden and unexpected dousing just prior to the end of the game.

But, DiNardo maintained he was not surprised that LSU had a winning season.

"I thought we had enough talent to do something like this, but I didn't think it was automatic," he said. "I think talent just gives you a chance."

Despite a surprising 3-1 start, LSU faltered and eventually stood at 4-3-1 with Alabama, Ole Miss and Arkansas remaining.

"Before the Alabama game we were talking about playing the last 12 quarters the best we could," said DiNardo. "I think our defense probably did, but our offense struggled against Alabama."

At 4-4-1, the season was on the brink. LSU could have finished at 4-6-1 as easily as it did 6-4-1.

DiNardo thought not.

"I thought we could win the last two," he said. "We played exceptionally well in the last two. They really came back strong.

"I didn't think we would win this game 28-0 or last week would be the way it was, but I thought we could win the last two."

The victory was vitally important in rebuilding the Tiger program.

It broke the losing streak and got rid of the albatross which has been around LSU's neck for six years.

Now the Tigers can start a winning streak.

"I think that's big time, but we will still have a lot of work to do as you go through it. Look what happened to South

■ LSU wide receiver Sheddrick Wilson (6) high steps it into the end zone after his 9-yard touchdown catch.

Carolina," he said of a team which went to a bowl under a new coach last season but finished 4-6-1 this season. "We can't have that happen to us. In the second year of a program you can't take a step back."

He admitted the victory was good to build on next year, but noted, "It's not automatic."

On Jan. 1, 1966, LSU defeated a highly-favored Arkansas team 14-7, in the Cotton Bowl in one of the Tigers' greatest wins.

Almost 30 years later, 47 players and coaches on that team sat in the stands to watch another LSU team defeat Arkansas in a game which could surpass that one in greatness.

Twenty or thirty years from now, fans may look back to 1995 as the year, Nov. 18 as the day and this 28-0 win as the victory which brought back the magic to LSU football.

Green Wave's Jinx Continues, LSU Wins 7-6

By Bud Montet
The Advocate

New Orleans, La. — *Dec. 1, 1956*

The Bengal Tigers of LSU continued their jinx over the Tulane Green Wave and grabbed a 7-6 victory from the Billow before 60,000 fans here this afternoon.

Today's victory assured LSU its dominance over the Greenies, a victory pact that has held good since 1949. The last time Tulane handed the Tigers a setback was in Baton Rouge in 1948 when they bested the Tigers, 46-0.

Since that time, LSU has won all the games with the exception of two ties.

Tulane, who was favored in today's game, scored first when they picked up a touchdown in the second quarter with Ronnie Quillian, the Baton Rouge youth, going two yards for the score.

LSU came back to dominate play in the second half as they took advantage of Tulane fumbles to get their score with Jimmy Taylor going over from the Tulane 1 for the touchdown and kicking the extra point to secure the victory.

A succession of Tulane fumbles in the second half kept the Bengals in Tulane's backyard during the second half of the game.

Prior to their scoring drive, LSU had driven to the Tulane 3-yard line where a fourth-down pass from M.C. Reynolds to Billy Hendrix failed. But on the first play after this attempt, Tulane's quarterback fumbled and LSU's Durwood Graham recovered the ball on the Tulane 3. Taylor scored two plays later.

For the rest of the game, the Tigers dominated play although they failed to score after reaching the Tulane 1-yard line early in the fourth quarter.

A few minutes later, Earl Leggett's recovery of a Green Wave fumble on the Tulane 30 gave the Bengals a chance which they muffed as they drove to the Tulane 13, where

Taylor fumbled and Tulane recovered.

The Green Wave dominated the statistics as they picked up 202 yards rushing to the Bengals' 128 and added 32 yards in the air while completing two of 12 passes. LSU failed to connect on any of the half dozen they attempted.

For the Bengals, the hard running of big Taylor sparked their ground attack as the Baton Rouge native picked up 86 yards in 26 carries.

J.W. Brodnax, the Tiger halfback, picked up 28 yards in 15 tries.

For LSU, the game was one of capitalizing on breaks as they received them.

After a scoreless first quarter, the Green Wave got a break as Brodnax fumbled on the LSU 36 and the Green Wave recovered. Freddie Wilcox rambled for five yards, then Boo Mason raced around the Tiger left end for 16 yards and a first down at the Bengal 16. Mason added three yards as the first period ended and on the first play of the second quarter Willie Hoff picked up two yards to the Bengal 11.

After Eugene Newton missed on a pass in the end zone, he kept for eight yards to the Bengal 3 and then Quillian raced over right guard for the first score of the game.

Emmet Zelenka failed to kick the extra point, but the Green Wave trotted off the field at the end of the first half leading, 6-0.

LSU scared the Green Wave fans midway in the second quarter when Taylor intercepted a Newton pass on the Bengal 4-yard line and ran it back 44 yards before being hauled down. However, the Bengals' threat was halted as a 15-yard penalty stymied the Bengals.

LSU took control of the game in the second half, playing most of the remaining game in the Tulane territory.

Driving from their 39 — after Paul Ziegler recovered a Green Wave fumble — to the Tulane 3, where they ran out of steam after being stopped on fourth down.

However, Graham's recovery of a Green Wave fumble on the Tulane 3 a few plays later gave LSU the chance they needed. LSU pushed the ball over with Taylor carrying on two plays.

Tulane made a bid to get back in front midway in the fourth period when they moved from midfield to the Bengal 20-yard line, but John Caruso missed on two long passes.

The victory gave the Bengals their third win of the season, their first SEC triumph of the 1956 season and their first win over Tulane for young Paul Dietzel.

LSU has six of their last eight games with the Green Wave. Their have been two ties, in 1950 and 1955. Today's victory saved them from one of the worst seasons ever suffered by a Tiger eleven.

Score by Periods

LSU	0	0	7	0 —	7
Tulane	0	6	0	0 —	6

■ Jimmy Taylor, an All-American in 1957 and All-Pro with the Green Bay Packers, carried for 86 yards on 26 carries.

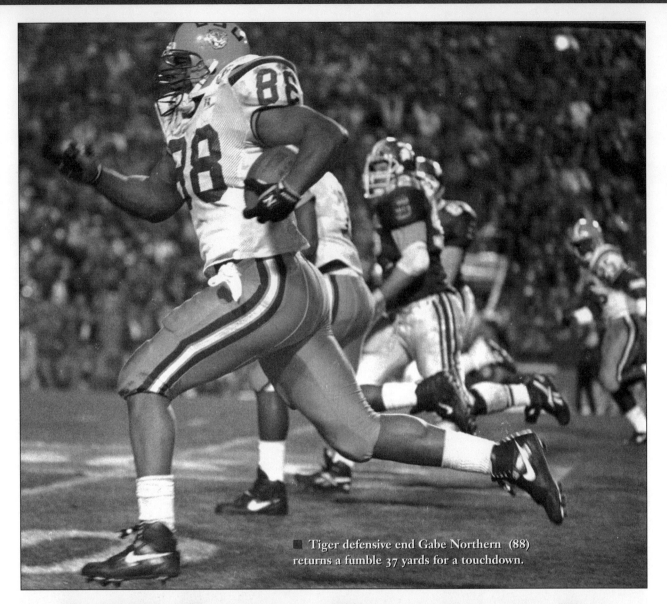

■ Tiger defensive end Gabe Northern (88) returns a fumble 37 yards for a touchdown.

LSU Routs Spartans In Independence Bowl, 45-26

BY DAVE MOORMANN
The Advocate

Shreveport, La. — *Dec. 29, 1995*

Michigan State scored on the game's second play from scrimmage. LSU scored on the second play of the third quarter.

LSU's Eddie Kennison returned a kickoff for a record 92-yard touchdown. Michigan State's Derrick Mason followed with a record 100-yard kickoff return.

■ **James Gillyard (7) bulldogs Michigan State quarterback Tony Banks (12) for a loss.**

If Michigan State produced the bizarre in the Poulan Weed Eater Independence Bowl, LSU answered with the unusual Friday.

Finally, about the time defensive end Gabe Northern recovered a third-quarter fumble and returned it for a 37-yard touchdown, LSU put an end to the counterpunching and walloped Michigan State, 45-26.

"That turned the game around," said LSU freshman quarterback Herb Tyler, who completed 10 of 20 passes for 164 yards and one touchdown.

Score by Periods

Michigan State	7	17	0	2	— 26
LSU	7	14	21	3	— 45

Maybe so, but freshman tailback Kevin Faulk certainly pointed LSU in the right direction in rushing 25 times for 234 yards, including touchdown runs of 51 and 5 yards.

Faulk was named the game's offensive most valuable player. Northern won the defensive award in LSU's first Independence Bowl appearance.

"At halftime we talked about, 'Let's just forget about the results of the game, let's just make sure we play with great intensity,' " LSU coach Gerry DiNardo said.

And so it did, as LSU claimed one of the most electrifying Independence Bowls in its 20-year history. LSU capped its first winning season and bowl appearance in seven years with a 7-4-1 record.

LSU won its second bowl in seven tries and its first since the 1987 Gator Bowl. Michigan State, playing its first football game against LSU, fell to 6-5-1.

LSU also scored on Kennison's 27-yard catch, freshman tailback Kendall Cleveland's 6-yard run and sophomore Wade Richey's 48-yard field goal. Kennison collected 249 all-purpose yards, including a team-high five catches for 124 yards.

"From the start of the game, I thought we had the better team," DiNardo said.

That was hard to tell, though, given the first-half fireworks that gave Michigan State a 24-21 halftime lead. At one point, four touchdowns were scored in a 93-second span of the second quarter.

"I didn't know when it was going to stop," DiNardo said. "I still thought we had the better team."

LSU finally showed it by dominating the second half in scoring 24 unanswered points before the sellout crowd of 48,835 at Independence Stadium. The Spartans' only second-half score came with 5:57 left when punter Chad Kessler took a safety in running time off the clock.

Michigan State managed just 125 of its 448 total yards in the second half. LSU amassed 436 total yards, including 201 in the second half.

"That was a wakeup call," LSU junior linebacker Pat Rogers said of the manner in which the Spartans scored against a defense that led the Southeastern Conference in allowing just 14.6 points per game.

LSU forced six turnovers overall, including an interception by junior linebacker Allen Stansberry, who made an Independence Bowl-record 18 total tackles. But no turnover was more prominent than the first fumble return for a touchdown in school history.

Northern and freshman strong safety Greg Hill forced a fumble from Michigan State quarterback Tony Banks. Northern scooped up the loose ball and raced into the end zone to give LSU a 35-24 lead at 9:20 of the third quarter.

"I just had some kind of determination that I was going to do something to put the team over the top," said Northern, who noted that he told someone on the ride from Baton Rouge that he would be defensive MVP. Northern and fellow senior defensive end James Gillyard each had an Independence Bowl-record three quarterback sacks.

Tyler said he sensed LSU would win when it scored early in

■ **Freshman Kevin Faulk (3) led the Tigers with 234 yards rushing on 25 carries and two touchdowns.**

■ **James Gillyard (7) sacks Michigan State quarterback Tony Banks again.**

the second half to take a 28-24 lead, and again on Northern's fumble return. Tyler highlighted the second half's opening possession that resulted in Faulk's 5-yard touchdown run at 14:29 of the third quarter.

After the Spartans were penalized for roughing Tyler, Kennison caught a 49-yard pass from Tyler on the first official play from scrimmage. Faulk followed with his score.

"In the locker room, I was telling my cousin (Derrick Beavers), I was going to cause a catastrophe with my feet," Faulk said.

Faulk did just that, as he rushed for the most yards by an LSU freshman, the most in LSU bowl history, and the second-most ever by an LSU player. LSU does not count bowl statistics in its record book.

In addition to his 51-yard touchdown run that tied the score, 21-21, at 13:11 of the second quarter, Faulk had a 40-yard run on LSU's first scoring drive and a 68-yard run in the second quarter that was the longest nonscoring run in

Independence Bowl history.

"I thought it was an outstanding and exciting football game in the first half," said Michigan State coach Nick Saban, who's in his first year as is DiNardo. "We just came out in the second half and seemed to be a little flat off the bat. For what reason, I don't know."

The first half surely didn't give an indication that either team would cool down. Michigan State scored on its second play when Banks fired a 78-yard touchdown pass to Muhsin Muhammad at 14:13. LSU retaliated with an 80-yard drive that ended in Cleveland's 6-yard run at 12:07.

The most explosive portion of the game began when Michigan State's Carl Reaves intercepted a pass and returned it 17 yards to the LSU 3-yard line to begin the second quarter. Fullback Scott Greene, who was benched for the first quarter because he missed curfew early Thursday morning, scored from there at 14:44.

Michigan State missed the extra point, but the scoring frenzy had begun. Kennison picked up a bouncing kickoff, slipped

■ **Kevin Faulk (3) escapes a pair of diving Michigan State defenders.**

a tackle in the middle of the field and outran two defenders down the right sideline to score at 14:30. Mason retaliated with his bowl-record 100-yard scamper at 14:17 in becoming the Big Ten Conference career leader in kickoff returns. Greene scored on a 2-pointer to put Michigan State ahead, 21-14.

Faulk's 51-yard dash came 66 seconds later, and although LSU fell behind one second before halftime on Chris Gardner's 37-yard field goal, the Tigers were to continue the assault in the second half.

"They say you practice like you play," Kennison said. "We played like we practiced."

Meanwhile, Saban blamed himself for what he said were Michigan State's poor practices this week.

"He's nice to have around," Tyler said of Kennison. "I hope he's around next year."

Kennison said he hasn't made a decision on whether to enter the NFL draft or return for his senior year.

Kennison's 27-yard touchdown catch at 7:13 of the third quarter gave LSU a 42-24 lead. The Tigers had a chance for even more points, but Andre Lafleur missed field-goal attempts of 37 and 38 yards in the third and fourth, quarters, respectively. That led Richey, with 8:45 left, to kick his first career field goal on his only try this season.

That ended LSU's scoring, but it only added to the heightened expectations that DiNardo knows exist now.

Asked what the Tigers must do in the future, DiNardo said, "Win more than seven games next year."

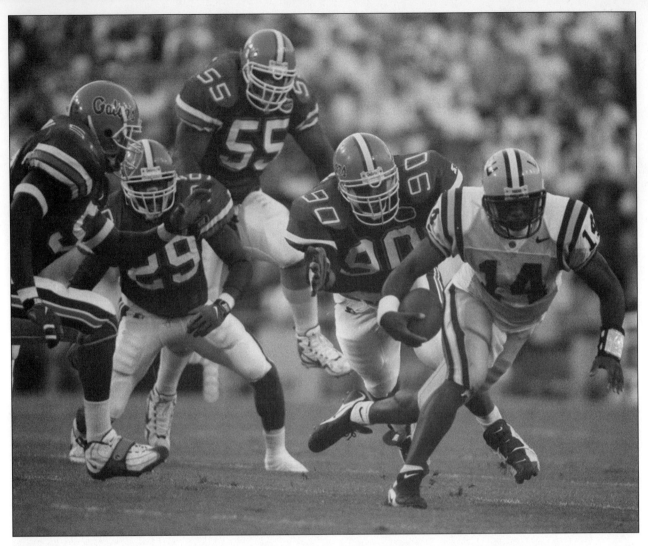

■ Herb Tyler ran past Florida's defense for two touchdowns, finishing with 50 yards rushing.

Pandemonium Reigns After Tigers Defeat No. 1 Florida

By Dave Moormann
The Advocate

Baton Rouge, La. — *Oct. 11, 1997*

Stunning isn't strong enough. Unthinkable, maybe. Pandemonium, for sure.

In an upset unlike any before in LSU's proud 104-year football history, the 14th-ranked Tigers shocked top-ranked Florida, 28-21, tonight and set off a wild, exhilarating scene in Tiger Stadium.

Many in LSU's second-largest paid crowd of 80,677 stormed the field and ripped down the goal posts in celebration of the monumental triumph.

■ **LSU's Cedric Donaldson returns a 31-yard interception for a touchdown which put LSU in front to stay.**

Never before had LSU beaten a No. 1 team, having gone 0-7-1 in such games, including losses to Florida in two of the previous three seasons.

"Other than getting a bill from (LSU Athletic Director) Joe Dean for the goal posts, it was a great night," LSU coach Gerry DiNardo said.

LSU took immediate control in bolting to a 14-0 first-quarter lead. The Tigers became the first team to score a first-quarter touchdown against Florida this season.

LSU also ended Florida's Southeastern Conference winning streak at 25 games, two short of the league record. In the process, it snapped Florida's SEC road win streak at a record-tying 19 games.

Florida's first loss of the season dropped them to 5-1 overall and 3-1 in the SEC, where it shares first place in the Eastern Division with Tennessee. LSU, which owns the same records, trails Auburn by one-half game in the West.

"The first drive set us off mentally," sophomore left offensive tackle Al Jackson said.

LSU established itself with a 58-yard march, even if the possession ended with Rondell Mealey's fumble. The Tigers stormed back with a pair of one-play touchdown drives to stun the Gators.

After Florida punted, LSU junior quarterback Herb Tyler sped around the right side on an option for a 40-yard touchdown that gave LSU a 7-0 lead at 8:42 of the first quarter.

Score by Periods

Florida	7	0	7	7 —	21
LSU	14	0	0	14 —	28

Tyler added an 11-yard rushing touchdown that proved to be the difference on another option run around the right side to put LSU ahead, 28-14, with 11:40 left.

"We just had the attitude of playing hard and executing and winning the game," said Tyler, who had been criticized in recent weeks for his erratic play. Tyler improved his career record as a starter to 19-3.

Tyler's second touchdown allowed LSU to weather Fred Taylor's 3-yard TD run with 6:44 to play. It was the last of Taylor's three touchdowns.

LSU ended Florida's last possession when junior strong safety Raion Hill came up with LSU's fourth interception of the night.

Senior cornerback Cedric Donaldson already had intercepted two passes, returning one for a 31-yard touchdown that put LSU in front, 21-14, at 13:13 of the fourth quarter.

Donaldson's first theft and 68-yard return set up freshman fullback Tommy Banks for a 7-yard touchdown run that put LSU ahead, 14-0, at 7:44 of the first quarter.

"(Florida sophomore quarterback Doug) Johnson is not as accurate as (Danny Wuerffel)," Donaldson said of the current New Orleans Saints quarterback who helped defending national champion Florida past LSU last season, 56-13. "He throws the ball all over the place. We knew he was going to mess up and throw one (interception). I ran out of gas (on the 68-yard return)."

Taylor slowed the Tiger express with a 2-yard touchdown run that cut the early deficit to 14-7 at 2:14 of the first quarter. LSU took that lead into halftime before Taylor tied the score, 14-14, on his 1-yard touchdown run at 12:17 of the third quarter.

But LSU broke the deadlock with Donaldson scoring on his team-best sixth interception of the season, and Tyler adding the decisive touchdown on his scamper. Florida's Bo Carroll fumbled a kickoff return to put LSU in position for Tyler to score.

"They just outplayed us, outcoached us, and they deserved to win," said Florida coach Steve Spurrier, who had guided the Gators in seven of the nine consecutive games they had won against LSU.

"We just got beat tonight," Johnson said. "They were the better team and more prepared."

LSU ended Florida's NCAA-record string of regular-season games with a touchdown pass at 62.

LSU will return to action Saturday at home against Ole Miss. Florida must visit eighth-ranked Auburn.

LSU rushed for 158 yards after gaining 28 yards on the ground last year at Florida. Kevin Faulk rushed 22 times for 78

■ **Mark Roman (8) celebrates after teammate Chris Cummings blocked a Florida field goal.**

yards; a year ago he gained 26 yards. Florida outgained LSU, 391-330, but it wasn't enough.

"It hit me as soon as the clock had 50 seconds on it," Faulk said. "It's really exciting."

It was a measure of vindication both for LSU and Tyler, with LSU coming off a 31-28 loss to Auburn on Sept. 20 and a 7-6 lackluster victory against Vanderbilt last week.

Tyler hadn't played particularly well in either game, and LSU was a decided underdog against Florida. He completed 10 of 17 passes for 172 yards without an interception Saturday.

"I don't know what the critics are going to say now," Jackson said.

"We wanted to hit them in the mouth," LSU junior defensive tackle Anthony McFarland said. "We wanted to play physical ... There's nothing like Saturday night in Tiger Stadium."

■ **LSU fan Bryan Allen leads the postgame celebration by tearing down one of the goalposts.**

LSU surprised Florida with an unusual defensive scheme that it branded "The Bandit" package in taking the name from the defensive group that played during LSU's 1958 national championship season.

When it went to that formation, LSU used a 3-3-5 alignment with backup players. LSU normally lines up in a 4-2-5 set.

After LSU opened up its 14-0 lead, Florida responded with an 80-yard scoring drive. Taylor capped it with his 2-yard scoring run into the right corner of the end zone.

Copying how LSU began the game, Florida started the second half by marching downfield for a touchdown that tied the score, 14-14, on Taylor's 1-yard run.

Taylor not only scored to end the seven-play, 80-yard drive, but he also figured prominently into the march.

Florida opened with Taylor's 53-yard reception and run. Taylor also rushed for 19 yards in moving into fifth-place on Florida's all-time rushing list.

LSU threatened on its next drive, but Florida blocked Wade Richey's 44-yard field-goal attempt. Richey finished with three failed field-goal tries, missing also from 37 and 39 yards out.

In scoring on its two one-play touchdown drives in the first quarter, LSU became the first team to take a lead on Florida this season.

Florida entered the game with a composite 91-3 first-quarter lead over its opponents. But LSU shocked the Gators.

Not only did LSU win the pregame coin toss, but it elected to receive and embarked on an impressive seven-play, 58-yard drive that began at its 20-yard line.

However the drive ended when Mealey, in what would be his only first-half carry, fumbled the football. After everyone was slow to react as it rolled backward, Willie Rodgers finally recovered and returned it on the Florida 25-yard line.

LSU forced Florida to punt after three plays, and on first down from the Florida 40-yard line, Tyler ran an option around right end.

He stumbled just past the line of scrimmage before recovering his balance and racing into the end zone to put LSU ahead, 7-0.

"A lot of people had talked about him," junior center Todd McClure said, "but we need Herb Tyler. He showed the quarterback he is."

Carroll's 44-yard kickoff return put Florida in good field position on its 45-yard line. Taylor gained 14 yards on first down before Johnson threw incomplete to Green. Johnson followed with his worst pass of the half, which Donaldson intercepted.

Some nifty running and strong blocking allowed Donaldson to return it 68 yards to the Florida 7-yard line. Donaldson didn't score, but Banks zipped up the middle on first down for a 7-yard touchdown. Banks' second touchdown of the season gave LSU a 14-0 lead.

Florida responded with a 13-play, 80-yard scoring drive that Taylor capped with his 2-yard run.

Both teams tried second-quarter field goals with futile results. A snap that rolled to the holder didn't help Richey, who missed a 39-yarder at 9:41.

Florida came back with a methodical 16-play, 51-yard drive. LSU's defense stiffened when Florida reached the Tigers' 27-yard line, and rather than go for the first down on fourth-and-12, the Gators had Collins Cooper attempt a 44-yard field goal.

Chris Cummings blocked the kick, giving LSU its third block in as many games. Kenny Mixon blocked an extra-point attempt on the final play to preserve LSU's one-point victory over Vanderbilt the previous week. Before that, Arnold Miller batted down a field-goal try in LSU's 56-0 victory over Akron.

In leading 14-7 at halftime, LSU led a top-ranked team after two quarters for the first time since jumping ahead of Florida State, 16-7, in 1991. FSU came back to win, 27-16.

Not only did LSU hold on this time, it made its way into history.

Beating Gators Tops the List

BY SAM KING

The Advocate

....

Baton Rouge, La. — *Oct. 11, 1997*

Go ahead, call it The Greatest.

The 999,999 people who will swear they were in Tiger Stadium on Oct. 11, 1997, to witness football's Mission Impossible will call LSU's 28-21 triumph over defending national champion and No. 1-ranked Florida the greatest victory, the greatest victory in Tiger Stadium and the greatest game every played by an LSU team.

It is all debatable.

Certainly LSU's 14-7 upset of No. 2-ranked Arkansas in the Jan. 1, 1966, Cotton Bowl was great. There is also the Heisman Trophy-winning run of Billy Cannon in a 7-3 victory over Ole Miss in this same stadium in 1959.

As for the greatest game in between these walls, you can't forget Charles McClendon's last year in 1979 when No. 1 Southern Cal needed the benefit of generous officials to get out alive. And even Bear Bryant and his No. 1 Tide won by only 3-0 the same year, although it was probably the most lopsided 3-0 rout these eyes ever witnessed.

How great it was when they had a sign to set our clocks back four seconds when you crossed the Louisiana-Mississippi state line after the Tigers recorded what many Rebel fans emphasized was a post-game, 17-16 victory in 1972.

The band played late. The fans swarmed the field. The crowd was wild.

It was also a similar scenario after a 61-17 rout of Ole Miss in 1970 with oranges filling the sky and field as LSU prepared to go to the Orange Bowl, the same as against Florida State, 55-21, in 1982.

But, on this humid October night in Tiger Stadium, there was a little of it all — plus the element of surprise.

It was a completely, shocking, stunning upset. It had the offensive and defensive thrills that would send a wave of pandemonium throughout the second-biggest crowd (80,677) in Tiger Stadium history.

Oh, how they relished the sweet taste of victory — those who weren't wearing that gaudy Orange and Blue stuff.

And, for the record, there was no porch for these football Tigers. They proved they can run with the biggest of dogs in college football. It is they who put the bite on No. 1. It is this team that became the first LSU club to defeat a top-ranked team.

They call it history.

You can also call Florida's 25-game SEC winning streak history. The Gators' string of 19 consecutive triumphs away from Florida Field are also gone with the win — LSU's win, that is.

Remember this night when a determined, battling team waged a total team effort to make this one of the most unforgettable nights, games and victories in Tiger football history.

The goal posts came down, the students stormed the field — wild, screaming and running with reckless abandon.

Damn, we of the media found out quickly how Florida quarterback Doug Johnson must have felt as LSU sent wave after wave of charges at him all night. They wrecked the poise and confidence of this team that had won the national championship only a year ago — after it virtually obliterated this same group of Tigers, 56-13. That's a 50-point swing. That's a big deal.

But, this was not the same LSU team, by any stretch of the imagination, that escaped the wrath of being upset by Vanderbilt a week ago — thanks only to Vandy's own inability to run a simple play.

Please welcome back the Tigers.

Welcome back Clarence LeBlanc — a defensive back out since the second game with an injury. What a comeback, what a heck of a game.

Don't welcome Cedric Donaldson back. He's not been anywhere. Just tell him thanks for two interceptions, one that he returned 31 yards for the Tigers' third TD.

Welcome back Herb Tyler ... wherever you have been. Why did you stay away so long? What was it you had, 10 completions in 17 attempts for 172 yards and scrambling for 50 on the ground, including touchdown runs of 40 and 11 yards. Superb ... just superb.

Believe me, Kevin Faulk's stats can't tell you what he meant. Seventy-eight yards on 22 carries never seemed so much. He's probably never faced a night so long — nor ever enjoyed one quite as much.

Give Carl Reese and Morris Watts, the coordinators much credit. Guess those guys can really give a clinic now on how to beat Florida now.

Give the fans also much credit for the never-ending roar.

After the triumph, Gerry DiNardo said, "I know I've never seen anything like it in my years here."

And I'm not sure I have either.

It was one for the history book.

Call it The Greatest.

You may as well.

Mostly everyone else will — especially the 999,999 other people who were in Tiger Stadium when LSU finally beat No. 1.

■ **Larry Foster (22) scored on a 29-yard touchdown reception in the third quarter.**

Tyler & Daring Tigers Destroy Auburn, 31-19

By Scott Rabalais
The Advocate

Auburn, Ala. — *Sept. 20, 1998*

If the Auburn Tigers thought LSU quarterback Herb Tyler couldn't beat them with his throwing arm, they were right.

The LSU senior needed more than that. He required nimble feet, a head full of big-game experience and a throwing arm that has rarely been more on target.

With all of those things working for him near peak efficiency, Tyler threw for three touchdowns and ran for another, leading No. 7-ranked LSU to a crucial 31-19 victory in its SEC opener at Jordan-Hare Stadium.

■ LSU's Clarence LeBlanc (18) reaches for a first-quater interception, which he returned for a touchdown.

"You're supposed to save your best for the big games," said Tyler, his right (throwing) hand heavily bandaged afterward, courtesy of a helmet he banged into in the first quarter. "We came out on top."

LSU improved to 2-0, 1-0 in the SEC and won the game that has meant so much to these two teams in recent SEC Western Division races. The Tigers now have the early half-game lead and tiebreaker on Auburn (1-2, 1-1 in the SEC), the team picked in the preseason to be LSU's closest SEC West pursuer.

"It was a great win," tailback Rondell Mealey said. "It was our first step in reaching our goals."

In this series marked by "earthquakes," interceptions, great comebacks and even a burning building outside Jordan-Hare two years ago, this game will add another quirky chapter. LSU won despite seemingly being unable to stop Ben Leard's third-down passing the entire first half and its seeming inability to ever convert an extra point opportunity.

But as LSU coach Gerry DiNardo pointed out, "When you come on the road in the SEC looking good is winning. At times we didn't look as good as we can.

Score by Periods

LSU		19	0	6	6 —	31
Auburn		7	10	2	0 —	19

"After the game I told the team we played hard for 60 minutes. I guess we'll be ranked No. 6 in the morning because someone (No. 2 Florida or No. 6 Tennessee) has to lose. I told them there's a lot of responsibility in being No. 6."

There's a lot of responsibility going into being an LSU quarterback, especially with a defense like Auburn's geared to stop the Tigers' most notorious weapon, tailback Kevin Faulk.

Auburn did limit Faulk to 21 carries for 88 yards. But time and again it was Tyler doing the damage: scrambling away from a rush or hitting Abram Booty and Larry Foster with touch sideline patterns.

"Their quarterback was totally the difference in the game," Auburn defensive coordinator Bill Oliver said. "I don't think

■ LSU quarterback Herb Tyler dives in for his first touchdown, after twisting his way to the end zone.

we got a sack."

No they didn't, but not for lack of opportunities. Tyler scrambled around for a net 12 yards on 11 carries and a touchdown. He passed 20 times, completing 16 for 174 yards and three touchdowns.

"It was typical Herb Tyler," said DiNardo, who ran to the 10,000 or so LSU fans in the north end zone after the game and acknowledged them by pumping his fist in the air. "He found a way to win."

Tyler improved to 25-5 as a starter, tying Warren Rabb for second-most victories in LSU history for a quarterback behind Tommy Hodson's 31.

"His maturity showed," LSU offensive coordinator Morris Watts said. "He never got down or bothered the entire game."

It looked as if this would go down as Auburn's self-destruction game in the first 5½ minutes. Turnovers on Auburn's first two plays led to a 13-0 LSU lead on a one-handed interception and 21-yard return by strong safety Clarence LeBlanc on Auburn's first offensive play and Tyler's juking 5-yard quarterback draw. That score was set up when linebacker Aaron Adams stripped Auburn tailback Michael Burks of Kenner, the ball recovered by inside linebacker Thomas Dunson.

"That's what Herb offers you," said Watts, describing a run in which Tyler zig-zagged around strong safety Rob Pate and dived into the end zone. "It's not a run everyone could make."

After the interception, LSU struggled to contain Auburn quarterback Ben Leard the rest of the half. Without much help from his running game but plenty from a confused-looking LSU defense, Leard completed 16 of 22 passes for 221 yards, including a 54-yard TD pass to wide-open fullback Heath Evans and a 10-yard TD pass to wide receiver Karsten Bailey.

After Evans' score, LSU went up, 19-7, late in the first quarter on a 19-yard Tyler-to-Faulk scoring pass with Faulk working out of the slotback position. Auburn pulled within 19-14 on Bailey's grab then made it 19-17 at halftime on a 29-yard Robert Bironas field goal as time expired.

Their early big lead all but gone, some LSU players began to worry.

"After we got up 13-0 some of them started to panic when Auburn came back," nose guard Anthony McFarland said. "But we knew it would be a 60-minute game."

LSU dominated field position in the third quarter but struggled to score. Tyler struggled, too, unable to get a first down on fourth-and-inches at the Auburn 18 and a fumble that Pate recovered at his 7.

But LSU took over at the Auburn 41 late in the third and finally produced some points. After three straight runs, Tyler rolled right to give an option fake, dropped back and found wide-open flanker Larry Foster streaking across the middle for a 29-yard score.

Auburn pulled within 25-19 after Charles Dorsey blocked his second Danny Boyd extra-point try and Brad Ware returned it 88 yards for two points. But LSU's defense continued to harass Leard in the second half. He completed 5 of 16 for 64 yards in the second half and was sacked five times.

"In the second half they were one step ahead of us offensively," Auburn coach Terry Bowden said. "When you are trying to keep the run in and it's not working too well, you're asking Ben to do a lot of things."

A diving interception by cornerback Chris Cummings at the LSU 46 gave the Tigers the ball with 10 minutes left. With Faulk running and Tyler passing, LSU reached the 1 but was pushed back to the 6 by a procedure penalty.

In last Saturday's 42-6 win over Arkansas State, Tyler overthrew tight end Kyle Kipps in the right flat of the end zone on fourth down. This time he rolled right and found the big tight end left open by an Auburn defender who came up to stop Tyler's run for the clinching points with 5:27 remaining.

"Last year Herb kind of struggled," against Auburn, said Faulk, recalling a bitter 31-28 loss in Baton Rouge. "This year he was hurt and continued to play his heart out."

Halftime Made All the Difference

By Sam King
The Advocate

Auburn, Ala. — *Sept. 20, 1998*

Two years after the great Barn Fire in Auburn, LSU's secondary was caught practicing fire drills in the midst of a game.

Or, at least that's what the confusion in the secondary looked like.

Ben Leard looked like Dameyune Craig.

LSU's great season looked like history.

The Tigers looked a gift horse in the mouth and squandered most of a charitable 13-point as Leard passed for 221 first-half yards and two touchdowns that left LSU holding a slim 19-17 lead.

Now, the rest of the story.

Let Auburn coach Terry Bowden tell you.

"I thought they changed in the second half," said Bowden. "I thought they did. I got a little frustrated, too. I'm going to have to go back and look.

"They changed some things and got me out of sync — I say me, because I was calling the plays. They got us out of sync.

"They did a great job. I was getting blitzed at different times," continued Bowden. "In the first half we kind of got momentum (on offense). We stayed one step ahead of them. But, in the second half, they were one step ahead of us."

That, in a nutshell, is why LSU left here with a 31-19 victory.

That is why the No. 7-ranked Tigers are 2-0 and have a good start on their quest of winning the Southeastern Conference Western Division.

One of the greatest assets of any coaching staff is being able to adjust at halftime.

It meant everything this afternoon.

Leard managed only five completions in 16 attempts for 64 yards and the Auburn rushing game that had managed only 16 yards in the first half ended with a net 21 yards for the game. That's big-time, major-college defense — although Leard was sacked for losses totaling 50 yards.

"We just turned it up a little bit," is what Anthony McFarland said of the second-half surge. "We made a few switches.

"We were getting in their face the first half, but they were throwing the ball. In the second half, we were able to get there a little quicker," continued McFarland. "We just tried to run a few more stunts up front and were able to get home."

He admitted, however, that Leard finding an open receiver — sometimes no defender even close — was getting to some of the players.

■ LSU defenders Mark Roman (8), Robert Davis (9) and Anthony McFarland (94) close in to help as Joe Wesley (48)and Arnold Miller (98) wrap up Auburn running back Michael Burks. LSU held Auburn to 21 total yards rushing.

In this wild and wacky series anything happens and it seems this year it was a case of turnabout being fair play. Last year Craig put two quick first-quarter scores on the board. This time, on Auburn's first offensive play of the game, Leard was intercepted by Clarence LeBlanc who raced into the end zone after less than three minutes of play.

On Auburn's next offensive play, Michael Burks fumbled with linebacker Thomas Dunson recovering. LSU capitalized and led by 13-0 with 9:34 still remaining.

The lead came almost too quickly and too easily.

But, if you've kept up with this series, you know no lead is ever completely, totally safe.

LSU's defense answered the challenge in the second half. The Tigers maintained field position most of the half and threatened, only to be repelled by an Auburn defense that was anything but poor.

As expected the battle in the trenches was big time and it wasn't until LSU's defensive front started making its stand with strong pressure on Leard that the Tigers were able to take control.

Not enough can be said of the very key, clutch and vital play of quarterback Herb Tyler, who connected with receivers on critical third-down plays or ran, scrambled and dazzled with some moves to get a first — or a touchdown as he did on the second TD of the game (from 5 yards out).

Flanker Larry Foster had the best game of his career with 10 catches, some absolutely astounding, in picking up 111 yards.

Abram Booty had three catches, two for first downs.

The defense was remarkable in adjusting and LSU continues its great ability to win on the road — all of which should help lead to better things.

"I got up and told the guys to just stay calm, that it isn't the worst thing for someone to be driving," said McFarland. "I told them to stay calm. We knew it was going to be a 60-minute game and later on the game would come to us.

"I said, 'Don't get in a frenzy. Stay calm. The game will come to us,' and eventually it did."

Color this one a big victory.

Although one game is not a season, this was a major decision the Tigers had to have to be able to achieve some lofty goals this season.

Now, it's up to them to make sure they don't squander such a good start.

Early Errors Cost Auburn

By Sam King
The Advocate

Auburn, Ala. — *Sept. 20, 1998*

"You can't spot the No. 7 team 14 and beat them," Auburn coach Terry Bowden said, mistakenly referring to the quick 13 points the hosts helped dish out to LSU in today's 31-19 loss.

"Spot 'em 14 and lose by 12 — that's as close as you're going to come."

To Bowden, you had to look no farther than the Tigers' veteran four-year starting quarterback Herb Tyler for the difference in the game.

"That experienced quarterback just made so many plays," Bowden said of Tyler, who not only completed 16 of 20 passes for three touchdowns and 174 yards, but came up with some critical scrambles for vital first-down yardage. "You've got to have a guy who, on every little third-and-four situation makes 4½ yards.

"I saw that over and over again. It's what we saw in Dameyune Craig last year."

Despite spotting LSU a two-touchdown lead, Auburn played some outstanding offense to get back in the game and trail by only 19-17 at half. Quarterback Ben Leard sparkled by completing 16 of 22 passes for 221 yards and two touchdowns, although two were intercepted, one returned by Clarence LeBlanc for the game's first touchdown.

"We were one step ahead," Bowden said of the first-half surge. "I guess we were doing some things they weren't expecting. We were one step ahead.

"We did well in the first half, but they made the adjustments necessary. They made some sacks in long yardage situations," he said.

Something else he pointed out: "They are a team that doesn't give up the naked bootleg like Ole Miss. Their style is not

■ LSU quarterback Herb Tyler (14) skips away from Auburn defenders Brad Ware (27) and Rob Pate (31) for a 5-yard touchdown run.

of a bump-and-run, play loose a little."

Bowden pointed out Auburn had a problem preparing for LSU since it had only played Arkansas State and they had nothing else to evaluate the new defense by.

"They did a good job of playing their base (defense), but they were also giving us some things we didn't know about," Bowden said.

For the second time in three games, Auburn finished with paltry rushing yardage: Auburn gained a net 18 against Virginia

and was limited to 21 by LSU — although that includes 50 yards of losses when Leard was sacked.

"We have got to run the ball," Bowden said. "Last year (with Craig), I could debate if we needed to run when we could throw like we did. But now what we've got to do is get past the line of scrimmage (rushing) a few more times."

Bowden was especially complimentary of LSU's passing game.

"Take (Abram) Booty and (Larry) Foster, I thought they both played good," Bowden said. "Booty is just so depend-

able. He came to our camp in high school. He's a lot better football player than he gets credit for being. He has good speed, runs perfect routes and sometimes makes some unbelievable catches.

"On third-and-ten, he catches for 12 — right at the line, I mean."

With LSU's passing game, their running game has to get tougher.

"Foster can really hurt you a lot," he said of the Tiger flanker, who snared 10 passes for 111 yards and one TD.

■ LSU's Chris Cummings (19) and Thomas Dunson (52) dive for a fumble in the first quarter.

GREATEST MOMENTS IN
LSU FOOTBALL HISTORY

Photo Credits

Chick-Fil-A Peach Bowl — 74, 75.

CompUSA Florida Citrus Bowl — 102, 103, 105.

The Birmingham News — 76,78,81.

FedEx Orange Bowl — 38, 40-41, 152, 153.

LSU Sports Information — 13, 14, 18, 19, 21, 44, 45, 57, 58, 64-65, 67, 68, 69, 70, 77, 84, 89, 107-right, 110, 167, 172.

Nokia Sugar Bowl — Back program covers (3), 24, 26-27, 28-29, 46, 47, 48-49, 49, 50, 50-51, 60, 62-63, 86, 87.

Southwestern Bell Cotton Bowl — Back cover program (1), 43, 166.

The Advocate — Front Cover, 2, 2-3, 4-5, 5-both, 6, 7-both, 8, 15, 16, 17, 20, 23, 30, 31, 35, 36, 37, 52, 53, 54-55, 55, 56, 66, 72, 80, 82-83, 91, 92, 93, 94-95, 96, 97, 98, 99, 100, 101, 104, 106, 107-left, 198, 109, 112, 113, 115, 116, 117, 118, 119, 120-both, 121, 122, 123-both, 124, 125, 126, 128, 129, 130, 131, 132-133, 134-135, 136, 137, 140, 142-143, 144, 145, 146, 147, 148-149, 150, 154, 155, 156, 157, 159, 160, 161, 162-163, 164, 164-165, 168, 169, 170, 171, 173, 174, 175, 176, 178-179, 181, 182, 183, 184-185, 186, 187, 188, 189, 190, 191, 193, 194, 195, 196-197, 198, 199, 200, 201, 202-203, 204, 206, 207, 208-209, 210-211, 212-213, 214-215.

T.J. Ribs — 33, 111.

LSU running back Domanick Davis (31) celebrates with Jerel Myers as Illinois' Joe Bevis walks away. Davis scored four touchdowns in the game.

LSU Piles Up Points to Hold Off Illinois

BY CARL DUBOIS
The Advocate

New Orleans, La. — *Jan. 1, 2002*

LSU, the Southeastern Conference football champion and winner of the 2002 Nokia Sugar Bowl? Yeah, right. And snow will fall in south Louisiana to start the New Year.

That's a response you might have heard two months ago, when the Tigers were all but out of the SEC Western Division race. But Tuesday night, as winter storm warnings spread throughout the suddenly icy Gulf Coast, LSU defeated Illinois 47-34 in the Sugar Bowl to cap a season that ends with a surprising array of engraved gold destined for the Tigers' trophy case.

Twelfth-ranked LSU (10-3) ends the season with a six-game winning streak, its strongest finish since1961. Seventh-ranked Illinois (10-2) missed a shot at being the first team in school history to win 11 games in a season.

In a matchup of teams playing in their first BCS bowl — each boasting the best offense in its history — LSU rolled to an impressive 34-7 halftime lead, then held off an inspired Illinois comeback attempt.

LSU senior quarterback Rohan Davey, voted the game's Most Outstanding Player by the media, completed 31 of 53 passes for 444 yards and three touchdowns. Davey said the win will boost LSU's recruiting and raise its national profile, something he and the other seniors will relish with pride.

"As a group we wanted to be remembered as a team that thrust LSU into the top 10, that thrust LSU into the national spotlight for next year," Davey said.

LSU coach Nick Saban said he was proud of the Tigers for regrouping and winning their last six games of the season after an up-and-down start.

"We certainly proved we should be in a BCS bowl game, and we carried the mantle of the SEC proudly tonight," Saban said.

LSU tailback Domanick Davis, filling in for injured LaBrandon Toefield, set a Sugar Bowl record with four rushing touchdowns. He scored the game's first three touchdowns to set the tone for LSU as it raced to a 27-0 lead.

Davis rushed 28 times for 122 yards. Late in the game, Saban said, he was worn out. LSU Sports Information Director Michael Bonnette said Davis was sick to his stomach in the locker room.

Later, Davis met with the media.

"There was no pressure on me," Davis said. "Early on I had told the team I was going to make the most out of my opportunity. I basically took the approach that I was going to go out there and have fun."

Score by Periods

LSU	7	27	7	6	—	47
Illinois	0	7	14	13	—	34

All-America wide receiver Josh Reed, who caught 14 passes for 239 yards and two touchdowns, said Davis' running helped create opportunities for LSU against the aggressive Illinois man-to-man defense.

"They blitz a lot, and that leaves a lot of one-on-one coverages," Reed said. "They had to put a lot of people in the box to stop the run, so we had to beat them on the outside."

They did, with Davey playing one of his best games. His only interception was unofficial, coming on a two-point conversion try.

"I couldn't have picked a better way to go out," Davey said of his last game in an LSU uniform.

The Illini didn't go quietly. After trailing by 27 points at halftime, Illinois rallied behind quarterback Kurt Kittner and pulled to within 13 points twice in the fourth quarter, the last time on a trick play with 5:41 left.

Taking advantage of a fumble by LSU wide receiver Michael Clayton, Illinois turned to a play that caught the Tigers flat-footed. Wide receiver Brandon Lloyd, who caught two of Kittner's four touchdown passes in the game, threw a 40-yard touchdown pass to wide receiver Walter Young to cut LSU's lead to 47-34.

But Illinois didn't get its hands on the ball again. LSU ran out the last 5:41.

"I'm proud of our guys," Illini coach Ron Turner said. "They've got a lot of fight and a lot of heart. The next step in our program is to learn how to win a game like this."

The Tigers set so many records — Sugar Bowl records and LSU bowl-game records — they'll still be sorting them out today. Among the most notable are 595 yards of total offense, a Sugar Bowl record, and 47 points, an LSU bowl high.

Before a crowd of 77,688 in the Louisiana Superdome, LSU won on New Year's Day for the first time since its 20-13 win over Wyoming in the 1968 Sugar Bowl.

The victory was also LSU's fifth straight bowl win, a school record. The Tigers won the Peach Bowl in 1996 and 2000 and the Independence Bowl in 1995 and 1997. But this was LSU's first Sugar Bowl win in the Superdome in three tries.

The Tigers beat a top-10 team for the second time this season. LSU beat Tennessee, ranked No. 2 at the time, 31-20 in the SEC Championship Game.

LSU finished with 10 wins for the fourth time, the first since 1996, when Gerry DiNardo's second LSU team was 10-2. But this was the Tigers' first time in 108 seasons to play 13 games.

LSU's only 11-win season came in 1958, when it won its only national championship.

Kittner came into the Sugar Bowl with a reputation as a comeback king, having led the Illini to 12 come-from-behind wins in four years, including four this season. But a rally from a 34-7 halftime deficit was too much to ask of him.

"Once we settled down, we played great football," Kittner said. "It was just a tough deficit to overcome.

"We started slow, and in Big Ten games we were able to fight back. Tonight most of our problems came with my passes getting batted down, bad throws and some dropped passes."

LSU defenders batted away five Kittner passes at the line of scrimmage, a point of emphasis for the Tigers going into the game, and sacked him three times. His second-half performance put a scare into LSU's defense.

"Coach always says never look at the scoreboard," LSU linebacker Bradie James said. "But it got to a point where I was saying, 'Tick, tick — please tick. These guys are coming.'"

Kittner struggled early in the game. At one point, he was 1-for-11 for 1 passing yard. He finished 14-for-35 for 262 yards and four touchdowns.

The LSU defense deflected 11 of Kittner's passes, five at the line.

"They told us in meetings that he throws a low ball, lots of quick stuff," LSU defensive end Chad Lavalais said. "We did a pretty good job on him in the first half. It's hard to get a rush with that three-step drop."

Davey, who missed the second half of LSU's 31-20 win over Tennessee in the SEC Championship Game with bruised ribs, was far more efficient. He spread his passes among Michael Clayton, Jerel Myers and Reed early, making the Illini pay for paying too much attention to Reed.

LSU scored 27 points in the second quarter, a Sugar Bowl record. The variety of offensive weapons played a big role in that explosion.

"I didn't think their guys could cover our guys consistently," Saban said. "The momentum of the game swung in our direction right there (in the second quarter)."

By rolling to a 34-7 halftime lead, LSU broke the Sugar Bowl record for points in a half. Davey completed 19 of 33 passes in the half for an LSU bowl record 246 yards. He also threw two touchdown passes.

Davis was the star, though, scoring LSU's first three touchdowns on runs of 4, 25 and 16 yards. He added his record fourth touchdown on another 4-yarder.

"I felt like I was in the zone," Davis said.

Thanks to an Illinois personal foul, LSU needed just three plays to drive 36 yards for his second touchdown. Davis picked up the final 25 after blowing past blitzing defensive end Derrick Strong.

2002: LSU vs. Illinois

Records set or tied by LSU on January 1, 2002 in the Sugar Bowl. Previous marks listed in parentheses:

Sugar Bowl Records

Team Records

Points in a quarter: 24 (2nd quarter)
(24, Tennessee, 1971, 1st quarter, vs. Air Force)

Points in a half: 34 (1st half)
(32, Notre Dame, 1992, 2nd half, vs. Florida)

Total points both teams: 81
(72, Florida, 52, vs. Florida State, 20, 1997)

Total offense yards: 595
(527, Arkansas, 1970 vs. Ole Miss)

First downs: 32
(30, Florida, 1994, vs. West Virginia)

Individual Records

Most points: 24, Domanick Davis, 4 touchdowns (20, Peter Warrick, Florida State — 3 touchdowns, 1 2-pt. PAT — vs. Virginia Tech, 2000)

Most rushing touchdowns: 4, Domanick Davis
(3, Peter Warrick, Florida State, vs. Virginia Tech, 2000 and Ike Hilliard, Florida, vs. Florida State, 1997)

Most completions: 31, Rohan Davey
(28, Shane Matthews, Florida, vs. Notre Dame, 1992 and Danny Wuerffel, Florida vs. Florida State, 1995)

Most passing yards: 444, Rohan Davey
(394, Danny Wuerffel, Florida vs. Florida State, 1995)

Most receiving yards: 239, Josh Reed
(178, Ray Perkins, Alabama vs. Nebraska, 1967)

Most pass receptions: 14, Josh Reed
(12, Chuck Dicus, Arkansas vs. Georgia, 1969)

LSU Bowl Records

Team Records

Points in a half: 34 (1st half)
(27, vs. Iowa State, 2nd half, 1971 Sun)

Points in a quarter: 27 (2nd quarter)
(21, vs. Michigan State, 3rd quarter, 1995 Independence)

Total points: 47
(45, vs. Michigan State, 1995 Independence)

Total offense yards: 595
(510, vs. Wake Forest, 1979 Tangerine)

Offense plays: 97
(86, vs. Stanford, 1977 Sun)

Individual Records

Rushing touchdowns: 4, Domanick Davis
(2, six players)

Passing touchdowns: 3, Rohan Davey
(3, Bert Jones vs. Iowa State, 1971 Sun; Tommy Hodson vs. South Carolina, 1987 Gator and Rohan Davey vs. Georgia Tech 2000 Peach)

Points: 24, Domanick Davis (3 touchdowns)
(19, Steve Van Buren – 3 touchdowns, 1 PAT — vs. Texas A&M, 1944 Orange)

Passing yards: 444, Rohan Davey
(229, Mike Hillman vs. Florida State, 1968)

Passes completed: 31, Rohan Davey
(20, Jeff Wickersham vs. Nebraska, 1985 Sugar)

Passes attempted: 53, Rohan Davey
(37, Jeff Wickersham vs. Nebraska, 1985 Sugar)

Pass receptions: 14, Josh Reed
(9, Andy Hamilton vs. Nebraska, 1971 Orange; Wendell Davis vs. S. Carolina, 1987 Gator; Josh Reed vs. Georgia Tech, 2000 Peach)

Receiving yards: 239, Josh Reed
(165, Andy Hamilton vs. Iowa State, 1971 Sun)